Lecture Notes in Electrical Engineering

Volume 744

The book series *Lecture Notes in Electrical Engineering* (LNEE) publishes the latest developments in Electrical Engineering - quickly, informally and in high quality. While original research reported in proceedings and monographs has traditionally formed the core of LNEE, we also encourage authors to submit books devoted to supporting student education and professional training in the various fields and applications areas of electrical engineering. The series cover classical and emerging topics concerning:

- Communication Engineering, Information Theory and Networks
- Electronics Engineering and Microelectronics
- Signal, Image and Speech Processing
- Wireless and Mobile Communication
- Circuits and Systems
- Energy Systems, Power Electronics and Electrical Machines
- Electro-optical Engineering
- Instrumentation Engineering
- Avionics Engineering
- Control Systems
- Internet-of-Things and Cybersecurity
- Biomedical Devices, MEMS and NEMS

For general information about this book series, comments or suggestions, please contact leontina.dicecco@springer.com.

To submit a proposal or request further information, please contact the Publishing Editor in your country:

China

Jasmine Dou, Editor (jasmine.dou@springer.com)

India, Japan, Rest of Asia

Swati Meherishi, Editorial Director (Swati.Meherishi@springer.com)

Southeast Asia, Australia, New Zealand

Ramesh Nath Premnath, Editor (ramesh.premnath@springernature.com)

USA, Canada:

Michael Luby, Senior Editor (michael.luby@springer.com)

All other Countries:

Leontina Di Cecco, Senior Editor (leontina.dicecco@springer.com)

** This series is indexed by EI Compendex and Scopus databases. **

More information about this series at http://www.springer.com/series/7818

Pantelimon Stănică · Sugata Gangopadhyay ·
Sumit Kumar Debnath
Editors

Security and Privacy

Select Proceedings of ICSP 2020

Editors
Pantelimon Stănică
Department of Applied Mathematics
Naval Postgraduate School
Monterey, CA, USA

Sugata Gangopadhyay
Department of Computer Science
and Engineering
Indian Institute of Technology Roorkee
Roorkee, India

Sumit Kumar Debnath
Department of Mathematics
National Institute of Technology
Jamshedpur
Jamshedpur, Jharkhand, India

ISSN 1876-1100   ISSN 1876-1119   (electronic)
Lecture Notes in Electrical Engineering
ISBN 978-981-33-6783-8   ISBN 978-981-33-6781-4   (eBook)
https://doi.org/10.1007/978-981-33-6781-4

This Springer imprint is published by the registered company Springer Nature Singapore Pte Ltd.
The registered company address is: 152 Beach Road, #21-01/04 Gateway East, Singapore 189721,
Singapore

Organization Committee

General Chair:

Pantelimon Stănică, Naval Postgraduate School, USA

Program Chairs:

Sumit Kumar Debnath, NIT Jamshedpur, India
Kouichi Sakurai, Kyushu University, Japan

Technical Program Committee Members:

Chris Mitchell, Royal Holloway, UK
Luca De Feo, IBM Research Zürich, Switzerland
Bimal Kumar Roy, ISI Kolkata, India
Kouichi Sakurai, Kyushu University, Japan
Pantelimon Stănică, Naval Postgraduate School, USA
Pratish Datta, NTT Research, USA
Partha Sarathi Roy, University of Wollongong, Australia
Minho Jo, Korea University, South Korea
Peter Scholl, Aarhus University, Denmark
Sabyasachi Dutta, University of Calgary, Canada
David Naccache, ENS, France
Sourav Sen Gupta, NTU, Singapore
Avishek Adhikari, Presidency University, India
Sourav Mukhopadhyay, IIT Kharagpur, India

J. D. Koli, DRDO, India
Arnab Patra, DRDO, India
Shoichi Hirose, University of Fukui, Japan
Jun Kurihara, University of Hyogo, Japan
Koji Nuida, The University of Tokyo, Japan
Mario Larangeira, Tokyo Institute of Technology/IOHK, Japan
Maharage Nisansala Sevwandi Perera, ATR, Japan

Organizing Committee

Chief Patron:

Prof. Karunesh Kumar Shukla, Director, National Institute of Technology Jamshedpur, India

Patron:

Dr. Sunil Kumar, Head, Department of Mathematics, National Institute of Technology Jamshedpur, India

Chairman:

Dr. Sourav Das, National Institute of Technology Jamshedpur, India

Convener & Organizing Secretary:

Dr. Sumit Kumar Debnath, National Institute of Technology Jamshedpur, India

Members:

Prof. Tarni Mandal, National Institute of Technology Jamshedpur, India
Dr. Ramayan Singh, National Institute of Technology Jamshedpur, India
Dr. Sripati Jha, National Institute of Technology Jamshedpur, India
Dr. Hari Shankar Prasad, National Institute of Technology Jamshedpur, India

Preface

This volume contains the refereed proceedings papers of the First International Conference on Security and Privacy (ICSP 2020), organized by the National Institute of Technology Jamshedpur, India, during November 05–06, 2020.

This volume includes topics on all aspects of security and privacy such as network security, secure cryptographic protocols, post-quantum cryptography, quantum cryptography, blockchain and cryptocurrency, IoT security and privacy, cloud security, privacy-preserving technologies, biometric security, security and privacy of Big Data, cloud and edge computing security, access control, steganography and steganalysis, leakage-resilient cryptography, cyber-physical security, machine learning in cybersecurity, etc.

The proceedings of the conference contain 14 contributed papers, accepted out of the 92 submitted papers. All the papers have been thoroughly reviewed by at least three reviewers and most of the reviews were done by members of the program committee. We thank all of the reviewers for their contribution. In addition to the contributed papers, we had eight invited lectures given by Bimal Kumar Roy (Head, R C Bose Centre for Cryptology and Security, Indian Statistical Institute, Kolkata, India), Pantelimon Stănică (Professor and Manager—Secure Communication Program, Naval Postgraduate School, USA), Kouichi Sakurai (Professor, National University Corporation Kyushu University, Mathematical Informatics, Japan), Carmit Hazay (Deputy Director and the Head of the Scientific Committee of the Center for Research in Applied Cryptography and Cyber Security, Bar-Ilan University, Israel), Luca De Feo (Researcher, IBM Research Zürich, Switzerland), Sourav Sen Gupta (Professor, Nanyang Technological University, Singapore), Sourav Mukhopadhyay (Professor, Indian Institute of Technology Kharagpur, India), Ratna Dutta (Professor, Indian Institute of Technology Kharagpur, India). We would like to extend our sincere thanks to these experts for sharing their opinion and expertise during the conference.

Monterey, USA
Roorkee, India
Jamshedpur, India

Pantelimon Stănică
Sugata Gangopadhyay
Sumit Kumar Debnath

Contents

About the Editors

Pantelimon Stănică is currently working as a Professor in the Department of Applied Mathematics, Graduate School of Engineering & Applied Sciences (GSEAS) at Naval Postgraduate School, Monterey, USA. He is also associated with the Institute of Mathematics of Romanian Academy as a researcher. He received his doctoral degree in mathematics from the State University of New York at Buffalo in 1998. He also received a doctorate in algebra from the Institute of Mathematics of the Romanian Academy in 1998. He has published over 150 research articles in internationally reputed journals and conferences and has co-authored a book on Cryptographic Boolean Functions (now in the second edition) and co-edited two conference proceedings. His research interests include number theory, cryptography, coding theory, combinatorics, finite fields, Boolean functions, valuation theory, class field theory, and theoretical computer science.

Sugata Gangopadhyay is currently working as a Professor in the Department of Computer Science and Engineering, Indian Institute of Technology Roorkee, India. He received his doctoral degree in mathematics from the Indian Institute of Technology Kharagpur, India, in 1998. He received an Outstanding Teacher Award in 2016 from IIT Roorkee and ONR-Global VSP award to visit Naval Postgraduate School, Monterey, California USA. He served in the program committee of NSUCRYPTO the International Students' Olympiad in Cryptography organized by Novosibirsk State University, Russia. He has published several research articles in internationally reputed journals and conferences. His research interests include cryptology, cryptographic Boolean functions, and stream cipher cryptanalysis.

Sumit Kumar Debnath is an Assistant Professor in the Department of Mathematics, National Institute of Technology Jamshedpur, India. He received his doctoral degree in cryptology & network security from the Indian Institute of Technology Kharagpur, India, in 2017. He has published several research articles in internationally reputed journals and conferences. He is a life member of the Cryptology

Research Society of India (CRSI). His research interests include multivariate cryptography, lattice-based cryptography, isogeny-based cryptography, quantum cryptography, secure two-party/multi-party computation, secure set intersection, electronic voting, functional encryption, identity-based cryptography, and oblivious transfer.

A Score-Level Fusion Method for Protecting Fingerprint and Palmprint Templates

Mulagala Sandhya, Y. Sreenivasa Rao, Sahoo Biswajeet, Vallabhadas Dilip Kumar, and Maurya Anup Kumar

1 Introduction

Biometric refers to our use to progress in the evaluation and examination of the physiological or behavioral properties of a person [1, 2]. However, uni-biometric frameworks which use only biometric characteristic for recognition often suffer negative results such as spoof attacks, lack of characteristics, low accuracy of recognition, and biometrics information variation [3]. A multi-biometric framework combines two or more springs with different biometric characteristics, such as fingerprint, palm print, face, iris, and finger vein, etc. [4]. We cannot reset or replace a compromised biometric template. An important protection template technique is cancelable biometrics, which performs a one-way transformation for verifying the original data [5]. Mathematically, this one-way processing cannot be inverted, and only changing transformation parameters can effectively revoke and replace this trading template. The accompanying four necessities that should be met by a legitimate model are diversity, revocability, irreversibility, and performance. Multimodal biometric fusion can be divided into two types: Fusion before matching and Fusion after matching. Fusion at the level of the sensor and the level of the features are essentially considered as fusion prior matching. Following matching, fusion at match score level and decision level can be fused [2]. The multi-biometric systems are the systems that use

M. Sandhya (✉) · S. Biswajeet · V. Dilip Kumar
Computer Science and Engineering, National Institute of Technology Warangal,
Warangal, India
e-mail: msandhya@nitw.ac.in

Y. Sreenivasa Rao
Department of Mathematics, National Institute of Technology Warangal, Warangal, India
e-mail: ysr@nitw.ac.in

M. Anup Kumar
Goa Institute of Management, Sanquelim, India
e-mail: anupmaurya88@gmail.com

more than one physiological or behavioral characteristic. Generally, multi-biometric systems are classified as Multi-sensor systems, Multi-algorithmic systems, Multi-Instance systems, Multi-sample systems, and Multimodal systems. The multi-modal systems establish an identity based on the evidence of multiple biometric traits. These systems offer considerable rise in the accuracy of a biometric system.

1.1 T-Norm & T-Conorms

We now present a brief overview of the triangular norms and triangular conorms.
T-norm:
Definition: A function $T : [0, 1]^2 \rightarrow [0, 1]$ is known as *triangular norm (t-norm)* if it satisfies the following properties for all $a, b, c \in [0, 1]$ [6]

(T1) $T(a, b) = T(b, a)$, i.e., the t-norm satisfies commutative property,

(T2) $T(T(a, b), c) = T(a, T(b, c))$, i.e., the t-norm satisfies associative property,

(T3) $a \leq b \rightarrow T(a, b) \leq T(b, c)$, i.e., the t-norm satisfies monotone property,

(T4) $T(a, 1) = a$, i.e.,1 is the neutral element.

T-conorm:
Definition: A function $S : [0, 1]^2 \rightarrow [0, 1]$ is called *triangular conorm(t-conorm)* if it satisfies the following properties for all $a, b, c \in [0, 1]$ [6]

(T1) $S(a, b) = s(b, a)$, i.e., the t-conorm satisfies commutative property,

(T2) $S(s(a, b), c) = s(a, s(b, c))$, i.e., the t-conorm satisfies associative property,

(T3) $a \leq b \rightarrow S(a, b) \leq S(b, c)$, i.e., the t-conorm satisfies monotone property,

(T4) $S(a, 0) = a$, i.e., 0 is the neutral element.

The rest of the paper is organized as follows: Sect. 2 provides related work, Sect. 3 gives the proposed score-level fusion method. Section 4 gives experimental results and analysis of proposed method. Section 5 concludes the paper.

2   Related Work

Barrero et al. [7] proposed architecture for protecting multi-biometric templates using homomorphic encryption. Barrero et al. [8] proposed a fingerprint and finger vein based fusion mechanism using bloom filters. Sandhya and Prasad [9] proposed a method for fusing two algorithms at score level for fingerprint templates using triangular norms. Chang et al. [10] developed a new framework BIOFUSE by the combination of fuzzy commitment and fuzzy vault using the format-preserving encryption scheme. Chin et al. [11] proposed a technique to generate an integrated template of fingerprint and palmprint using random tiling and discretization. Sandhya and Prasad [12] provided a clear review of template protection schemes in the literature and provided various sources of available datasets for the ongoing research on template protection schemes carried out worldwide. Dinca and Hancke [13] provided a survey on fusion methods and security highlighting the open challenges in this area of research work. Multi-biometric Systems offer improved accuracy, fault tolerance, and resistance to spoofing, at the same time add complexity for developers in terms of gathering sample inputs and how the templates are used to decide the user is genuine or an imposter. Hence we proposed a method for fusing fingerprints and palmprints at score level thereby improving performance with added security.

3 Proposed Method

The proposed method for fusing fingerprint & palm print at score level contains the following steps as shown in Fig. 1. Minutiae are the most significant points present in the fingerprint which helps in deciding the uniqueness of a fingerprint. We extracted them using the Verifinger SDK tool.

3.1 Binary String Generation from Fingerprint Image

Let f_p be a fingerprint image, we extract a set of minutiae represented by (x, y, θ, δ), θ is the orientation of the point, and δ is the type of minutia, (x, y) is the x and y coordinate location. A local structure p_{jk} constructed by the pair of minutia formed in fingerprint image by matching each minutia with all other minutiae points. For instance, Fig. 2 shows minutia pair m_j and m_k. If m_j is paired with m_k to form p_{jk}, then symmetric minutia pair of p_{kj} is excluded to maintain a strategic distance without redundancy. Assume that in a fingerprint image f_p, there are N_1 minutiae; a group of $C_2^{N_1}$ minutiae pairs are built. The following are characterized for every pair, p_{jk} with translation and rotation-invariant properties.

- Edge length, for example, l_{jk}.
- Every minutia angle to the edge, for example, α_j and α_k.
- Generally each minutiae is of type δ_k and δ_j. Therefore, a overall total of $C_2^{N_1}$ characteristics such as $l_{jk}, \alpha_j, \alpha_k, \delta_j, \delta_k$ can be removed in fingerprint image f_p from minutia $C_2^{N_1}$ couples formed by N_1 Minutiae.
- For example consider an integer value 300 i.e. $V_{jk}=300$ then the 300th position of the set [0, 2¬Lf-1] is indexed by '1' and remaining positions are indexed with '0'. Then we integrate all these binary strings into a single vector Bf which is of length 2Lf which is shown in Fig. 3.

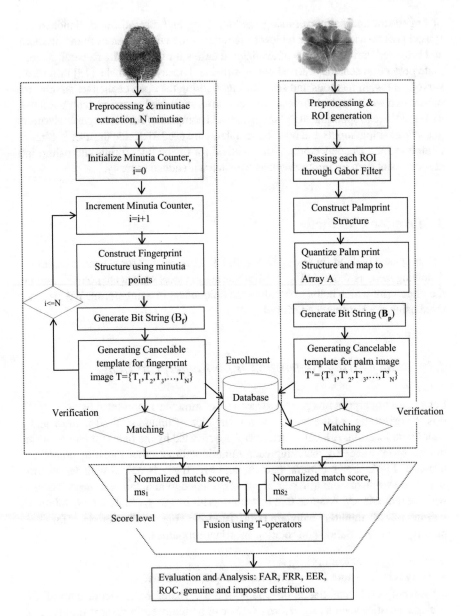

Fig. 1 Flowchart of the proposed method

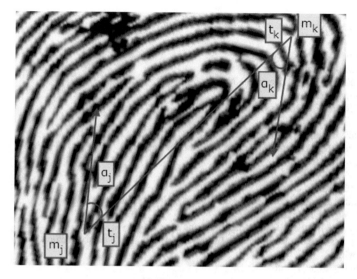

Fig. 2 Minutia pair p_{jk}—example of local minutia structure

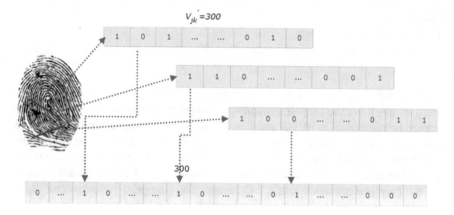

Fig. 3 Minutiae pair, a local minutia structure example

3.2 Palm Print Feature Extraction and Transformation

Passing ROI through Gabor filter

A Gabor filter, balanced by a Gaussian envelope is composed as

$$G(x, y, \sigma, \theta) = \frac{1}{2\pi\sigma^2} \, e^{-\frac{x^2 + y^2}{2\sigma^2}} e^{j2\pi(x\cos\theta + y\sin\theta)}$$

Algorithm 1 Generation of Finger print Match Score

Input:
1: Minutiae locations (x_i, y_i)
2: Orientation of minutiae points θ_i
3: Total number of minutiae points N
4: Random matrix R
Output: Normalized match score
5: begin
6: Initialize minutiae counter $i \leftarrow 0$;
7: $N \leftarrow$ Number of minutiae points in a fingerprint image;
8: **while** $i \leq N$ **do**
9:     for each j $\leftarrow N - 1$ points
10:     l_{ij}: Length of the edge
11:     α_i and α_j : Angle between orientation of each minutiae and edge
12:     δ_i and δ_j : Type of each Minutiae
13:     $V_{ij} \leftarrow l_{ij}||\alpha_i||\alpha_j||\delta_i||\delta_j$, which contains $L_f = L_1 + L_2 + L_3 + 2$;
14:     L_f bits represents 2^{L_f} ranging from 0 to $2^{L_f}-1$ to get B_f binary vector
15: **end while**
16: **while** $i \leq Size(B_f)$ **do**
17:     $V \leftarrow DFT(B_f)$;
18:     $T(i) \leftarrow R \times V$;
19:     $i \leftarrow i + 1$;
20: **end while**
21: Match score ms_1 generation;
22: **end**

---

where θ and σ signify the orientation of Gabor filter and bandwidth, respectively, and $j = \sqrt{-1}$. We use the palmprint images filtered by Gabor. Wavelengths are considered orientations $\theta = \{0, 90\}$ and $\sigma = \{5, 10\}$, resulting in four filters from Gabor and for each ROI, a phased image is provided. After plotting the graph concerning phase and magnitude, we can convert the graph into a 2-D matrix and then convert the 2-D matrix into a 1-D vector to get B_p. Certain quantization steps can be used for the graph to convert it into a 2-D matrix. The palmprint feature vector B_p is bolstered non-invertible transformation based on the DFT that produces an identical feature-length vector of B_p.

Cancelable template generation

Let the bit string length B_p be m. n^1-point discrete fourier transformation is applied to B_p. Complex vector V^1 is produced as follows [9]

$$V' = \sum_{s=0}^{n^1-1} B_p e^{-\frac{j2\pi is}{n'}}, \qquad i = 0, 1, \ldots, n^1 - 1$$

Thus, the size of V^1 is $n^1 \times 1$. A random matrix (R) of dimension $m \times n^1$ for V^1 is generated. To obtain T^1, we multiply R^1 and V^1, where T^1 is the template that can be cancelable. Thus the size of T^1 is $m \times 1$.

$$R'_{m \times n} \times V'_{n \times 1} = T'_{m \times 1}$$

In addition, we create N canceled vector templates in $T^1 = (T_1, T_2, \ldots, T_N)$ representing palm print, where N is the number of canceled vector templates.

Algorithm 2 Generation of Palm Print Match Score

Input:
1: ROI of palmprint I
2: Random matrix R
Output: Normalized match score
3: begin
4: Input ROI's I to Gabor Filter to get a graph between phase and magnitude
5: Convert the Graph into 2-D binary matrix
6: Convert 2-D matrix to 1-D binary vector B_p
7: **while** $i \leq Size(B_p)$ **do**
8:     $V' \leftarrow DFT(B_p)$;
9:     $T'(i) \leftarrow R' \times V'$;
10:     $i \leftarrow i + 1$;
11: **end while**
12: Match score ms_2 generation;

3.3 Score-Level Fusion

Table 1, where p covering the T-operative space, which is indicated by the T-conorms implemented in our fusion method [9].

Table 1 Fusion of match scores of fingerprint and palmprint implemented using T-conorms

S.No.	T-conorm	$S(S_1, S_2)$
1.	Zadeh (max rule)	$\max(S_1, S_2)$
2.	Goguen, Bandler	$S_1 + S_2 - S_1.S_2$
3.	Dombi $(0 < p < +\infty)$	$\dfrac{1}{1 + ((\frac{1-S_1}{S_2})^{-p} + (\frac{1-S_2}{S_2})^{-p})^{-\frac{1}{p}}}$
4.	Dubois $(p\epsilon[0, 1])$	$1 - \dfrac{(1-S_1)(1-S_2)}{\max(1-S_1, 1-S_2, p)}$
5.	Sugeno-Weber $((-1 < p < +\infty))$	$\min(S_1 + S_2 + p.S_1.S_2, 1)$
6.	Yu Yandong $((-1 < p < +\infty))$	$\min(S_1 + S_2 + p.S_1.S_2, 1)$

3.4 Transformed Domain Matching

Let, Y^T be the feature vector of the template and Y^Q be the feature vector of query (T and Q superscripts mean template and query, respectively). The Y^T and Y^Q are both complex vectors. The similarity is calculated using the following equation:

$$S(Y^T, Y^Q) = 1 - \frac{||Y^T - Y^Q||_2}{||Y^T||_2 + ||Y^Q||_2} \tag{1}$$

where $|| \cdot ||_2$ represents the 2-norm. The similarity scores $S(Y^T, Y^Q)$ is in the range [0, 1]. The greater the score of similarity, the template, and query feature vectors are similar.

4 Experimental Results & Analysis

4.1 Experimental Setup

To test the proposed method, we used databases FVC 2002 (DB1, DB2) for fingerprints and HandV2 for palmprint images.

4.2 Accuracy

Two cases will be considered to assess the accuracy of our proposed fusion method. First, when each user is assigned a different key, i.e., each user is assigned a specific key that is unique to each user. This process is referred to as plain verification. The EER value for this scenario is ideal, i.e., for all two FVC 2002 DB1 and FVC 2002 DB2, it shows the EER as 0%. Second, stolen or lost key, where the attacker has the key of the user and he is trying to verify. The EER value for this scenario is greater than 0, like in the case of FVC 2002 DB1 is 6.58% & for FVC 2002 DB2 is 9.95%. Figures 4a, b represent EER values of the proposed method.

The ROC curve for the proposed fusion method is shown in Fig. 5a, b for FVC 2002 DB1 and DB2, respectively.

Table 2 represents the EER reported for the proposed method by using score-level fusion of the match scores using T-norms by fusing FVC DB1 and DB2 databases. with Handv2 databases. We have run the two types of fusion mechanism for 200 samples (100 users) on FVC 2002 DB1 and DB2 where Score level Fusion is giving better results compared to Feature-Level Fusion, i.e., the lowest EER we are achieving is for FVC 2002 DB1 which is 6.58%.

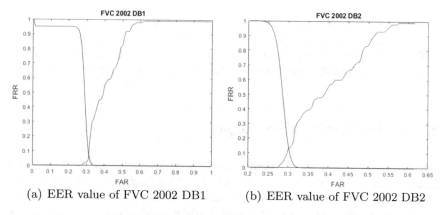

(a) EER value of FVC 2002 DB1

(b) EER value of FVC 2002 DB2

Fig. 4 **a** EER value of FVC 2002 DB1. **b** EER value of FVC 2002 DB2

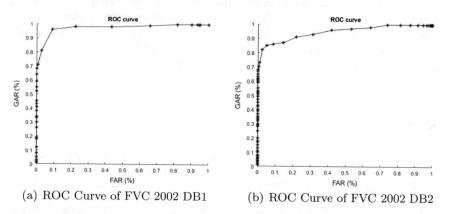

(a) ROC Curve of FVC 2002 DB1

(b) ROC Curve of FVC 2002 DB2

Fig. 5 **a** ROC Curve of FVC 2002 DB1. **b** ROC Curve of FVC 2002 DB2

Table 2 EER values against different fusion methods

Samples(N)	Fusion method used	$EER(\%)$ for FVC 2002 DB	
		DB1	DB2
200	Feature-level fusion	36.5	37.03
200	Score-level fusion	6.58	9.95

4.3 Security Analysis

Consider the following cases for security analysis:

- *Inverse attack*: For each fingerprint image, all minutiae are considered, where each minutia has a different position, orientation with respect to other minutiae which makes it difficult to generate the binary vector. Here, it's hard to reconstruct B_f and B_p.

- *Non-invertibility*: Non-invertibility claims that it is almost impossible to construct an original fingerprint image & palm-print image from the transformed template. By using the help of DFT and multiplying with the random matrix, we can provide one-way functionality to our template. Hence making our solution secure.

5 Conclusion and Future Scope

We have used Fingerprint and Palmprint as the multi-biometric traits and used minutiae position and Gabor filter, respectively, for generating binary vectors. In this method, we are not directly storing distance between minutia, orientation, type, etc., for fingerprint and phase and magnitude for palmprint. But we are storing the attributes such that if any template got leaked the information like distance between two minutia points, orientation will not be revealed directly to the attacker. Then we used DFT to create a cancelable template for each of the vectors and then calculate the match score for both the respective vectors. The match score for both the vectors are fused using the T-operators to give the resultant match score.

References

1. Jain AK, Nandakumar K, Nagar A (2008) Biometric template security. EURASIP J Adv Signal Process 113
2. Ross A, Govindarajan R (2004) Feature level fusion in biometric systems. In: Proceedings of the 2004 biometric consortium conference, p 2
3. Rathgeb C, Gomez-Barrero M, Busch C, Galbally J, Fierrez J (2015) Towards cance-lable multi-biometrics based on bloom filters: a case study on feature level fusion of face and iris. In: Proceedings of the 2015 international workshop on biometrics and forensics (IWBF), pp 1-6
4. Jagadeesan A, Duraiswamy K (2010) Secured cryptographic key generation from multimodal biometrics: feature level fusion of fingerprint and iris. Int J Comput Sci Inf Secur 7:28–37
5. Lin K, Han F, Yang Y, Zhang Z (2011) Feature level fusion of fingerprint and finger vein biometrics. Adv Swarm Intell 6729:348–355
6. Ratha N, Chikkerur S, Connell J, Bolle R, Generating cancelable fingerprint templates. IEEE Trans Pattern Anal Mach Intell 29(4):561–572
7. Gomez-Barrero M, Maiorana E, Galbally J, Campisi P, Fierrez J (2017) Multi-biometric template protection based on homomorphic encryption. Pattern Recognit 67:149–163
8. Gomez-Barrero M, Rathgeb C, Li G, Ramachandra R, Galbally J, Busch C (2018) Multi-biometric template protection based on bloom filters. Inf Fusion 42:37–50
9. Sandhya M, Prasad MVNK, Multi-algorithmic cancelable fingerprint template generation based on weighted sum rule and T-operators. Pattern Anal Appl 21:397–412
10. Chang D, Garg S, Ghosh M, Hasan M (2021) BIOFUSE: a framework for multi-biometric fusion on biocryptosystem level. Inf Sci 546:481–511
11. Chin YJ, Ong TS, Teoh ABJ, Goh KOM (2014) Integrated biometrics template protection technique based on fingerprint and palmprint feature-level fusion. Inf Fusion 18:161–174

12. Sandhya M, Prasad MVNK (2017) Biometric template protection: a systematic literature review of approaches and modalities. In: Jiang R, Al-maadeed S, Bouridane A, Crookes P, Beghdadi A (eds) Biometric security and privacy. Signal Processing for Security Technologies, Springer, Cham
13. Dinca LM, Hancke GP (2017) The fall of one, the rise of many: a survey on multi-biometric fusion methods. IEEE Access 5:6247–6289

Combining Human Ear and Profile Face Biometrics for Identity Recognition

Partha Pratim Sarangi and Madhumita Panda

1 Introduction

In recent years, the human ear biometrics has become the most reliable and fast means of identity recognition such as identification and verification of individuals for providing protection to device accesses control, secure commercial transaction, public security, and privacy protection [1, 17]. Hence, ear biometric is rapidly gaining popularity and attracting researchers to explore the field of identity recognition, forensics, and surveillance applications. However, ear-based unimodal biometric systems always suffer from inevitable challenges in uncontrolled environments such as noisy data, poor contrast, illumination variation, pose changes, and partial occlusion. These issues act as impediments in the way of improvements in overall recognition accuracy. As a consequence, ear recognition still requires many studies to overcome the above-described challenges and improvements in recognition performance.

By combining multiple biometric modalities into the recognition process, the above-described problems of ear biometric system can be overwhelmed and successively the recognition performance can be improved. Over the past decade, many studies have been proposed in the field of ear-based multimodal biometrics in [2, 3, 5, 10, 11, 15]. Recently a few number of research articles have been proposed to improve performance by combining ear and profile face modalities [6, 10, 14]. In addition, fusion of ear and profile face modalities has been studied in [20] for person age and gender recognition. There are several advantages observed in ear and profile face based multimodal biometrics such as reducing the failure-to-acquire rate, sensor cost, computational time, and additional acquisition time. In spite of that fusion of

P. P. Sarangi (✉)
School of Computer Engineering, KIIT Deemed to be University, Bhubaneswar, Odisha, India
e-mail: ppsarangi@gmail.com

M. Panda
Department of Master of Computer Applications, Seemanta Engineering College, Jharpokharia, Odisha, India

© The Author(s), under exclusive license to Springer Nature Singapore Pte Ltd. 2021   13
P. Stănică et al. (eds.), *Security and Privacy*, Lecture Notes in Electrical Engineering 744,
https://doi.org/10.1007/978-981-33-6781-4_2

ear and profile face modalities acquired from a single camera is still an understudied area that motivates us to explore in this direction.

In this work, we have tried to overcome the issues of unimodal ear biometric system by introducing a robust ear and profile face based multimodal biometric recognition system. In order to minimize the effect of illumination and pose variation, Gabor filters bank has been successfully used in face recognition [13, 21]. Gabor filter bank is a set of different scale and orientation representations which are very similar to the visual system of a human being. In this work, we employed the Gabor filter bank to extract the local texture features of different scales and orientations from ear and profile face with the objective of minimizing the effect of illumination and pose variation. As the Gabor feature vectors have higher dimension, it is necessary to reduce feature vector size along with extracting discriminative features. After that fusion of two reduced feature sets is performed. All these tasks are achieved at the time of feature-level fusion. Here, we explored three feature-level fusion schemes, namely serial, CCA, and KCCA for comparing the recognition performance of our system. Finally, well-known nearest neighbor classifier is applied for the verification and identification of individuals. The experimental results demonstrate that the proposed method using the KCCA fusion scheme provides an improved recognition performance in comparison to existing ear and profile face based multimodal methods on UNDE and UND-J2 datasets.

The remaining parts of this paper are organized as follows. Section 2 describe related work. Section 3 explains the proposed multimodal recognition system and three feature-level fusion schemes. Experiments and results analysis are described in Sect. 4 and finally, conclusion and future work are highlighted in Sect. 5.

2 Related Work

The most recent, well structured, and comprehensive survey on ear biometrics was published in [1, 17]. Despite the several research work, the performance of identity recognition is not up to the levels due to certain challenges under uncontrolled conditions.

Recently many multimodal biometrics with ear as one of the major modalities have been proposed to overcome the limitations of ear biometrics. However, only a few multimodal studies have been published based on the fusion of ear and profile face biometric modalities. These biometrics are captured by a single sensor in one short. First et al. [18] proposed an ear and profile face based multimodal approach in which both modalities were extracted from the single side face images. They used kernel canonical correlation analysis (KCCA) to extract non-linear discriminative features that achieved a better identification rate than the canonical correlation analysis (CCA) based approach. In [19], the authors used kernel Fisher discriminant analysis (KFDA) to fuse profile face and ear images. Their results showed the weighted-sum rule based feature-level fusion technique considerably increased identification rates in comparison to the ear and profile face modality alone. Rathore et al. [6] proposed a

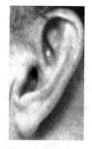

Fig. 1 Pipeline of the proposed method

multimodal biometric approach using ear and profile face. They used three enhancement schemes separately for both biometrics and for each images SURF descriptors were extracted. They employed both feature- and score-level fusion of ear and profile face images for multimodal recognition. From their results, it is observed the score level fusion outperforms feature-level fusion based personal recognition.

From these research works, it is observed that many potential improvements in this multimodal framework can be explored in order to improve recognition accuracy. Therefore, we tried an efficient multimodal approach using ear and profile face with KCCA based fusion level fusion (Fig. 1).

3 Proposed Multimodal Biometrics Framework

This section describes the framework of the proposed feature-level fusion of ear and profile face based multimodal human identity recognition. The main steps of the proposed method are (1) extract ear and profile face from the side face image, (2) do preprocessing, (3) to separately transform ear and profile face images into a number of Gabor images of different scales and orientations, (4) decrease the sampling rate by a constant factor to reduce the size of all Gabor images, (5) to normalize individual feature vectors of both modalities using z-score normalization, (6) to combine the two feature vectors using KCCA, and (7) to perform verification and identification operation for identity recognition using kNN classifier. The pipeline of the proposed framework is shown in Fig. 2.

3.1 ROI Extraction

In this work, both the ear and profile face regions are cropped from the side face image which is acquired by using a camera. At first, we automatically localized the ear part from the side face image by using our previous work [12] in which modified

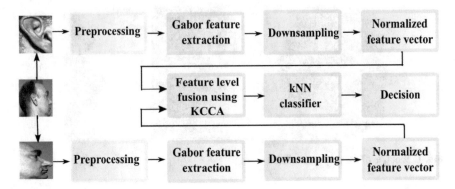

Fig. 2 Pipeline of the proposed method

Hausdorff distance based template matching is used. Then from the remaining part of the side face image, profile face is manually cropped. The ear and profile face images are two modalities extracted from the side face image simultaneously using a single sensor as shown in Fig. 1. Proper localization of ear and profile face regions from the side face images are very important which crucially affects the recognition performance of the biometric systems.

3.2 Preprocessing

In order to minimize the presence of noise and variation of illumination, we applied the Gaussian low-pass filter on the side face images. To perform this operation, we convolve Gaussian kernel (G) on the side face image (I) using Eq. 1.

$$I' = I * G(u, v, \sigma),$$
$$G(u, v, \sigma) = \frac{1}{\sqrt{2\pi}\sigma} exp\left(-\frac{u^2 - v^2}{2\sigma^2}\right), \tag{1}$$

where σ is the standard deviation of Gaussian kernel.

3.3 Feature Extraction Using Gabor Filters

Gabor filters are well known for the analysis of image texture information due to their biological property that are very similar to simple cells in visual cortex. Gabor filters have been extensively used in many biometrics modalities for extracting local texture features because it efficiently handles the effect of illumination and pose variation. Gabor filter bank is a popular choice for the feature extraction in face biometrics

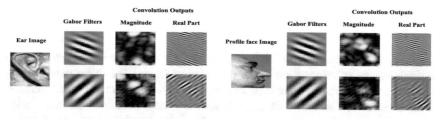

Fig. 3 Convolution outputs of ear and profile face images with two Gabor filters

in [21] in which the authors demonstrated that it is very robust to illumination changes. In our work, Gabor filter bank has been employed for local texture feature extraction for both ear and profile face modalities. A 2D Gabor filter is expressed as the product of a Gaussian kernel function and sinusoid wave as given in Eq. (2).

$$g(x, y; \lambda, \theta, \phi, \gamma) = \exp\left(-\frac{x'^2 + \gamma^2 y'^2}{2\sigma^2}\right) \cos\left(2\pi \frac{x'}{\lambda} + \phi\right) \qquad (2)$$

where $x' = x \cos\theta + y \sin\theta$, $y' = -x \sin\theta + y \cos\theta$, λ represents the wavelength of sinusoidal wave, θ denotes the orientation of a Gabor function, ϕ is the phase offset, σ is the standard deviation of the Gaussian envelope, and γ is the spatial aspect ratio that signifies the ellipticity of the Gabor function. Gabor filter bank contains a set of Gabor filters with different frequencies and orientations which are used for extracting texture features. These set of 2D filters convolve on our ear and profile face images to generate Gabor images. The five scales and eight orientations of the Gabor filter bank are mostly used, as mentioned in [13]. Figure 3 shows the convolution outputs of two Gabor filters of different scales and orientations on ear and profile face images.

Equations (3) and (4) express five scales $u = (0, 1, \ldots, 4)$ and eight orientations $v = (0, 1, \ldots, 7)$ for the Gabor filter bank respectively.

$$\omega_u = \frac{\pi}{2} \times \sqrt{2}^{-u} \qquad (3)$$

$$\theta_v = \frac{\pi}{8} \times v \qquad (4)$$

Then, each ear and profile face image $I_e(x, y)$, $I_{pf}(x, y)$ perform convolution with a set of 40 Gabor filters to generate 40 Gabor wavelet coefficients $G_{u,v}(x, y)$. The size of each $G_{u,v}(x, y)$ is then downsampled by a factor of k to reduce the size of Gabor image by $(k \times k)$, after that normalization is performed by zero mean and unit variance and then a vector $\mathbf{z}_{u,v}$ is generated. Finally, all of the normalized Gabor feature vectors $(\mathbf{z}_{u,v})$ are concatenated to form a robust feature vector $\mathbf{z}$. Eq. (5) presents the Gabor feature vector $\mathbf{z}$ for each ear and profile face image as follows.

$$\mathbf{z} = [\mathbf{z}_{0,0}^T, \mathbf{z}_{0,1}^T, \ldots, \mathbf{z}_{4,7}^T] \qquad (5)$$

3.4   Feature-Level Fusion

In multimodal biometrics, multiple sources of information are combined to form a single source of information which is termed as fusion. The feature-level fusion combines more than one feature vectors to a single feature vector. In the literature, it has been mentioned that multimodal biometric systems that combine information at an early stage preserve more discriminative information than the use of fusion at a later stage in the pipeline [7]. To take this advantage, we have compared the performance of three feature-level fusion schemes such as serial, CCA, and KCCA based on a recognition system of verification and identification. We briefly describe these three fusion schemes in the following sections.

3.5   Serial Feature Fusion

It is a simple scheme of feature-level fusion, in which more than one feature vectors are directly concatenated one after another to form a single feature vector. In this case, if the feature components are not compatible then the fusion of feature vectors may adversely affect the recognition performance of the biometric systems [11]. The effect of large dimensionality of the combined feature vectors increases the computational and storage space cost. To overcome these issues, prior to feature-level fusion we performed dimensionality reduction using PCA and normalization of reduced feature vectors using z-score normalization. Afterward, supervised linear subspace transformation is performed using linear discriminative analysis (LDA) [8, 9] to further minimize the size of fused feature vector equal to the number of subjects minus one and extracting discriminative feature for classification.

3.5.1   Fusion Using Canonical Correlation Analysis

Canonical correlation analysis (CCA) is an unsupervised powerful statistical analysis scheme to extract correlated feature components between two multivariate feature vectors and generate a combined feature vector with lesser dimension. Recently, CCA has been used to combine ear- and palmprint-based multimodal biometrics in [2]. However, the problem of CCA is the unsupervised linear subspace fusion method, which cannot extract more complex and nonlinear correlation relationship between two feature vectors.

3.5.2   Kernel Canonical Correlation Analysis

Kernel canonical correlation analysis (KCCA) is the generalization of CCA-based fusion method. It is a supervised statistical analysis in which kernel-based nonlinear correlation statistical analysis is performed in effect extract more discrimination features. In this scheme, first kernel matrices are determined for nonlinear mapping of feature vectors. The most common kernels that satisfy Mercer's theorem are namely polynomial, polylinear, and Gaussian kernel. In this work, we have explored all three kernels, in the results, it is demonstrated that the polynomial kernel offers better result than the other two kernels.

4 Experiments

In this section, we evaluate the performance of our approach by performing comprehensive experiments on two publicly available side face datasets. The experimental results are compared for three feature-level fusion schemes namely, serial fusion, CCA fusion, and KCCA fusion.

4.1 Datasets

All the experiments are performed using University of Notre Dame collection E (UND-E) and Collection J2 (UND-J2) datasets [16]. UND-E dataset contains 464 color side face images of 114 classes with each class having a minimum of 3 to a maximum of 9 samples. All of the images were acquired from a distance with change in poses, varying illumination conditions, and in different days. Similarly, the UND-J2 dataset comprises 2430 color side face images from 415 classes, each class having 2–22 samples taken under poor contrast, varying lighting conditions with different poses. Due to variation in the number of samples from each class in both datasets, the experiments were performed with 3 samples selected from each class. Hence, maximum of 114 subjects from UND-E and 273 subjects from UND-J2 were used in this experiment. Figure 4 illustrates ear and profile face samples from different subjects of the UND-E and UND-J2 datasets, respectively.

In the experiment, we randomly select three samples for each subject from UND-E and UND-J2 datasets. In practice, an all-to-all test strategy is commonly used for the distribution of training and test sets in biometrics literature [2, 4]. In which, subject-wise every sample at a time is selected as a test sample and the remaining samples are used as training samples. Then, the total number of training and test sets formed is equal to the number of samples available from each subject. In this way, we obtain three different training and testing sets without any overlapping between them. Hence, UND-E datasets were provided with (114×2) training and (114×1) testing samples. Similarly, UND-J2 were provided with (273×2) training and (273×1) testing samples.

In our work, the size of ear and profile face image is (152×112) then size of $\mathbf{z}$ is $(152 \times 112) \times (5 \times 8) = 680960$. As the dimension of each Gabor feature vectors is very large, the size of the ear and profile face images has been downsampled by a

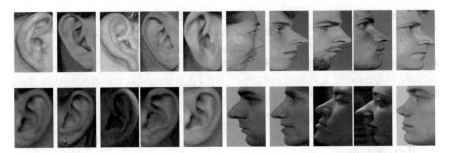

Fig. 4 Sample ear and profile face images of same subjects from UND-E dataset (top row) and UND-J2 dataset (bottom row)

factor of $k = 4 \times 4 = 16$ to reduce the feature vector $\mathbf{z} = 42560$. In [13], the authors have shown that a Gabor filter bank with five scales and eight orientations has the best performance. Therefore, we choose to use Gabor filters of five scales and eight orientations in our experiments. Similarly, the polynomial kernel function with an exponent of 2.3 and σ of 1 is used in KCCA.

4.2   Result Analysis of the Feature-Level Fusion Using Proposed Methods

The results of the proposed method are analyzed in this section. The performance of a biometric verification system can be measured in terms of accuracy (ACC) and equal error rate (EER). Accuracy is defined as $ACC = 100 - \frac{(FAR+FRR)}{2}$. Another performance measure is EER, which is the rate at which FAR and FRR are equal. In practice, a biometric system with low EER leads to more accurate results. The performance of the biometric verification system is also represented graphically using the receiver operating characteristic (ROC) curve. On the contrary, the performance of a biometric identification system is measured in terms of identification rate or rank, which is defined as the number of test samples successfully identified out of all test samples using a similarity distance measure. Generally, the identification ranks are illustrated graphically by means of the cumulative match characteristic (CMC) curve.

The performance results of the proposed method on UND-E and UND-J2 datasets are shown in Table 1. From the results, it is observed that the proposed method using KCCA fusion provides higher accuracy (99.17% and 99.4%) with EER (1.73% and 0.59%), and Rank-1 identification rate (99.12% and 98.12%) on UND-E and UND-J2 datasets, respectively, than serial- and CCA-based fusion. The receiver operating characteristic (ROC) curve of the verification operation of the proposed method using three different fusion schemes on UND-E and UND-J2 datasets are shown in Fig. 5a, b respectively. Similarly, the Cumulative Match Curve (CMC) of the

Table 1 Average results of identity recognition by combining ear and profile face

Dataset	Feature-level fusion	Accuracy (%)	EER	Rank-1 (%)	Rank-3 (%)
UND-E	Serial fusion	97.58	2.41	97.37	99.02
	CCA fusion	98.26	1.73	98.25	100
	KCCA fusion	**99.17**	**0.82**	**99.12**	**100**
UND-J2	Serial fusion	97.82	2.17	97.80	99
	CCA fusion	98.55	1.45	97.8	99.6
	KCCA fusion	**99.4**	**0.59**	**98.25**	**99.7**

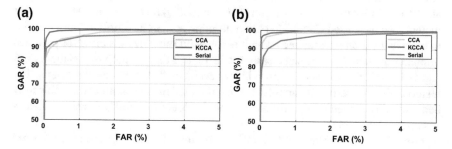

Fig. 5 ROC curve for UND-E and UND-J2 datasets

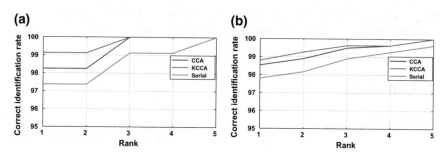

Fig. 6 Identification rates for UND-E and UND-J2 datasets

identification mode of the proposed method using three different fusion schemes on UND-E and UND-J2 datasets are shown in Fig. 6a, b, respectively. From the CMC graph, it is clearly observed that the identification rate of the proposed method using CCA and KCCA fusion is 100% in Rank-3 on UND-E and UND-J2 datasets are shown in Fig. 6a, b, respectively. It can be clearly observed from the results that non-linear kernel-based canonical correlation analysis (KCCA) methods are performing fundamentally better than their corresponding linear LDA- and CCA-based fusion schemes. To the best of our knowledge, the proposed multimodal method offers promising identity recognition performance on UND-E and UND-J2 datasets than other existing ear-based multimodal methods mentioned so far in the literature.

4.3 *Performance Comparison With Existing Multimodal Ear and Profile Face Approaches*

In the previous studies, we found only two similar works: Rathore et al. [6] and Sarangi et al. [10] have been published. However, in the first work, the authors have been studied only for personal verification and the second work for identification operation. As shown in Table 2, we compare average verification and identification results (Accuracy, EER, and Rank-1) of our CCA and KCCA fusion methods with recently published works on UND-E and UND-J2 datasets. In Rathore et al. [6], the authors combined feature vectors of three enhancement techniques and Sarangi et al. [10] combined two local descriptors (LDP and LPQ) for ear and profile face. In our method, we have used Gabor filters of 5 different scales and 8 different orientations to represent ear and profile face which is robust to minimize the effect of pose and illumination variation. We can clearly see in Table 2 that the proposed Gabor+CCA and Gabor+KCCA methods achieve higher accuracy than previous algorithms. The results of these experiments showed that our proposed method is offering significantly better identity recognition performance than the direct feature-level fusion schemes of two previous works.

From the experimental results, it is demonstrated that the proposed method based on feature-level fusion of ear and profile face can significantly improve the performance of personal identity verification and identification operations. In addition, all the proposed feature-level fusion schemes have achieved higher accuracy and rank-1 identification rates than the existing ear based unimodal and multimodal biometrics.

5 Conclusion

In this paper, we have proposed an improved multimodal ear and profile face biometrics for reliable identity recognition in uncontrolled environments. The proposed method utilized Gabor filter bank that contains different scales and orientations of Gabor filters to extract local texture information separately for ear and profile face images. These Gabor feature vectors of the corresponding Gabor filters are normalized and combined to form a global feature vector which is very robust to minimize the effect of illumination and pose variations. In order to extract more discriminative features, three fusion schemes such as serial, CCA, and KCCA have been explored. From extensive experiments, it was found that the KCCA-based fusion outperforms the other two fusion schemes. In the proposed method ear and profile face feature vectors are fused using KCCA into a single vector. Finally, identity verification and identification of individuals are performed using kNN classifier. Experimental results were tested on UND-E and UND-J2 datasets to demonstrate the effectiveness of our approach. The results achieved by our approach are significantly improved than the state-of-the-art ear and profile face based multimodal methods for both datasets.

Table 2 Performance comparison with other recent methods using feature-level fusion of ear and profile face biometrics

Dataset	Author	Results	Feature-level fusion
UND-E	Rathore et al. [6]	Accuracy (%)	97.54
		EER (%)	4.28
		Rank-1 (%)	–
	Sarangi et al. [10]	Accuracy (%)	–
		EER (%)	–
		Rank-1 (%)	99.12
	Proposed method using CCA	Accuracy (%)	98.26
		EER (%)	1.73
		Rank-1 (%)	98.25
	Proposed method using KCCA	Accuracy (%)	99.17
		EER (%)	0.82
		Rank-1 (%)	99.12
UND-J2	Rathore et al. [6]	Accuracy (%)	95.71
		EER (%)	5.09
		Rank-1 (%)	–
	Proposed method using CCA	Accuracy (%)	97.95
		EER (%)	2.04
		Rank-1 (%)	98.12
	Proposed method using KCCA	Accuracy (%)	99.4
		EER (%)	**0.59**
		Rank-1 (%)	98.53

In future, we will investigate an efficient multimodal biometric system by exploring various learned features using different CNN models along with other effective fusion schemes. In addition, we aim to design automated multimodal biometrics that can amalgamate multiple biometrics such as ear, frontal face, and profile face for yielding better recognition results.

References

1. Emeršič Ž, Štruc V, Peer P (2017) Ear recognition: more than a survey. Neurocomputing 255:26–39
2. Hezil N, Boukrouche A (2017) Multimodal biometric recognition using human ear and palmprint. IET Biom

3. Huang Z, Liu Y, Li X, Li J (2015) An adaptive bimodal recognition framework using sparse coding for face and ear. Pattern Recognit Lett 53:69–76
4. Kumar A, Wu C (2012) Automated human identification using ear imaging. Pattern Recognit 45(3):956–968
5. Kumar AM, Chandralekha A, Himaja Y, Sai SM (2019) Local binary pattern based multimodal biometric recognition using ear and FKP with feature level fusion. In: 2019 IEEE international conference on intelligent techniques in control, optimization and signal processing (INCOS). IEEE, pp 1–5
6. Rathore R, Prakash S, Gupta P (2013) Efficient human recognition system using ear and profile face. In: 6th IEEE international conference on biometrics: theory, applications and systems (BTAS). IEEE, pp 1–6
7. Ross A, Jain AK (2004) Multimodal biometrics: an overview. In: 12th European conference on signal processing. IEEE, pp 1221–1224
8. Sarangi PP, Mishra B, Dehuri S (2017) Ear recognition using pyramid histogram of orientation gradients. In: 4th IEEE international conference on signal processing and integrated networks (SPIN). IEEE, pp 590–595
9. Sarangi PP, Mishra B, Dehuri S (2017) Pyramid histogram of oriented gradients based human ear identification. Int J Control Theory Appl 10(15):125–133
10. Sarangi PP, Mishra BP, Dehuri S (2018) Multimodal biometric recognition using human ear and profile face. In: 4th international conference on recent advances in information technology (RAIT). IEEE, pp 1–6
11. Sarangi PP, Mishra BSP, Dehuri S (2018) Fusion of PHOG and LDP local descriptors for kernel-based ear biometric recognition. Multimed Tools Appl 78:9595–9623
12. Sarangi PP, Panda M, Mishra BP, Dehuri S (2016) An automated ear localization technique based on modified hausdorff distance. In: International conference on computer vision and image processing. Springer, pp 229–240
13. Shen L, Bai L, Fairhurst M (2007) Gabor wavelets and general discriminant analysis for face identification and verification. Image Vis Comput 25(5):553–563
14. Toygar Ö, Alqaralleh E, Afaneh A (2018) Symmetric ear and profile face fusion for identical twins and non-twins recognition. Signal Image Video Process 1–8
15. Toygar Ö, Alqaralleh E, Afaneh A (2020) On the use of ear and profile faces for distinguishing identical twins and non-twins. Expert Syst 37(1):e12389
16. University of Notre Dame Ear Database, Collection E and Collection J2. http://www.nd.edu/cvrl/CVRL/DataSets.html
17. Wang Z, Yang J, Zhu Y (2019) Review of ear biometrics. Arch Comput Methods Eng 1–32
18. Xu X, Mu Z (2007) Feature fusion method based on KCCA for ear and profile face based multimodal recognition. In: IEEE international conference on automation and logistics. IEEE, pp 620–623
19. Xu XN, Mu ZC, Yuan L (2007) Feature-level fusion method based on KFDA for multimodal recognition fusing ear and profile face. In: International conference on wavelet analysis and pattern recognition (ICWAPR), vol 3. IEEE, pp 1306–1310
20. Yaman D, Irem Eyiokur F, Kemal Ekenel H (2019) Multimodal age and gender classification using ear and profile face images. In: Proceedings of the IEEE conference on computer vision and pattern recognition workshops
21. Zou J, Ji Q, Nagy G (2007) A comparative study of local matching approach for face recognition. IEEE Trans Image Process 16(10):2617–2628

Computation And Communication Efficient Chinese Remainder Theorem Based Multi-Party Key Generation Using Modified RSA

Arjun Singh Rawat and Maroti Deshmukh

1 Introduction

In day-to-day life people are dealing with many remote applications related to two participants or multi-participant group conversation. These applications encapsulated with security advancement makes people conversationally reliable with security, but still, these applications are not reliable in terms of communication and computation cost, thus, many researchers also working on these. Inefficient communication and computation cost create congestion on a network and delay on a sender and receiver side as well. There are many key agreement and key generation schemes, which provide not only security but also efficient communication and computation. The key agreement protocol is a cryptographic scheme [1] that follows the process of exchanging public keys with each other by hiding the private key over an unsecured channel, after exchanging the public information the participants agree on the common session key and perform encryption and decryption process [2–4]. The process of the key exchange protocol based on two participants is shown in Fig. 1, where User-A shares its public key to User-B, in the same way User-B shares its public key to User-A. After exchanging the information both agree on a common session key for further process of encryption and decryption.

One of the common public-key cryptography based key agreement protocols is Diffie–Hellman key exchange, developed in 1976 [5]. This approach is not cost-effective in terms of computation cost taking huge time, but gives better security with the advancement of discrete logarithm problems, but with large key size, for

A. S. Rawat (✉) · M. Deshmukh
National Institute of Technology, Srinagar, Uttarakhand, India
e-mail: arjunsinghrawat005@gmail.com

M. Deshmukh
e-mail: marotideshmukh@nituk.ac.in

© The Author(s), under exclusive license to Springer Nature Singapore Pte Ltd. 2021
P. Stănică et al. (eds.), *Security and Privacy*, Lecture Notes in Electrical Engineering 744,
https://doi.org/10.1007/978-981-33-6781-4_3

Fig. 1 Key exchange
protocol

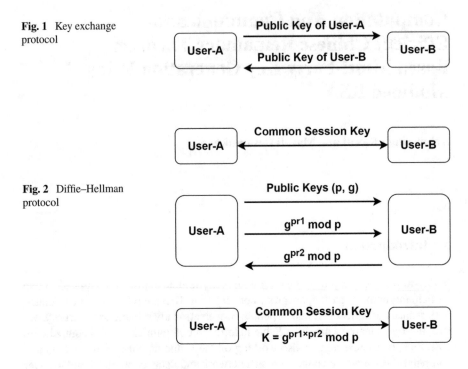

Fig. 2 Diffie–Hellman
protocol

breaking that algorithms at least requiring of polynomial time. The Diffie–Hellman key exchange is shown in Fig. 1, the process has the following steps:

1. User-A and User-B agree upon public keys as a large prime number p and generator or the primitive root g less than p.
2. Both User-A and User-B, respectively, generate the random private keys as pr_1 and pr_2 less than large prime p.
3. User-A shares the public key ($g^{pr_1} \bmod p$) to User-B.
4. User-B shares the public key ($g^{pr_2} \bmod p$) to User-A.
5. After sharing the public keys both users agree upon a common session key $K = (g^{pr_1 \times pr_2} \bmod p)$ (Fig. 2).

According to this approach, to identify the value of the common session key there should be a requirement of polynomial time because of the discrete logarithm problem, by applying the brute force attack there would be a need for exponential time to break. The key generation protocol is the public-key cryptography, the popular key generation protocol is RSA [6], widely used as secure data transmission, where the encrypted key is public and decrypted key different from the encrypted key is private. The protocol is shown in Fig. 3, the process in the following steps:

The algorithm steps are as follows for 2 participants:

1. There are two participants Q and R.
2. Let participant Q generates the two large random prime numbers n_1 and n_1, where their product evaluation as, $n = n_1 \times n_2$.

3. Now participant Q calculates the $\phi(n) = (n_1 - 1) \times (n_2 - 1)$.
4. Participant Q chooses the random public key e, where $1 < e < \phi(n)$ and gcd $(e, \phi(n)) = 1$.
5. Participant Q chooses the random private key d, where $1 < d < \phi(n)$ and $d \times e \equiv 1 \mod \phi(n)$.
6. Participant R, sends the message m in encrypted form to the participant Q as $c = (m^e \mod n)$, c is represented as cipher text.
7. Participant Q decrypts the cipher text as $(c^d \mod n)$ and retrieves the original message m.

There are many algorithms to speed up the process of the RSA algorithm, one of them is the Chinese remainder theorem, giving the unique solution to simultaneous congruences related to coprime modulo. The process of the Chinese remainder theorem as follows:

1. Let $p_1, \ldots, p_n$, are large prime numbers, be pairwise coprime $(\gcd(p_i, p_j) = 1$, whenever $i \neq j)$ to each other, and $1 \leq i, j \leq n$. The $pu_1, \ldots, pu_n$, are the random integers.
2. System of n equations of simultaneous congruences has a unique solution for $e \, modulo \, P$, where $P = p_1 \times p_2 \times \cdots \times p_n$.

$$e \equiv pu_1 \ (\mathrm{mod} \ p_1)$$

$$\ldots$$

$$e \equiv pu_n \ (\mathrm{mod} \ p_n)$$

3. Defining $a_j = P/p_j$ and $a'_j = a_j^{-1}(\mathrm{mod} \ p_j)$
4. The solution as follows: $e = \sum_{j=1}^{n} pu_j \times a_j \times a'_j(\mathrm{mod} \ P)$

The remaining paper as follows. Section 2, representing as a literature review of the group key agreement protocol. Section 3 represents the methodology of proposed work. Section 4 represents the experimental result and complexity analysis. Section 5 represents the conclusion of entire paper work.

2 Related Work

Rawat and Deshmukh [7] discussing the computation and communication efficient group key exchange protocol for low configuration system with minor degradation in security, the computation cost reduced by applying the modular multiplication instead of a modular exponential operation, for reducing the communication cost the approach used the divide and conquer approach, but still had a major issue in security.

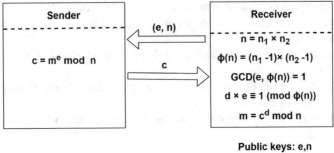

Fig. 3 Key generation as RSA

Mandal and Mohanty [8] discussed the multi-participant group key exchange protocol by achieving the perfect forward secrecy, the approach based on central authority as trusted third-party authority for managing the group operations. Michael et al. [9] discussed the improved Diffie–Hellman group key establishment protocol as well as comparative analysis on the basis of multiplication cost, exponentiation cost, and time complexity. Naresh and Murthy [10] discussed the optimized improved group Diffie–Hellman approach by comparing the number of rounds, number of messages, number of exponential operations. Murthy and Naresh [11] discussed the improved Diffie–Hellman key establishment protocol by any time sharing of multiple shared key with the help of case optimized complexity with polynomial time as well as the comparative analysis with Diffie–Hellman group key exchange protocol. Rawat and Deshmukh [12] discussing the common key generation for not only group but also small subgroups by applying the divide and conquer approach based on tree with the help of Elliptic curve Diffie–Hellman as well as proving the better security.

3 Proposed Model

The major problem with the existing approaches was they are less secure and inefficient in terms of computation and communication cost for multiple participants (group). The proposed approach is based on the client and server mechanism, providing secure communication, by applying modified RSA using the Chinese remainder theorem for group communication. The Chinese remainder theorem provides a common key for a group without violating the security in less computation cost and modified RSA providing secure communication for the group. The Chinese remainder theorem and modified RSA based multiple participants are described in two different phases as a common key generation for the group, group communication.

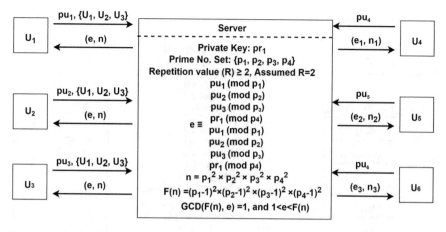

Fig. 4 Generating common key using multi-party modified RSA

3.1 Common Key Generation for the Group

In this phase, the algorithm is illustrated for the three participants as shown in Fig. 4. The common key generation for the group in the following steps:

1. There are six participants $U_1, U_2, U_3, U_4, U_5, U_6$, and a server S, out of which three participants U_1, U_2, U_3 sending the group request to the server S, by performing the multi-party RSA algorithm, U_4, U_5, U_6 are the individual users, performing the simple RSA algorithms for communication.

2. Participants U_1, U_2, U_3 send their public keys pu_1, pu_2, pu_3, respectively, along with group request $\{U_1, U_2, U_3\}$ to the Server S. The pu_4, pu_5, pu_6 are the public keys sent by the individual users U_4, U_5, U_6 to the Server S.

3. Server S separately generates the random private key pr_1 and prime numbers p_1, p_2, p_3, p_4. The server generates as many prime numbers as the number of participants in the group plus server. In the given illustration, the group size is 3, hence 4 prime numbers generated.

4. Server S performs the Chinese remainder theorem as $e \equiv pu_1 \bmod p_1$, $e \equiv pu_2 \bmod p_2$, $e \equiv pu_3 \bmod p_3$, $e \equiv pr_1 \bmod p_4$.

5. Repetition R, where $R > 1$, is for applying the Chinese remainder theorem repeatedly, assuming $R = 2$ (increased the value of R, reducing the threat of factorizing attack), then $e \equiv pu_1 \bmod p_1$, $e \equiv pu_2 \bmod p_2$, $e \equiv pu_3 \bmod p_3$, $e \equiv pr_1 \bmod p_4$, $e \equiv pu_1 \bmod p_1$, $e \equiv pu_2 \bmod p_2$, $e \equiv pu_3 \bmod p_3$, $e \equiv pr_1 \bmod p_4$.

6. Server S, multiplying all random prime numbers, including repeated prime numbers as $n = p_1 \times p_2 \times p_3 \times p_4 \times p_1 \times p_2 \times p_3 \times p_4$.

7. Server S shares the common public-key pair (e, n) to the participants U_1, U_2, U_3. The public-key pairs (e_1, n_1), (e_2, n_2), (e_3, n_3), respectively, are shared with the individual users U_4, U_5, U_6, respectively.

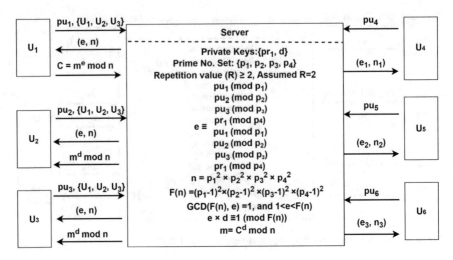

Fig. 5 Group communication using multi-party modified RSA

3.2 Group Communication

In this phase, after getting the common key, the group communication is performed as shown in Fig. 5. The group communication is illustrated in the following steps:

1. Server S separately generates the $F(n) = (p_1 - 1) \times (p_2 - 1) \times (p_3 - 1) \times (p_4 - 1) \times (p_1 - 1) \times (p_2 - 1) \times (p_3 - 1) \times (p_4 - 1)$.
2. If $\gcd(F(n), e) \equiv 1$ and $1 < e < F(n)$ then only the next step is followed, otherwise change the value of pr_1 again, until we get $\gcd(F(n), e) \equiv 1$ and $1 < e < F(n)$.
3. Server S calculates the private key d by satisfying the constraint as $d \times e \equiv 1 \mod F(n)$.
4. If any participant of a group $\{U_1, U_2, U_3\}$ wants to share a message m to the group, firstly, that message is shared in encrypted form to the server S as $C = m^e \mod n$.
5. Later, the server S decrypts the cipher text as $m = C^d \mod n$, and shares that decrypted message m in encrypted form as $m^d \mod n$ to the group's participants U_2 and U_3.

4 Performance Analysis

In performance analysis, we are comparing the proposed approach with the existing approaches in relation to group key generation with the parameters such as rounds, message, multiplication, exponentiation as shown in Table 1, where the proposed approach has a zero exponential operation, making it more computation efficient than all other existing approaches, as the computation cost of exponentiation operation is

Table 1 Complexity analysis

Approach	Rounds	Messages	Multiplication	Exponentiation	Time complexity
Michael et al. [9]	$k+1$	$2k-1$	–	$5k-6$	$O(k)$
Naresh and Murthy [10]	$k+1$	$k+1$	–	k	$O(k)$
Murthy and Naresh [11]	1	$2k$	k^2	k^2	$O(k^2)$
Mandal and Mohanty [8]	$k+1$	$k+1$	–	k	$O(k)$
Rawat and Deshmukh [7]	$\log_2(k)+1$	$2k-2$	$2\log k+c$	–	$O(k)$
Proposed approach	2	$2k$	$2Rk+1$	–	$O(R)$

dominant over multiplication. The proposed approach's multiplication cost, $2Rk + 1$, is a little bit more expensive than some of the existing approaches, where k is the number of participants in a group and R is the number of repetitions applied in the proposed approach. The number of messages interchanged is $2k$, which is almost equivalent to the existing approaches. The number of rounds required by this approach is 2, more efficient than the existing approaches. The time complexity of this new approach is also more efficient than all, taking $O(R)$ as unit cost.

5 Conclusion and Future Scope

The proposed approach is Chinese remainder theorem based multi-party key generation using modified RSA protocol. The Chinese remainder theorem provided a common key for the group without violating the security in less computation cost and modified RSA provided the secure communication for the group. The approach is computation and communication efficient for generating the common key for the group, because there is no use of modular exponentiation operation in key generation, only by applying the modular multiplication operation we make the approach computationally efficient. The key generation of a group is more suitable for a low configuration system, because there is no expensive operation. In complexity analysis, we found that our approach is giving better results in exponentiation, time complexity, rounds, a little bit expensive in multiplication cost, and equivalent performance in message transmission than the existing approach making it a communication-efficient protocol. The approach is giving much security than other existing approaches and is also very helpful for the low configuration system in terms of key generation of a group. The modified RSA reduced the threat of the factoring attack as the repetition R value is increased. The major limitation of the approach is that it is not suitable for a low configuration system when communication starts, because it uses expensive modular exponential operations for encryption and decryption, but it provided better security for the group. In the future we will also improve the computation cost in the communication phase with equal security.

References

1. Boyd C, Mathuria A (2013) Protocols for authentication and key establishment. Springer Science and Business Media
2. Forouzan BA, Mukhopadhyay D (2011) Cryptography and network security (Sie). McGraw-Hill Education
3. Stallings W (2006) Cryptography and network security, 4/E. Pearson Education India
4. Stinson DR (2005) Cryptography: theory and practice. Chapman and Hall/CRC
5. Diffie W, Hellman M (1976) New directions in cryptography. IEEE Trans Inform Theory 22(6):644–654
6. Khatarkar S, Kamble R (2015) A survey and performance analysis of various RSA based encryption techniques. Int J Comput Appl 114(7)
7. Rawat AS, Deshmukh M (2019) Efficient extended diffie-hellman key exchange protocol. In International conference on computing. power and communication technologies (GUCON). IEEE
8. Mandal S, Mohanty S (2014) Multi-party key-exchange with perfect forward secrecy. In 2014 international conference on information technology. IEEE
9. Michael S, Tsudik G, Michael W (1996) Diffie-Hellman key distribution extended to group communication. In Proceedings of the 3rd ACM conference on computer and communications security
10. Naresh VS, Murthy NVES (2010) Diffie-Hellman technique extended to efficient and simpler group key distribution protocol. Int J Comput Appl 4(11):1–5
11. Murthy NVES, Naresh VS (2010) Extended diffie-Hellman technique to generate multiple shared keys at a time with reduced keos and its polynomial time complexity. IJCSI Int J Comput Sci Issues 7
12. Rawat A, Deshmukh M (2020) Tree and elliptic curve based efficient and secure group key agreement protocol. J Inform Secur Appl 55:102599

Efficient Random Grid Visual Cryptographic Schemes having Essential Members

Bibhas Chandra Das, Md Kutubuddin Sardar, and Avishek Adhikari

1 Introduction

The essence of visual cryptography is that the encryption of a visual secret is done in such a way that the reconstruction can be performed only via sight-reading. So one can easily conclude that visual cryptography does not require many sophisticated cryptographic techniques like polynomial based secret image sharing [18–20, 26], yet it produces strong schemes for many practical scenarios. For this reason, throughout time many researchers have developed a strong interest in this specific area of cryptography.

The seminal paper by Naor and Shamir [17] is considered as the starting point of the (k, n)-visual cryptographic scheme. They proposed a way to distribute a secret image S among n members, where any k (or more) of them can superimpose their shares to reconstruct S. Obviously, the reconstruction comes with loss of contrast but still it is human readable. Then in 2017 Arungam et. al. [16] extended the idea of (k, n)-VCS to incorporate one essential member. This work was further extended by Sabyasachi et. al. [9] by extending it to a $(t, k, n)^*$-VCS, with t essential members. Some notable works on classical VCS may be found in [1–8, 10–14, 27, 29].

A thorough study of the literature will suggest that at the very initial stage the works in this area experienced huge pixel expansion with very little contrast. Researchers engaged themselves to deal with this problem and introduced the best solution,

B. Chandra Das
Institute for Advancing Intelligence (IAI), TCG CREST, Kolkata, India
e-mail: bibhas.iitm@gmail.com

M. K. Sardar
Department of Pure Mathematics University of Calcutta, Kolkata, India
e-mail: mks.pubm@gmail.com

A. Adhikari (✉)
Department of Mathematics, Presidency University, Kolkata, India
e-mail: avishek.adh@gmail.com

© The Author(s), under exclusive license to Springer Nature Singapore Pte Ltd. 2021
P. Stănică et al. (eds.), *Security and Privacy*, Lecture Notes in Electrical Engineering 744,
https://doi.org/10.1007/978-981-33-6781-4_4

namely Random Grid Visual Cryptography (RGVCS). In RGVCS, there is no pixel expansion and we can reach the optimal level for contrast. The basic idea of RGVCS is that each pixel of the secret image here is considered to be a random grid with an associated color. The literature study of RGVCS can be found in [15, 22, 24, 25].

In this paper, we have proposed a (t, k, n) scheme for black and white RGVCS for both "OR" and "XOR" models. Besides constructing the scheme, we have described the closed forms of the corresponding light contrasts. We have deviated a bit from the traditional "OR" operation to "XOR" operation with a motif of increasing the light contrast. The only thing that we have to keep in mind for the scheme with the "XOR" operation is that the reconstruction will no longer be visual. The experimental results presented indicate the efficiency of our proposed schemes.

The rest of the paper is organized as follows. We have started with Sect. 2 to describe the notations and basic concepts of VCS as well as RGVCS which we will need for construction and security analysis of our proposed scheme. In Sect. 3, we have given the construction of schemes with detailed theoretical security analysis. Section 4 deals with the experimental results to justify the theoretical results that we proved for analyzing the security of our scheme. Also, we have performed a comparison of the light contrast of our scheme with that of the modified versions of the schemes that are already proposed. The theoretical study together with the experimental results shows the significance of our scheme in the area of RGVCS. The paper concludes with Sect. 5, where we have pointed out the future direction of research.

2 Preliminaries

This section presents the notations that we will widely use to describe our proposed schemes. To start with let us assume a secret pixel S is to be shared among a set of n members, $\mathscr{P} = \{M_1, M_2, \ldots, M_n\}$. By Γ_{Qual}, we will denote the collection of all subsets of $\mathscr{P}$ who are eligible to reconstruct S by superimposing their shares. On the other hand, Γ_{Forb} denotes the collection of all those subsets of $\mathscr{P}$ who are not eligible to reconstruct S. Elements of Γ_{Qual} are called qualified set while elements of Γ_{Forb} are called forbidden set. The ordered pair $(\Gamma_{\text{Qual}}, \Gamma_{\text{Forb}})$ is called an access structure for $\mathscr{P}$ corresponding to S. Now a given access structure is called monotone when Γ_{Qual} is monotone increasing and Γ_{Forb} is monotone decreasing. For such an access structure, Minimal Qualified set and Maximal Forbidden set are defined as $\Gamma_0 = \{A \in \Gamma_{\text{Qual}} | A' \notin \Gamma_{\text{Qual}}, \forall A' \subset A\}$, $Z_M = \{B \in \Gamma_{\text{Forb}} | B \cup \{i\} \in \Gamma_{\text{Qual}}, \forall i \in \mathscr{P} \setminus B\}$. These two sets are, respectively, denoted by Γ_0 and Z_M. For our schemes, we talk about a special kind members, namely essential members. A member $a \in \mathscr{P}$ is said to be essential if there exists $X \subseteq \mathscr{P}$ such that $X \cup \{a\} \in \Gamma_{\text{Qual}}$ but $X \notin \Gamma_{\text{Qual}}$. The notation of a (k, n) threshold access structure is adapted from [24]. For our purpose, we have incorporated the idea of essential members with the notation of a (k, n) threshold access structure and have defined (t, k, n) access structure. By that, we mean that it is a (k, n) access structure where t of the n members are essential. Clearly enough, the values of the parameters for which $0 \leq t \leq k \leq n$ admit a meaningful (t, k, n) visual cryptographic scheme. Note that in such an access structure, a maximal forbidden set may be of the two types. Type I: Sets containing $k - 1$ members including all the essential members. Type II: Sets having a size exactly $n - 1$ which contains all but one of the t essential members.

Now the notations related to grid based VCS are adapted from [24]. We have considered a binary transparency Y in which each pixel is either transparent (0) or opaque (1). Generally, the value of each pixel is determined by a coin flip where it is assumed that probability of $y = 0$ is λ. Keeping in mind the fact that the pixel with $y = 0$ lets through light and the pixel with $y = 1$ stops it, the light transmission of y, denoted by $t(y)$, is defined to be $Pr(y = 0)$. The light transmission of a random grid, denoted by $\mathcal{T}(Y)$, is λ when $t(y) = \lambda$ for each pixel $y \in Y$ [24]. From this definition of light transmission, we can observe that for a random grid X with $\mathcal{T}(X) = \lambda$, $X \otimes X$ is a random grid with $\mathcal{T}(X \otimes X) = \mathcal{T}(X) = \lambda$. Also for two independent random grids with $\mathcal{T}(X) = \lambda_1$ and $\mathcal{T}(Y) = \lambda_2$, we have $\mathcal{T}(X \otimes Y) = \lambda_1 \lambda_2$. With this setting in our hand, we can now define the formal model of a (t, k, n) random grid based visual cryptographic scheme.

Notation: As in [21], let $S(0)$ $(S(1))$ denote the area of all of the transparent (opaque) pixels in the secret image S, i.e., (u, v)th pixel $S[u, v]$ of the secret S is in $S(0)$ $(S(1))$ if and only if $S[u, v] = 0$ $(S[u, v] = 1)$ where $S = S(0) \cup S(1)$ and $S(0) \cap S(1) = \emptyset$. Likewise, we denote the area of pixels in random grid G corresponding to $S(0)(S(1))$ by $G[S(0)]$ $(G[S(1)])$, i.e., (u, v)th pixel $G[u, v]$ of the random grid G is in $G[S(0)]$ $(G[S(1)])$ if and only if $G[u, v]$'s corresponding pixel $S[u, v]$ is in $S(0)(S(1))$. Needless to mention, $G = G[S(0)] \cup G[S(1)]$ and $G[S(0)] \cap G[S(1)] = \emptyset$.

Definition 1 For valid parameters t, k and n, an $H' \times W$ binary secret image S and set of n members the set of random grids $\mathcal{G} = \{G_1, G_2, \ldots, G_n\}$ forms an "OR" based (t, k, n)-RGVCS if:

1. $\mathcal{T}(G_v) = \frac{1}{2}$ for all $1 \leq v \leq n$.
2. For each $F = \{M_{u_1}, M_{u_2}, \ldots, M_{u_p}\} \in \mathcal{F}, \mathcal{T}(G^F[S(0)]) = \mathcal{T}(G^F[S(1)])$, where $G^F = G_{u_1} \otimes G_{u_2} \otimes \cdots \otimes G_{u_p}$, i.e., $t(G^F[u, v] \mid S[u, v] = 0) = t(G^F[u, v] \mid S[u, v] = 1), \forall u, v$.
3. For $Q \in \Gamma_0, \mathcal{T}(G^Q[S(0)]) > \mathcal{T}(G^Q[S(1)])$ where $G^Q = G_1 \otimes G_2 \otimes \cdots \otimes G_q$, i.e., $t(G^Q[u, v] \mid S[u, v] = 0) > t(G^Q[u, v] \mid S[u, v] = 1), \forall u, v$.

Definition 2 The light contrast for any given set $H \subseteq \mathcal{P}$, denoted as α_{OR}^H, is defined as $\alpha_{OR}^H = \mathcal{T}(G^H[S(0)]) - \mathcal{T}(G^H[S(1)])$.

3 Proposed Scheme

In this section, we propose an efficient (t, k, n)-RGVCS for both monotone and non-monotone access structures. We will first start with describing the constructions and then discuss their light corresponding light transmission. To our knowledge, this is the first ever (t, k, n)-RGVCS.

3.1 Construction

For a secret $H' \times W$ binary image S, the dealer first constructs the shares for the members and distributes them in the following manner.

- The dealer first identifies the essential members and marks them as $M_1, M_2, \ldots,$ M_t. The rest of the members are marked as $M_{t+1}, M_{t+2}, \ldots, M_{n-1}, M_n$.
- For each secret pixel $S[u, v]$ of S, the dealer selects $k - 1 - t$ members randomly from $M_{t+1}, M_{t+2}, \ldots, M_{n-1}$, and together with $M_1, M_2, \ldots, M_t$ form a set A of size $k - 1$.
- The dealer assigns 0 or 1 random grids to the members of A.
- For the remaining members the share is generated as $g(s, x) = s \oplus x,$ for $s, x \in \{0, 1\}$, where $\oplus$ denotes binary "XOR" operation.

Algorithm 1 is the detailed construction of the share generation phase of our proposed scheme.

Algorithm 1: Algorithm toward constructing a (t, k, n)-RGVCS

Input: A black and white secret image S of size $H' \times W$, and the access structure (t, k, n) with meaningful triplet (t, k, n) and set $\mathcal{P}$ of n members.

Output: n shares $G_1, G_2, \ldots, G_n$ each of size $H' \times W$.

1 From the set $\mathcal{P}$ of n members, select the t essential members. Denote them as $M_1, M_2, \ldots, M_t$. Denote the remaining members as $M_{t+1}, M_{t+2}, \ldots, M_{n-1}, M_n$.

2 **for** $(u = 1; u \leq H'; u + +)$ **do**

3   **for** $(v = 1; v \leq W; v + +)$ **do**

4   Generate $(k - 1)$ random grids $r_1[u, v], r_2[u, v], \ldots, r_{k-1}[u, v]$

5   Randomly select $k - t - 1$ members, say $M_{l_1}, M_{l_2}, \ldots, M_{l_{k-t-1}}$ from $\{M_{t+1}, M_{t+2}, \ldots, M_{n-1}\}$. Let

       $A = \{M_1, M_2, \ldots, M_t, M_{l_1}, M_{l_2}, \ldots, M_{l_{k-t-1}}\}$

       Construct $b_1[u, v], b_2[u, v], \ldots, b_k[u, v]$ as

6             $b_1[u, v] = r_1[u, v]$

            $b_p[u, v] = g(r_p[u, v], b_{p-1}[u, v]) \; \forall p = 2, 3, \ldots, k - 1$

            $b_k[u, v] = g(S[u, v], b_{k-1}[u, v])$

7   **for** $(q = 1; q \leq t; q + +)$ **do**

8           $G_q[u, v] \leftarrow r_q[u, v]$

9   **end**

10   **for** $(q = 1; q \leq k - t - 1; q + +)$ **do**

11          $G_{l_q}[u, v] \leftarrow r_{t+q}[u, v]$

12   **end**

13       $G_s[u, v] \leftarrow b_k[u, v]$, for all $s \in \{1, 2, \ldots, n\} \setminus \{1, 2, \ldots, t, l_1, l_2, \ldots, l_{k-t-1}\}$.

14   **end**

15 **end**

16 Member M_i is given the share $G_i, i = 1, 2, \ldots, n$.

Now in the secret reconstruction phase, the member can adapt one of the following two methods:

1. Either they can superimpose their shares to reconstruct the secret image. The way the random grid is defined superimposition corresponds to classical "OR" operation. Algorithm 1 together with this type of secret reconstruction gives us a scheme for strong monotone access structure.

2. On the other hand, if the members can provide some computational power they can use "XOR" operation in the place of "OR" operation. Algorithm 1 together with this type of secret reconstruction gives us a scheme for non-monotone access structure.

3.2 Discussion on Light Transmission

Now we will prove theoretically that the proposed scheme is a valid (t, k, n) scheme by showing that it satisfies the conditions of Definition 1.

Before going to the direct proof we will start by proving three lemmas which in turn will take us to the final conclusion.

Lemma 1 *The light transmission* $\mathscr{T}(G_u) = \dfrac{1}{2}$ *for* $1 \leq u \leq n$.

Proof Note that each G_i is either a random grid or constructed by applying f on $k - 1$ random grids. In both the cases, the randomness is not hampered. $\blacksquare$

Lemma 2 *For a given* (t, k, n)-RGVCS, *let* F *be a maximal forbidden set of members. Then* $\mathscr{T}(G^F[S(0)]) = \mathscr{T}(G^F[S(1)])$, *where* G^F *is obtained by applying any reconstruction function "OR" or "XOR" on* $G_{l_1}, G_{l_2}, \ldots, G_{l_m}$.

Proof First of all, let us denote the two types of maximal forbidden sets that we mentioned earlier as Type I and Type II sets, respectively. One can now easily observe that the Type I sets are nothing but the sets of size $\leq k - 1$ of a (k, k)-scheme. The light transmission of this set depends on the choice of A. The length of the intersection of A and F can vary from t to $k - 2$ when $M_n \in F$. But when $M_n \notin F$ the the length of intersection can vary from t to $k - 1$. If we consider the classical "OR" reconstruction then the total light transmission of F is given as $t(G^F[u, v] \mid S[u, v] = 0) =$

$$t(G^F[u, v] \mid S[u, v] = 1) = \frac{1}{\binom{n-1-t}{k-1-t}} \left[\sum_{h=t}^{k-2} \frac{\binom{k-2-t}{h-t} \times \binom{n-k+1}{k-1-h}}{2^{h+1}} \right], \text{ if } M_n \in F$$

$$= \frac{1}{\binom{n-1-t}{k-1-t}} \left[\frac{1}{2^{k-1}} + \sum_{h=t}^{k-2} \frac{\binom{k-1-t}{h-t} \times \binom{n-k}{k-1-h}}{2^{h+1}} \right], \text{ if } M_n \notin F.$$

But for Type II sets, their behavior does not vary for different choices of $\mathscr{A}$. So for them the light transmission will be

$$t(G^F[u, v] \mid S[u, v] = 0) = \frac{1}{2^{k-1}} = t(G^F[u, v] \mid S[u, v] = 1).$$

The same type of calculation follows for "XOR" operation. $\blacksquare$

Lemma 3 *For a given* (t, k, n)-RGVCS, *let* Q *be a minimal qualified set of members. Then* $\mathscr{T}(G^Q[S(0)]) > \mathscr{T}(G^Q[S(1)])$, *where* G^Q *is obtained by applying any reconstruction function "OR" or "XOR" on* $G_{l_1}, G_{l_2}, \cdots, G_{l_k}$.

Proof We will proceed again here as in the previous lemma. Here $\mid Q \cap A \mid$ can vary from t to $k - 1$. So depending on number of different choices of $\mathscr{A}$ for classical reconstruction method "OR" the light transmission for Q is

$$t(G^Q[u, v] \mid S[u, v] = 0) = \frac{1}{\binom{n-1-t}{k-1-t}} \left[\frac{1}{2^{k-1}} + \sum_{h=t}^{k-2} \frac{\binom{k-1-t}{h-t} \times \binom{n-k}{k-1-h}}{2^{h+1}} \right], \text{ if } M_n \in Q$$

$$= \frac{1}{\binom{n-1-t}{k-1-t}} \left[\frac{k-t}{2^{k-1}} + \sum_{h=t}^{k-2} \frac{\binom{k-t}{h-t} \times \binom{n-1-k}{k-1-h}}{2^{h+1}} \right], \text{ if } M_n \notin Q.$$

$$\text{And } t\,(G^Q[u,v] \mid S[u,v] = 1) = \frac{1}{\binom{n-1-t}{k-1-t}} \left[\sum_{h=t}^{k-2} \frac{\binom{k-1-t}{h-t} \times \binom{n-k}{k-1-h}}{2^{h+1}} \right], \text{ if } M_n \in Q$$

$$= \frac{1}{\binom{n-1-t}{k-1-t}} \left[\sum_{h=t}^{k-2} \frac{\binom{k-t}{h-t} \times \binom{n-1-k}{k-1-h}}{2^{h+1}} \right], \text{ if } M_n \notin Q.$$

Subtracting this two we get the light contrast for Q as $\alpha_{OR}^Q = \frac{1}{\binom{n-1-t}{k-1-t}} \cdot \frac{1}{2^{k-1}}$, $M_n \in Q$, and $\alpha_{OR}^Q = \frac{1}{\binom{n-1-t}{k-1-t}} \cdot \frac{k-t}{2^{k-1}}$, $M_n \notin Q$. Now to conclude the theorem we notice that the validity condition $k > t$ makes the light contrast a strictly positive quantity. Similar arguments can be followed to show that for "XOR" reconstruction the light contrast becomes exactly 1. Now we are in good shape two state the following results:

Theorem 1 *Let S be a secret image. Then for a (t, k, n) threshold access structure our scheme in Algorithm 1 gives a (t, k, n)-RGVCS with light contrast for a minimal qualified set:*

$$\alpha_{OR}^Q = \frac{1}{\binom{n-1-t}{k-1-t}} \cdot \frac{1}{2^{k-1}}, \text{ if } M_n \in Q, \text{ and } \alpha_{OR}^Q = \frac{1}{\binom{n-1-t}{k-1-t}} \cdot \frac{k-t}{2^{k-1}}, \text{ if } M_n \notin Q \text{ for}$$

classical "OR" reconstruction method and exactly 1 for "XOR" -based reconstruction method.

Proof From Lemmas 1–3, the proof is very much obvious.

The following table shows a practical example for the calculations we have just described theoretically.

Now in a nutshell the security of our proposed scheme is given in form of the following theorem.

Theorem 2 *Let S be a secret image and n be the number of members, t of them are essential. Let the threshold value be k. Then our scheme produces a (t, k, n)-RGVCS. If $\bar{\alpha}_{OR}^Q$ denotes the light contrast of a minimal qualified set $Q \subseteq \mathcal{P}$ then $\bar{\alpha}_{OR}^Q$ is given by $\bar{\alpha}_{OR}^Q = \frac{1}{\binom{n-t}{k-1-t}} \cdot \frac{1}{2^{k-1}}$ for classical "OR" reconstruction and 1 for "XOR" reconstruction method.*

3.3 Comparison Among the Schemes Proposed by Wu and Sun [28] and Shyu [23]

To the best of our knowledge, our proposed (t, k, n)-random grid visual crypto-graphic scheme for black and white images is the first proposed scheme in the literature of visual cryptography for essential access structures. That is why, it is not possible for us to have a direct comparison with the existing schemes. However, as particular cases, we can construct (t, k, n)-RGVCS, from the random grid based schemes for general access structures. In this section, we are comparing our proposed Algorithm 1 with the customized schemes, obtained as a particular case from general access structures proposed in [23, 28]. To the best of our knowledge, these schemes are the most efficient schemes that exist in the literature for general access structures.

The following theorem is obtained if we apply the scheme proposed in [28] on the essential access structure for (t, k, n):

Theorem 3 (customized from *[28]*) *For an essential (t, k, n) access structure with a given black and white secret image S and valid parameters t, k, and n, the scheme described in [28] produces a (t, k, n)-RGVCS with light contrast:*

$$\alpha_w = \frac{1}{\binom{n-t}{k-t}} \cdot \frac{1}{2^{k-1}}.$$

Analogously, we can obtain the following theorem, if we apply the scheme pro-posed by Shyu [23] on the essential access structure for valid parameters $t, k,$ and n:

Theorem 4 (customized from *[23]*) *For an essential (t, k, n) access structure with a black and white secret image S along with the valid parameters t, k, and n, the scheme described in [23] generates a (t, k, n)-RGVCS with light contrast: $\alpha_s = \frac{1}{2^{\mathcal{K}}}$,*

where $\mathcal{K} = 1 + \sum_{h=t}^{k-1} \binom{k-t}{h-t} \binom{n-k}{k-h} h.$

Remark 1 Note that the light contrast for our proposed scheme is better than that of the schemes proposed in [23, 28]. Numerical evidence as shown in Table 1 demon-strates that our scheme performs better in terms of light contrast than the existing schemes.

Table 1 Calculation of the light contrast with access structure (2, 4, 6)-RGVCS. Here, $n_2(A)$ and $n_3(A)$ denote, respectively, the number of choices of A for which $|H \cap A|$ is 2 and 3.

Set of members: H	$n_2(A)$	$n_3(A)$	$\mathcal{T}(G^H[S(0)])$	$\mathcal{T}(G^H[S(1)])$	α_{OR}^H
$\{M_1, M_2, M_3\}$	2	1	0.2500	0.2500	0.0000
$\{M_1, M_2, M_6\}$	3	0	0.2500	0.2500	0.0000
$\{M_2, M_3, M_4, M_5, M_6\}$	3	0	0.2500	0.2500	0.0000
$\{M_1, M_2, M_3, M_4\}$	1	2	0.1670	0.0830	0.0830
$\{M_1, M_2, M_3, M_6\}$	2	1	0.2080	0.1670	0.0420

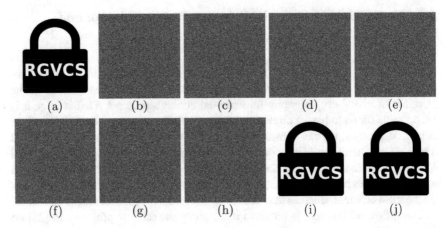

Fig. 1 The results for (2, 3, 5)-XRGVCS are implied. Here **(a)** the secret. stands for the random grid **(b)** G_1, **(c)** G_2, **(d)** G_3, **(e)** G_4, **(f)** G_5. The stacked images **(g)** $G_1 \oplus G_2$, **(h)** $G_1 \oplus G_2 \oplus G_3 \oplus G_4$, **(i)** $G_1 \oplus G_2 \oplus G_3 \oplus G_4 \oplus G_5$, **(j)** $G_1 \oplus G_2 \oplus G_3$, where the operation "$\oplus$" represents binary "XOR"

Remark 2 From the construction of our scheme, it is clear that we are doing nothing but repeated application of (k, k) scheme. So, to start with, we put $t = 0, k = n$ in our construction as described in Algorithm 1 and apply "XOR" operation in the secret reconstruction phase to get the following theorem.

4 Experiment and Discussions

In this section, we have shown the experimental as well as simulation results to validate our theoretical results. Before we proceed, let us first fix up few notations. Corresponding to an essential (t, k, n) access structure with valid parameters t, k, and n, let us denote $\mathcal{R}$ to be the set of all n random grids that are generated through the proposed Algorithm 1. Let $H \subseteq \mathcal{R}$ be such that $1 \leq h(=| H |) \leq n$. Python code is being used for experimental verification. The analytic light contrasts α_{OR}^H and α_{XOR}^H are compared in Tables 4 and 5. The comparison table of numerical values as

Table 2 Table of comparisons: proposed "OR"- and "XOR" -based schemes (See Fig. 3)

Access structures	OR		XOR	
	In	Out	In	Out
Q0: (1, 2, 3)	0.5000	0.5000	1.0000	1.0000
Q1: (1, 2, 4)	0.5000	0.5000	1.0000	1.0000
Q2: (1, 2, 5)	0.5000	0.5000	1.0000	1.0000
Q3: (1, 3, 4)	0.1250	0.2500	0.5000	1.0000
Q4: (1, 3, 5)	0.0830	0.1670	0.3330	0.6670
Q5: (1, 3, 6)	0.0630	0.1250	0.2500	0.5000
Q6: (1, 4, 5)	0.0420	0.1250	0.3330	1.0000
Q7: (1, 4, 6)	0.0210	0.0630	0.1670	0.5000
Q8: (2, 3, 4)	0.2500	0.2500	1.0000	1.0000
Q9: (2, 3, 5)	0.2500	0.2500	1.0000	1.0000
Q10: (2, 3, 6)	0.2500	0.2500	1.0000	1.0000
Q11: (2, 4, 5)	0.0630	0.1250	0.5000	1.0000
Q12: (2, 4, 6)	0.0420	0.0830	0.3330	0.6670
Q13: (3, 4, 5)	0.1250	0.1250	1.0000	1.0000
Q14: (3, 5, 6)	0.0310	0.0630	0.5000	1.0000
Q15: (3, 6, 7)	0.0100	0.0310	0.3330	1.0000

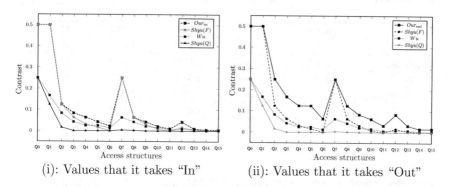

(i): Values that it takes "In"   (ii): Values that it takes "Out"

Fig. 2 (i) and (ii) display the graphical representation of simulation data from the Table 1

well as the graphical representations of light contrast of our scheme with that of the already proposed general access structures restricted to customized (t, k, n) scenario are shown in Tables 1 and 2 and in Figs. 2 and 3 (Fig. 1 and Table 3).

The theoretical results α_{XOR}^{H} and the related experimental results $e\alpha_{XOR}^{H}$ and their differences are summarized in Table 5. Note that for each cases, $\alpha_{XOR}^{H} - e\alpha_{XOR}^{H} < 0.004$. This explains why the experimental outputs of the light contrast are very similar to the analytical values.

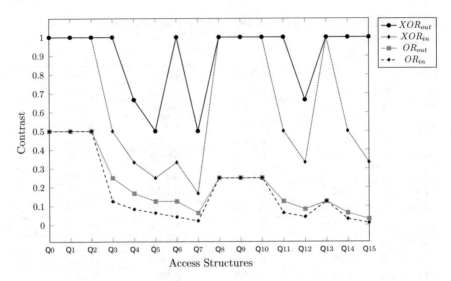

Fig. 3 Graphical representation of values, as shown in Table 2, for our "OR"- and "XOR"-based schemes

Table 3 Comparison of contrasts for different access structures (1, 2, 4) (See Fig. 4)

Set of members	Shyu (Q)	Shyu (F)	Wu	Our	
				In	Out
S0: $\{M_1\}$	0.0000	0.0000	0.0000	0.0000	0.0000
S1: $\{M_1, M_2\}$	0.1250	0.5000	0.1670	0.5000	1.0000
S2: $\{M_1, M_4\}$	0.1250	0.5000	0.1670	0.5000	1.0000
S3: $\{M_1, M_2, M_3\}$	0.1250	0.5000	0.1670	0.5000	NS
S4: $\{M_1, M_2, M_4\}$	0.1250	0.5000	0.1670	0.5000	NA
S5: $\{M_1, M_2, M_3, M_4\}$	0.1250	0.5000	0.1250	0.5000	NA

Table 4 The proposed (1, 2, 4)-RGVCS

Set of members: H	α_{OR}^H	$e\alpha_{OR}^H$	α_{XOR}^H	$e\alpha_{XOR}^H$
$\{M_1, M_2\}$	0.5000	0.5004	1.0000	1.0000
$\{M_1, M_4\}$	0.5000	0.5004	1.0000	1.0000
$\{M_2, M_3\}$	0.000	0.0000	0.0000	0.0000
$\{M_1, M_2, M_3\}$	0.5000	0.5000	NA	NA
$\{M_1, M_2, M_4\}$	0.5000	0.5000	NA	NA
$\{M_2, M_3, M_4\}$	0.0000	0.0000	NA	NA
$\{M_1, M_2, M_3, M_4\}$	0.5000	0.5004	NA	NA

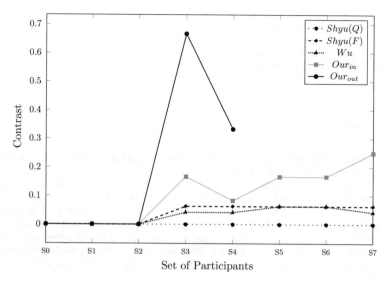

Fig. 4 (1, 2, 4)-RGVCS (See Table 3)

Table 5 The proposed (2, 3, 5)-RGVCS

Set of members: H	α_{OR}^{H}	$e\alpha_{OR}^{H}$	α_{XOR}^{H}	$e\alpha_{XOR}^{H}$
$\{M_1, M_2\}$	0.0000	0.0004	0.0000	0.0003
$\{M_1, M_2, M_3\}$	0.2500	0.2495	1.0000	1.0000
$\{M_1, M_2, M_5\}$	0.2500	0.2495	1.0000	1.0000
$\{M_2, M_3, M_4\}$	0.0000	0.0002	0.0000	0.0007
$\{M_1, M_2, M_3, M_4\}$	0.2500	0.2495	NA	NA
$\{M_1, M_2, M_3, M_5\}$	0.2500	0.2495	NA	NA
$\{M_2, M_3, M_4, M_5\}$	0.0000	0.0002	NA	NA
$\{M_1, M_2, M_3, M_4, M_5\}$	0.2500	0.2495	NA	NA

5 Conclusion

This paper puts forward efficient direct constructions of both "OR"- and "XOR"-based (t, k, n) schemes for random grid visual cryptographic schemes for black and white images. In the paper, we provide closed forms of light contrasts for both "OR" and "XOR" models. Our theoretical as well as experimental simulated results show that our algorithms work efficiently. As a a challenging future research work in the field of RGVCS, we will consider the problem of obtaining closed forms of the optimal light contrasts for both "OR" and "XOR" based VCSs for (t, k, n) access structure.

Acknowledgements The second author is thankful to the Council of Scientific and Industrial Research (CSIR), Government of India for providing financial support (Award No.09/028(0975)/ 2016-EMR-1). The research of the third author is partially supported by DST-SERB Project MATRICS vide Sanction Order: MTR/2019/001573.

References

1. Adhikari A, Sikdar S (2003) A new $(2, n)$-color visual threshold scheme for color images, INDOCRYPT'03. Lecture Notes in Computer Science. vol 2904. Springer, pp 148–161
2. Adhikari A, Bose M (2004) A new visual cryptographic scheme using latin squares. IEICE Trans Fundam Electron Commun Comput Sci 87(5):1198–1202
3. Adhikari A, Dutta TK, Roy BK (2004) A new black and white visual cryptographic scheme for general access structures. In: Progress in cryptology—INDOCRYPT 2004, 5th international conference on cryptology in India, Chennai, India, 20–22 Dec 2004, Proceedings, pp 399–413
4. Adhikari A, Bose M, Kumar D, Roy BK (2007) Applications of partially balanced incomplete block designs in developing $(2, n)$ visual cryptographic schemes. IEICE Trans 90-A(5):949–951
5. Adhikari A (2014) Linear algebraic techniques to construct monochrome visual cryptographic schemes for general access structure and its applications to color images. Des Codes Cryptogr 73(3):865–895
6. Adhikari MR, Adhikari A (2014) Basic modern algebra with applications. Springer
7. Blundo C, Bonis AD, Santis AD (2001) Improved schemes for visual cryptography. Des Codes Cryptogr 24(3):255–278
8. Blundo C, De Santis A, Stinson DR (1999) On the contrast in visual cryptography schemes. J Cryptol 12(4):261–289
9. Dutta S, Adhikari A (2014) XOR based non-monotone t-$(k, n)^*$ -visual cryptographic schemes using linear algebra. In: Information and communications security—16th international conference, ICICS 2014, Hong Kong, China, 16–17 Dec 2014, Revised Selected Papers, pp 230–242
10. Dutta S, Rohit RS, Adhikari A (2016) Constructions and analysis of some efficient t-$(k, n)^*$-visual cryptographic schemes using linear algebraic techniques. Des Codes Cryptogr 80(1):165–196
11. Dutta S, Roy PS, Adhikari A, Sakurai K (2017) On the Robustness of visual cryptographic schemes, IWDW 2016: digital forensics and watermarking. Springer, LNCS, pp 251–262
12. Dutta S, Adhikari A (2017) Contrast optimal XOR based visual cryptographic schemes. In Information theoretic security—10th international conference, ICITS 2017, Hong Kong, China, Nov 29–Dec 2, 2017, Proceedings, pp 58–72
13. Dutta S, Adhikari A, Ruj S (2018) Maximal contrast color visual secret sharing schemes. Des Codes Cryptogr
14. Ryo Ito HK, Takana H (1999) Image size invariant visual cryptography. IEICE Trans Fundam, E82-A(10):2172–2177
15. Kafri O, Keren E (1987) Encryption of pictures and shapes by random grids. Opt Lett 12(6):377–379
16. Lakshmanan R, Arumugam S (2017) Construction of a (k, n)-visual cryptography scheme. Des Codes Cryptogr 82(3):629–645
17. Naor M, Shamir A (1995) Visual cryptography, pp 1–12. Springer, Berlin, Heidelberg, Berlin, Heidelberg
18. Sardar MK, Adhikari A (2020) A new lossless secret color image sharing scheme with small shadow size. J Vis Commun Image Represent 102768
19. Sardar MK, Adhikari A (2020) New lossless secret image sharing scheme for gray scale images with small shadow size. COMSYS-2020, ISBN 978-981-15-7833-5

20. Sardar MK, Adhikari A (2020) Essential secret image sharing scheme with small and equal sized shadows. Signal Process: Image Commun 87:115923
21. Shyu SJ (2007) Image encryption by random grids. Pattern Recognit 40(3):1014–1031
22. Shyu SJ (2009) Image encryption by multiple random grids. Pattern Recognit 42(7):1582–1596
23. Shyu SJ (2013) Visual cryptograms of random grids for general access structures. IEEE Trans Circuits Syst Video Technol 23(3):414–424
24. Shyu SJ (2015) Visual cryptograms of random grids for threshold access structures. Theor Comput Sci 565:30–49
25. Shyu SJ, Chen MC (2015) Minimizing pixel expansion in visual cryptographic scheme for general access structures. IEEE Trans Circuits Syst Video Technol 25(9):1557–1561
26. Thien C-C, Lin J-C (2002) Secret image sharing. Comput Graph 26(5):765–770
27. Verheul ER, van Tilborg HCA (1997) Constructions and properties of k out of n visual secret sharing schemes. Des Codes Cryptogr 11(2):179–196
28. Wu X, Sun W (2012) Visual secret sharing for general access structures by random grids. IET Inform Secur 6(4):299–309
29. Yang C (2004) New visual secret sharing schemes using probabilistic method. Pattern Recognit Lett 25(4):481–494

Further Results on Bent–Negabent Boolean Functions

Sihem Mesnager, Bachir ben Moussat, and Zepeng Zhuo

1 Introduction

Bent functions are Boolean functions with the highest possible nonlinearity in an even number of variables. They were introduced by Rothaus [19] and already studied first by Dillon [9] and next by many researchers for more than three decades ago. Since 1974, bent functions have been extensively developed for their own sake as interesting combinatorial objects but also due to their significantly important role in cryptography (design of stream ciphers, see, e.g., [3]), coding theory (Reed–Muller codes, Kerdock codes (see, e.g., [7]), two-weight codes [1], codes with a few weights [12], association schemes [17]), sequences (see, e.g., [13]), and graph theory (see, e.g., [16]). The classification of bent functions is still elusive, and therefore not only their characterization, but also their generation is a challenging problem.

A number of recent research works in the theory of bent functions have been devoted to the construction of bent functions. One distinguishes two kinds of con-

S. Mesnager (✉) · B. ben Moussat
Department of Mathematics, University of Paris VIII, F-93526 Saint-Denis, France
e-mail: smesnager@univ-paris8.fr

B. ben Moussat
e-mail: bachir.benmoussat@etud.univ-paris8.fr

S. Mesnager
Laboratory Geometry, Analysis and Applications, LAGA, University Sorbonne Paris Nord, CNRS, UMR 7539, Villetaneuse, F-93430, 91120 Palaiseau, Telecom Paris, France

B. ben Moussat
Laboratory Geometry, Analysis and Applications, LAGA, University Sorbonne Paris Nord, CNRS, UMR 7539, Villetaneuse, France

Z. Zhuo
School of Mathematical Science, Huaibei Normal University, Anhui 235000, Huaibei, China
e-mail: zzp781021@sohu.com

© The Author(s), under exclusive license to Springer Nature Singapore Pte Ltd. 2021   47
P. Stănică et al. (eds.), *Security and Privacy*, Lecture Notes in Electrical Engineering 744,
https://doi.org/10.1007/978-981-33-6781-4_5

structions of bent functions: primary constructions, which do not need to use previously constructed functions for designing new ones and secondary constructions (of new functions from two or several already known ones). A book devoted to bent functions is [11] and a jubilee survey on bent functions is [4].

The Walsh–Hadamard transform has been exploited extensively for the analysis of Boolean functions and used in coding theory and cryptology [3]. A Boolean function on an even number of variables is bent if and only if the magnitude of all the values in its Walsh–Hadamard spectrum is the same (flat Walsh–Hadamard spectrum). The Walsh–Hadamard transform is an example of a unitary transformation on the space of all Boolean functions. Riera and Parker [18] extended the concept of a bent function to some generalized bent criteria for a Boolean function, where they required that a Boolean function has flat spectrum with respect to one or more transforms from a specified set of unitary transforms. The set of transforms they chose is not arbitrary but is motivated by a choice of local unitary transforms that are central to the structural analysis of pure n-qubit stabilizer quantum states. The transforms they applied are n-fold tensor products of the identity $I = \begin{pmatrix} 1 & 0 \\ 0 & 1 \end{pmatrix}$, the Walsh–Hadamard matrix $H = \frac{1}{\sqrt{2}} \begin{pmatrix} 1 & 1 \\ 1 & -1 \end{pmatrix}$, and the nega-Hadamard matrix $N = \frac{1}{\sqrt{2}} \begin{pmatrix} 1 & i \\ 1 & -i \end{pmatrix}$, where $i^2 = -1$. The Walsh–Hadamard transform can be described as the tensor product of several H's, and the nega-Hadamard transform is constructed from the tensor product of several N's. The nega-Hadamard transform of Boolean functions was first proposed by Parker [14]. As in the case of the Walsh–Hadamard transform, a Boolean function is called negabent if the spectrum under the nega-Hadamard transform is flat. There are some papers about negabent functions in the last few years [10, 20–24, 26–28]. Many bent functions are known, and also some negabent functions are known. For an even number of variables, a function is bent–negabent if it is both bent and negabent. An interesting topic is to investigate the intersection of these two sets, i.e., to construct Boolean functions which are both bent and negabent. The bent–negabent functions were first introduced by Riera and Parker [18]. Some quite interesting results have been found in this topic by the authors mentioned above but there is still a gap between our interest and the results on the literature. The goal of this paper is to push further the study of negabent and bent–negabent by deriving results which help to design more such functions.

The paper is organized as follows. Section 2 aims to bring a background on the notions related to Boolean function needed in the paper. In Sect. 3, we discuss secondary constructions of bent–negabent functions and exhibit one construction based on the well-known indirect construction of bent functions. In Sect. 4, a secondary construction of bent function is revisited and a new method to design secondary construction is exhibited. Section 5 shows how one can design bent–negabent functions from quadratic Boolean functions. In Sect. 6, we provide a characterization of bent–negabent functions in terms of their second-order derivatives. In Sect. 7, we study the sum-of-squares indicator and derive tight lower and upper bounds. Negabent are those whose lower bound on the sum-of-squares indicator is reached.

2 Preliminaries

Let $\mathbb{F}_2$ denote the finite field with two elements. We denote by $\mathcal{B}_n$ the set of all Boolean functions of n-variable, i.e., of all the functions from $\mathbb{F}_2^n$ into $\mathbb{F}_2$. The set of integers, real numbers, and complex numbers are denoted by $\mathbb{Z}$, $\mathbb{R}$, and $\mathbb{C}$, respectively. The addition over $\mathbb{Z}$, $\mathbb{R}$, and $\mathbb{C}$ is denoted by $+$. The addition over $\mathbb{F}_2^n$ for all $n \geq 1$ is denoted by $\oplus$ (or $+$ if there is no ambiguity). If $z = a + bi \in \mathbb{C}$, then $|z| = \sqrt{a^2 + b^2}$ denotes the absolute value of z, and $\overline{z} = a - bi$ denotes the complex conjugate of z, where $i^2 = -1$, $a, b \in \mathbb{R}$.

The Hamming weight $wt(x)$ of an element $x = (x_1, x_2, \ldots, x_n) \in \mathbb{F}_2^n$ is the number of ones in x, i.e., $wt(x) = \sum_{i=1}^{n} x_i$. We say that a Boolean function is balanced if its truth table contains an equal number of 0's and 1's, that is, if its Hamming weight equals $wt(f) = 2^{n-1}$. The Hamming distance between two functions $f(x)$ and $g(x)$, denoted by $d(f, g)$, is the Hamming weight of $f \oplus g$, i.e., $d(f, g) = wt(f \oplus g)$.

Any Boolean function, $f \in \mathcal{B}_n$, is generally represented by its algebraic normal form (ANF)

$$f(x_1, \cdots, x_n) = \bigoplus_{u \in \mathbb{F}_2^n} \lambda_u \left(\prod_{i=1}^{n} x_i^{u_i} \right),$$

where $\lambda_u \in \mathbb{F}_2$ and $u = (u_1, u_2, \ldots, u_n) \in \mathbb{F}_2^n$. The algebraic degree of f, denoted by $deg(f)$, is the maximal value of $wt(u)$ such that $\lambda_u \neq 0$. A Boolean function is affine if there exists no term of degree strictly greater than 1 in the ANF and the set of all affine functions is denoted by A_n. An affine function with constant term equal to zero is called a linear function. Any linear function on $\mathbb{F}_2^n$ is denoted by $x \cdot \omega = x_1\omega_1 \oplus x_2\omega_2 \oplus \cdots \oplus x_n\omega_n$, where $x, \omega \in \mathbb{F}_2^n$. The nonlinearity of an n-variable function $f(x)$ is $nl(f) = \min_{g \in A_n}(d(f, g))$, i.e., the distance from the set of all n-variable affine functions.

The derivative of $f \in \mathcal{B}_n$ at $\beta \in \mathbb{F}_2^n$, denoted as $D_\beta f$, is defined as $D_\beta f(x) = f(x) + f(x + \beta)$ for all $x \in \mathbb{F}_2^n$. The second-order derivatives $D_\alpha D_\beta f$ at $(\alpha, \beta) \in \mathbb{F}_2^n \times \mathbb{F}_2^n$ of a Boolean function f are defined by $D_\alpha D_\beta f(x) = f(x + \alpha + \beta) - f(x + \alpha) - f(x + \beta) + f(x)$.

The Walsh–Hadamard transform of $f \in \mathcal{B}_n$ at $u \in \mathbb{F}_2^n$ is defined by

$$W_f(u) = \sum_{x \in \mathbb{F}_2^n} (-1)^{f(x) \oplus u \cdot x}.$$

The nega-Hadamard transform of $f \in \mathcal{B}_n$ at $u \in \mathbb{F}_2^n$ is the complex-valued function:

$$N_f(u) = \sum_{x \in \mathbb{F}_2^n} (-1)^{f(x) \oplus u \cdot x} i^{wt(x)}.$$

Let n be an even positive integer, a function $f \in \mathcal{B}_n$ is a bent function if $|W_f(u)| = 2^{n/2}$ for all $u \in \mathbb{F}_2^n$. Similarly, f is called negabent function if $|N_f(u)| = 2^{n/2}$ for all $u \in \mathbb{F}_2^n$. If f is both bent and negabent, we say that f is *bent–negabent*.

The concept of a dual bent function is well known. If $f \in \mathcal{B}_n$ is bent, then the dual function $\widetilde{f}$ of f, defined on $\mathbb{F}_2^n$ by $W_f(x) = 2^{n/2}(-1)^{\widetilde{f}(x)}$, is also bent and its own dual is f itself. If f is bent–negabent, then the dual has the same property. We refer to Carlet [3], and Cusick and Stănică [6] for more on cryptographic Boolean functions and to [11] for more about bent functions.

The nega-cross-correlation of f and g at $u \in \mathbb{F}_2^n$ is denoted by

$$C_{f,g}(u) = \sum_{x \in \mathbb{F}_2^n} (-1)^{f(x) \oplus g(x \oplus u)} (-1)^{u \cdot x}.$$

In case $f = g$, then the nega-cross-correlation is called the nega-autocorrelation of f at u and denoted by $C_f(u)$. A Boolean function $f \in \mathcal{B}_n$ is negabent if and only if $C_f(u) = 0$ for all $u \neq \mathbf{0}$. If $f(x)$ is an affine function, then for all $u \neq \mathbf{0}$ the nega-autocorrelation $C_f(u) = 0$. This implies that any affine function is negabent.

Definition 1 ([28]) Let $f, g \in \mathcal{B}_n$, the *sum-of-squares* indicator of the nega-cross-correlation between f and g is defined by

$$\sigma_{f,g} = \sum_{u \in \mathbb{F}_2^n} C_{f,g}^2(u).$$

If $f = g$ then $\sigma_{f,f}$ is called the *sum-of-squares* indicator of the nega-autocorrelation of f and denoted by σ_f, i.e.,

$$\sigma_f = \sum_{u \in \mathbb{F}_2^n} C_f^2(u).$$

Note that $C_f(\mathbf{0}) = 2^n$. Thus, $\sigma_f \geq C_f^2(\mathbf{0}) = 2^{2n}$. A Boolean function $f \in \mathcal{B}_n$ is negabent if and only if $C_f(u) = 0$ for all $u \in \mathbb{F}_2^n \setminus \{0\}$. Hence, $\sigma_f \geq 2^{2n}$, where the equality holds if and only if f is negabent function.

3   Secondary Constructions of Bent–Negabent Functions

A secondary construction of bent functions is due to Carlet [2] and is commonly referred to as the indirect sum construction.

Theorem 1 ([2]) *Let $f_1(x)$ and $f_2(x)$ be two r-variable bent functions (r even) and let $g_1(y)$ and $g_2(y)$ be two s-variable bent functions (s even). Let $(x, y) \in \mathbb{F}_2^r \times \mathbb{F}_2^s$. Then the function $h(x, y) = f_1(x) \oplus g_1(y) \oplus (f_1 \oplus f_2)(x)(g_1 \oplus g_2)(y)$ is bent and its dual $\widetilde{h}(x, y)$ is obtained from $\widetilde{f_1}(x)$, $\widetilde{f_2}(x)$, $\widetilde{g_1}(y)$ and $\widetilde{g_2}(y)$ by the same formula as $h(x, y)$ is obtained from $f_1(x)$, $f_2(x)$, $g_1(y)$ and $g_2(y)$.*

In this section, we use $h(x, y)$ to construct bent–negabent function. Here we first analyze the nega-Hadamard transform of the function $h(x, y)$.

Lemma 1 *Let* $f_1(x), f_2(x) \in \mathcal{B}_r, g_1(y), g_2(y) \in \mathcal{B}_s.$ *Define* $h(x, y) = f_1(x) \oplus g_1(y) \oplus (f_1 \oplus f_2)(x)(g_1 \oplus g_2)(y).$ *Then the nega-Hadamard transform of* $h(x, y)$ *at* $(u, v) \in \mathbb{F}_2^{r+s}$ *is given by*

$$N_h(u, v) = \frac{1}{2} N_{f_1}(u)[N_{g_1}(v) + N_{g_2}(v)] + \frac{1}{2} N_{f_2}(u)[N_{g_1}(v) - N_{g_2}(v)]. \quad (1)$$

Proof By definition, we have

$$N_h(u, v) = \sum_{(x,y)\in\mathbb{F}_2^{r+s}} (-1)^{h(x,y)\oplus u\cdot x\oplus v\cdot y} i^{wt(x)+wt(y)}$$

$$= \sum_{(x,y)\in\mathbb{F}_2^{r+s}:(g_1\oplus g_2)(y)=0} (-1)^{f_1(x)\oplus g_1(y)\oplus u\cdot x\oplus v\cdot y} i^{wt(x)+wt(y)}$$

$$+ \sum_{(x,y)\in\mathbb{F}_2^{r+s}:(g_1\oplus g_2)(y)=1} (-1)^{f_2(x)\oplus g_1(y)\oplus u\cdot x\oplus v\cdot y} i^{wt(x)+wt(y)}$$

$$= \sum_{y\in\mathbb{F}_2^s:(g_1\oplus g_2)(y)=0} (-1)^{g_1(y)\oplus v\cdot y} i^{wt(y)} \left(\sum_{x\in\mathbb{F}_2^r}(-1)^{f_1(x)\oplus u\cdot x} i^{wt(x)} \right)$$

$$+ \sum_{y\in\mathbb{F}_2^s:(g_1\oplus g_2)(y)=1} (-1)^{g_1(y)\oplus v\cdot y} i^{wt(y)} \left(\sum_{x\in\mathbb{F}_2^r}(-1)^{f_2(x)\oplus u\cdot x} i^{wt(x)} \right)$$

$$= N_{f_1}(u) \sum_{y\in\mathbb{F}_2^s:(g_1\oplus g_2)(y)=0} (-1)^{g_1(y)\oplus v\cdot y} i^{wt(y)}$$

$$+ N_{f_2}(u) \sum_{y\in\mathbb{F}_2^s:(g_1\oplus g_2)(y)=1} (-1)^{g_1(y)\oplus v\cdot y} i^{wt(y)}$$

$$= N_{f_1}(u) \sum_{y\in\mathbb{F}_2^s}(-1)^{g_1(y)\oplus v\cdot y} \left(\frac{1 + (-1)^{(g_1\oplus g_2)(y)}}{2} \right) i^{wt(y)}$$

$$+ N_{f_2}(u) \sum_{y\in\mathbb{F}_2^s}(-1)^{g_1(y)\oplus v\cdot y} \left(\frac{1 - (-1)^{(g_1\oplus g_2)(y)}}{2} \right) i^{wt(y)}$$

$$= \frac{1}{2}\left[N_{f_1}(u) \left(\sum_{y\in\mathbb{F}_2^s}(-1)^{g_1(y)\oplus v\cdot y} i^{wt(y)} + \sum_{y\in\mathbb{F}_2^s}(-1)^{g_2(y)\oplus v\cdot y} i^{wt(y)} \right) \right.$$

$$\left. + N_{f_2}(u) \left(\sum_{y\in\mathbb{F}_2^s}(-1)^{g_1(y)\oplus v\cdot y} i^{wt(y)} - \sum_{y\in\mathbb{F}_2^s}(-1)^{g_2(y)\oplus v\cdot y} i^{wt(y)} \right) \right]$$

$$= \frac{1}{2} N_{f_1}(u)[N_{g_1}(v) + N_{g_2}(v)] + \frac{1}{2} N_{f_2}(u)[N_{g_1}(v) - N_{g_2}(v)].$$

This completes the proof.   □

In (1), if $f_1(x) = f_2(x)$ or $g_1(y) = g_2(y)$, then $N_h(u, v) = N_{f_1}(u)N_{g_1}(v)$.

Corollary 1 *Let r and s be two even positive integers. Let $f_1(x) \in \mathcal{B}_r$ and $g_1(y) \in \mathcal{B}_s$ be two bent–negabent functions. Then $h(x, y) = f_1(x) \oplus g_1(y)$ is also a bent–negabent function.*

In the following, we propose a necessary and sufficient condition so that the indirect sum construction generates bent–negabent functions in $r + s$ variables, using r and s variable bent–negabent functions as the input functions.

Theorem 2 *Let $f_1(x)$, $f_2(x)$ be two r-variable bent–negabent functions (r even) and let $g_1(y)$, $g_2(y)$ be two s-variable bent–negabent functions (s even). Let $(x, y) \in \mathbb{F}_2^r \times \mathbb{F}_2^s$. Define*

$$h(x, y) = f_1(x) \oplus g_1(y) \oplus (f_1 \oplus f_2)(x)(g_1 \oplus g_2)(y).$$

Then $h(x, y)$ is bent–negabent if and only if $\frac{N_{f_1}(u)}{N_{f_2}(u)} = \pm 1$ or $\frac{N_{g_1}(v)}{N_{g_2}(v)} = \pm 1$, for all $(u, v) \in \mathbb{F}_2^r \times \mathbb{F}_2^s$.

Proof From Theorem 1, we know that $h(x, y)$ is bent. Thus, we need to prove that $\frac{N_{f_1}(u)}{N_{f_2}(u)} = \pm 1$ or $\frac{N_{g_1}(v)}{N_{g_2}(v)} = \pm 1$ if and only if $h(x, y)$ is negabent, that is, $|N_h(u, v)| = 2^{(r+s)/2}$ for all $(u, v) \in \mathbb{F}_2^r \times \mathbb{F}_2^s$.

For simplicity, set $z = N_h(u, v)$, $z_1 = N_{f_1}(u)$, $z_2 = N_{f_2}(u)$, $z_3 = N_{g_1}(v)$, and $z_4 = N_{g_2}(v)$. By Lemma 1, for all $(u, v) \in \mathbb{F}_2^r \times \mathbb{F}_2^s$, we have

$$2z = z_1(z_3 + z_4) + z_2(z_3 - z_4), \tag{2}$$

and

$$2\overline{z} = \overline{z_1}(\overline{z_3} + \overline{z_4}) + \overline{z_2}(\overline{z_3} - \overline{z_4}). \tag{3}$$

Combining (2) and (3), we have

$$\begin{aligned}
4|z|^2 = 4z\overline{z} &= [z_1(z_3 + z_4) + z_2(z_3 - z_4)][\overline{z_1}(\overline{z_3} + \overline{z_4}) + \overline{z_2}(\overline{z_3} - \overline{z_4})] \\
&= z_1\overline{z_1}(z_3\overline{z_3} + z_3\overline{z_4} + \overline{z_3}z_4 + z_4\overline{z_4}) + z_1\overline{z_2}(z_3\overline{z_3} - z_3\overline{z_4} + \overline{z_3}z_4 - z_4\overline{z_4}) \\
&\quad + \overline{z_1}z_2(z_3\overline{z_3} + z_3\overline{z_4} - \overline{z_3}z_4 - z_4\overline{z_4}) + z_2\overline{z_2}(z_3\overline{z_3} - z_3\overline{z_4} - \overline{z_3}z_4 + z_4\overline{z_4}) \\
&= |z_1|^2(|z_3|^2 + z_3\overline{z_4} + \overline{z_3}z_4 + |z_4|^2) + z_1\overline{z_2}(|z_3|^2 - z_3\overline{z_4} + \overline{z_3}z_4 - |z_4|^2) \\
&\quad + \overline{z_1}z_2(|z_3|^2 + z_3\overline{z_4} - \overline{z_3}z_4 - |z_4|^2) + |z_2|^2(|z_3|^2 - z_3\overline{z_4} - \overline{z_3}z_4 + |z_4|^2).
\end{aligned}$$

Suppose $h(x, y)$ is negabent $|N_h(u, v)| = 2^{(r+s)/2}$ for all $(u, v) \in \mathbb{F}_2^r \times \mathbb{F}_2^s$ and $|z_1| = |z_2| = 2^{r/2}$, $|z_3| = |z_4| = 2^{s/2}$, we obtain

$$(z_1 \overline{z_2} - \overline{z_1} z_2)(z_3 \overline{z_4} - \overline{z_3} z_4) = 0,$$

that is, $z_1 \overline{z_2} = \overline{z_1} z_2$ or $z_3 \overline{z_4} = \overline{z_3} z_4$. Therefore, we have

$$N_{f_1}(u) \overline{N_{f_2}(u)} = \overline{N_{f_1}(u)} N_{f_2}(u)$$

or

$$N_{g_1}(v) \overline{N_{g_2}(v)} = \overline{N_{g_1}(v)} N_{g_2}(v),$$

that is,

$$\frac{N_{f_1}(u)}{N_{f_2}(u)} = \frac{\overline{N_{f_1}(u)}}{\overline{N_{f_2}(u)}} = \overline{\left(\frac{N_{f_1}(u)}{N_{f_2}(u)}\right)}$$

or

$$\frac{N_{g_1}(v)}{N_{g_2}(v)} = \frac{\overline{N_{g_1}(v)}}{\overline{N_{g_2}(v)}} = \overline{\left(\frac{N_{g_1}(v)}{N_{g_2}(v)}\right)},$$

then $\frac{N_{f_1}(u)}{N_{f_2}(u)}$ or $\frac{N_{g_1}(v)}{N_{g_2}(v)}$ is a real number. Since $|N_{f_1}(u)| = |N_{f_2}(u)| = 2^{r/2}$, $|N_{g_1}(v)| = |N_{g_2}(v)| = 2^{s/2}$, we obtain $\frac{N_{f_1}(u)}{N_{f_2}(u)} = \pm 1$ or $\frac{N_{g_1}(v)}{N_{g_2}(v)} = \pm 1$.

Conversely, since $|z_1| = |z_2| = 2^{r/2}$, $|z_3| = |z_4| = 2^{s/2}$, and $\frac{z_1}{z_2} = \pm 1$ or $\frac{z_3}{z_4} = \pm 1$, which implies that $4|z|^2 = 2^{(r+s+2)}$, that is, $|z| = 2^{(r+s)/2}$. Therefore, we have $|N_h(u, v)| = 2^{(r+s)/2}$. This implies that $h(x, y)$ is a negabent function. $\square$

The sufficient condition for the function $h(x, y)$ to be bent–negabent has been given in [26].

Theorem 3 *([26]) Let $f_1(x)$, $f_2(x)$ be two n-variable bent–negabent functions (n even) and let $g_1(y)$, $g_2(y)$ be two m-variable bent–negabent functions (m even). Let $(x, y) \in \mathbb{F}_2^n \times \mathbb{F}_2^m$. Define $h(x, y) = f_1(x) \oplus g_1(y) \oplus (f_1 \oplus f_2)(x)(g_1 \oplus g_2)(y)$. If $D_1(\widetilde{f_1 \oplus \sigma_2})(x) = D_1(\widetilde{f_2 \oplus \sigma_2})(x)$, then $h(x, y)$ is bent–negabent.*

In the following, we show that the condition $D_1(\widetilde{f_1 \oplus \sigma_2})(x) = D_1(\widetilde{f_2 \oplus \sigma_2})(x)$ is equivalent to the condition $\frac{N_{f_1}(u)}{N_{f_2}(u)} = \pm 1$. We also need the following lemmas.

Lemma 2 *([15])Let n be even and $f(x) \in \mathcal{B}_n$. Then, $f(x)$ is negabent if and only if $f(x) \oplus s_2(x)$ is bent, where $s_2(x) = \bigoplus_{1 \leq i < j \leq n} x_i x_j$.*

Lemma 2 provides a connection between bent and negabent.

Lemma 3 *([24]) Let $f(x) \in \mathcal{B}_n$, then*

$$N_f(u) = \frac{W_{f \oplus s_2}(u) + W_{f \oplus s_2}(\overline{u})}{2} + i \cdot \frac{W_{f \oplus s_2}(u) - W_{f \oplus s_2}(\overline{u})}{2}.$$

Lemma 3 explores a direct link between the Walsh–Hadamard transform and the nega-Hadamard transform. These properties are an important tool to analyze the properties of negabent functions.

Theorem 4 *Let $f_1(x)$ and $f_2(x)$ be two r-variable negabent functions (r even). Then $\frac{N_{f_1}(u)}{N_{f_2}(u)} = \pm 1$ if and only if $D_1(\widetilde{f_1 \oplus s_2})(u) = D_1(\widetilde{f_2 \oplus s_2})(u)$, $u \in \mathbb{F}_2^r$.*

Proof Since $\frac{N_{f_1}(u)}{N_{f_2}(u)} = \pm 1$, then $N_{f_1}(u) = \pm N_{f_2}(u)$. By Lemma 3, we have

$$\frac{W_{f_1 \oplus s_2}(u) + W_{f_1 \oplus s_2}(\overline{u})}{2} + i \cdot \frac{W_{f_1 \oplus s_2}(u) - W_{f_1 \oplus s_2}(\overline{u})}{2}$$
$$= \pm \frac{W_{f_2 \oplus s_2}(u) + W_{f_2 \oplus s_2}(\overline{u})}{2} \pm i \cdot \frac{W_{f_2 \oplus s_2}(u) - W_{f_2 \oplus s_2}(\overline{u})}{2}.$$

Hence

$$\frac{W_{f_1 \oplus s_2}(u) + W_{f_1 \oplus s_2}(\overline{u})}{2} = \pm \frac{W_{f_2 \oplus s_2}(u) + W_{f_2 \oplus s_2}(\overline{u})}{2},$$

$$\frac{W_{f_1 \oplus s_2}(u) - W_{f_1 \oplus s_2}(\overline{u})}{2} = \pm \frac{W_{f_2 \oplus s_2}(u) - W_{f_2 \oplus s_2}(\overline{u})}{2},$$

then

$$W_{f_1 \oplus s_2}(u) = \pm W_{f_2 \oplus s_2}(u), \; W_{f_1 \oplus s_2}(\overline{u}) = \pm W_{f_2 \oplus s_2}(\overline{u}).$$

Recall that $W_f(u) = 2^{r/2}(-1)^{\widetilde{f}(u)}$, we get

$$(-1)^{\widetilde{f_1 \oplus s_2}(u) \oplus \widetilde{f_1 \oplus s_2}(\overline{u})} = (-1)^{\widetilde{f_2 \oplus s_2}(u) \oplus \widetilde{f_2 \oplus s_2}(\overline{u})}.$$

Thus, $D_1(\widetilde{f_1 \oplus s_2})(u) = D_1(\widetilde{f_2 \oplus s_2})(u)$.

Conversely, since $D_1(\widetilde{f_1 \oplus s_2})(u) = D_1(\widetilde{f_2 \oplus s_2})(u)$, then

$$\widetilde{f_1 \oplus s_2}(u) \oplus \widetilde{f_2 \oplus s_2}(\overline{u}) = \widetilde{f_1 \oplus s_2}(\overline{u}) \oplus \widetilde{f_2 \oplus s_2}(u).$$

Hence

$$W_{f_1 \oplus s_2}(u) W_{f_2 \oplus s_2}(\overline{u}) = W_{f_1 \oplus s_2}(\overline{u}) W_{f_2 \oplus s_2}(u).$$

Since $f_1 \oplus s_2$, $f_2 \oplus s_2$ are bent functions, we have $|W_{f_1 \oplus s_2}(u)| = |W_{f_2 \oplus s_2}(u)| = 2^{r/2}$, then $W_{f_1 \oplus s_2}(u) = \pm W_{f_2 \oplus s_2}(u)$, $W_{f_1 \oplus s_2}(\overline{u}) = \pm W_{f_2 \oplus s_2}(\overline{u})$. Thus, according to the similar discussion above, we obtain $\frac{N_{f_1}(u)}{N_{f_2}(u)} = \pm 1$. □

The functions $f(x)$ and $g(x)$ are said to have *complementary nega-autocorrelation* if for all nonzero $u \in \mathbb{F}_2^n$, $C_f(u) + C_g(u) = 0$. The relationship between the nega-autocorrelations of $f(x)$, $g(x)$ and their nega-Hadamard transforms has been given in [22] as follows.

Lemma 4 *([22]) The functions* $f(x), g(x) \in \mathcal{B}_n$ *have complementary nega-autocorrelations if and only if*

$$|N_f(u)|^2 + |N_g(u)|^2 = 2^{n+1}.$$

The following corollary is a direct consequence from Definition 1, Theorem 2, and Lemma 4.

Corollary 2 *Let* $f_1(x), f_2(x) \in \mathcal{B}_n$. *If* $\frac{N_{f_1}(u)}{N_{f_2}(u)} = 1$ *for all* $u \in \mathbb{F}_2^n$, *then the following statements are equivalent.*

1. $f_1(x), f_2(x)$ *are negabent functions.*
2. $|N_{f_1}(u)|^2 + |N_{f_2}(u)|^2 = 2^{n+1}.$
3. $f_1(x)$ *and* $f_2(x)$ *have complementary nega-autocorrelations.*

4 A Secondary Construction Revisited

Recently, a secondary construction of bent functions whose duals satisfy a certain property [25] [Theorem 5.1] has been proposed:

Theorem 5 *Let* f *from* $\mathbb{F}_2^n$ *to* $\mathbb{F}_2$ *be bent. Let* $\beta_1, \ldots, \beta_r$ *be points of* $\mathbb{F}_2^n$. *Let* F *be a Boolean function from* $\mathbb{F}_2^r$ *to* $\mathbb{F}_2$. *Suppose that its dual* $\tilde{f}$ *satisfies: there exists Boolean functions* $g_1, \ldots, g_r$ *from* $\mathbb{F}_2^n$ *to* $\mathbb{F}_2$ *such that*

$$\tilde{f}\left(u + \sum_{i=1}^{r} w_i \beta_i\right) = \tilde{f}(u) + \sum_{i=1}^{r} w_i g_i(u) \tag{4}$$

for every $u \in \mathbb{F}_2^n$ *and* $(w_1, \ldots, w_r) \in \mathbb{F}_2^r$. *Then, the Boolean function* h *from* $\mathbb{F}_2^n$ *to* $\mathbb{F}_2$ *defined at any point* $x \in \mathbb{F}_2^n$ *as*

$$h(x) = f(x) + F(\beta_1 \cdot x, \ldots, \beta_r \cdot x)$$

is bent and its dual is at any point $x \in \mathbb{F}_2^n$ *equal to*

$$\tilde{h}(x) = \tilde{f}(x) + F(g_1(x), \ldots, g_r(x)).$$

Let us now show that Condition (4) of the above theorem can be rewritten in terms of derivatives of the dual function of f. Recall that the derivative at point $\beta \in \mathbb{F}_2^n$ of a Boolean function f from $\mathbb{F}_2^n$ to $\mathbb{F}_2$, denoted as $D_\beta f$, is defined at any point $x \in \mathbb{F}_2^n$ as $D_\beta f(x) = f(x) + f(x + \beta)$. We introduce now a notation to denote derivatives of higher order. Let k be a positive integer and $\beta_1, \cdots, \beta_k$ be k elements of $\mathbb{F}_2^n$. Then, the kth-derivative of f at $(\beta_1, \ldots, \beta_k) \in \left(\mathbb{F}_2^n\right)^k$ is denoted by $D_{\beta_1, \ldots, \beta_k}^k f = D_{\beta_1} \cdots D_{\beta_k} f$. Now, note that, for $w \in \mathbb{F}_2$,

$$f(x + w\beta) = f(x) + D_{w\beta}f(x) = f(x) + wD_\beta f(x).$$

If we iterate the above identity, we get that, for $(w_1, \ldots, w_r) \in \mathbb{F}_2^r$,

$$f\left(x + \sum_{i=1}^{r} w_i\beta_i\right) = f(x) + \sum_{i=1}^{r} w_i D_{\beta_i}f(x) + \sum_{k=2} \sum_{a \in \mathbb{F}_2^r, wt(a)=k} w^a D^k_{\beta_a}f(x),$$

where $w^a = \prod_{i=1}^{r} w_i^{a_i}$ and $\beta_a = (\beta_{a_{i_1}}, \ldots, \beta_{a_{i_k}}) \in \mathbb{F}_2^k$ where $1 \le i_1 < \cdots < i_k \le r$ are the indexes such that $a_i = 1$. Therefore, Condition (4) is equivalent to say that, for $k \ge 2$, any kth-derivative with respect to any subset of $\{\beta_1, \ldots, \beta_r\}$ of the dual function $\tilde{f}$ of f vanishes on $\mathbb{F}_2^n$. Therefore, Theorem 5 can be rewritten as follows.

Theorem 6 *Let f from $\mathbb{F}_2^n$ to $\mathbb{F}_2$ be a Boolean bent function. Let $\beta_1, \ldots, \beta_r$ be points of $\mathbb{F}_2^n$. Suppose that, for any positive integer $2 \le k \le r$, all the kth-order derivatives of the dual of f relatively to subsets of $\{\beta_1, \ldots, \beta_r\}$ of size k vanish on $\mathbb{F}_2^n$. Let F be a Boolean function from $\mathbb{F}_2^r$ to $\mathbb{F}_2$. Then, the Boolean function h from $\mathbb{F}_2^n$ to $\mathbb{F}_2$ defined at any point $x \in \mathbb{F}_2^n$ as*

$$h(x) = f(x) + F(\beta_1 \cdot x, \ldots, \beta_r \cdot x)$$

is bent and its dual is

$$\tilde{h}(x) = \tilde{f}(x) + F(D_{\beta_1}\tilde{f}(x), \ldots, D_{\beta_r}\tilde{f}(x)).$$

5   Bent–Negabent Functions From Quadratic Functions

5.1   *Generalities*

Let f be a quadratic Boolean function whose algebraic normal form

$$f(x) = \sum_{1 \le i < j \le n} a_{ij}x_i x_j + \sum_{i=1}^{n} b_i x_i + c = x \cdot (\mathbf{M}x) + b \cdot x + c, \qquad (5)$$

where $\mathbf{M} = (a_{ij})_{1 \le i, j \le n}$ is a square matrix of size n whose entries are in $\mathbb{F}_2$ and whose entries are equal to 0 if $i \ge j$, $b \in \mathbb{F}_2^n$, and $c \in \mathbb{F}_2$. We denote $\mathbf{B}^\star$ the transpose matrix of $\mathbf{B}$ and $\mathbf{B}^{-1}$ the inverse of $\mathbf{B}$ (if $\mathbf{B}$ is of full rank). Finally, we denote $\mathbf{I}$ the identity matrix of size n. Define a symmetric square matrix of size n as $\mathbf{A} = \mathbf{M} + \mathbf{M}^\star$. Then, one has

Theorem 7 *([15]) f is bent if and only if $\mathbf{A}$ is of maximal rank.*

One can compute explicitly the dual of f.

Proposition 1 *A quadratic Boolean function f of the form (5) is bent if and only if $\mathbf{A} = \mathbf{M} + \mathbf{M}^\star$ is of full rank and the dual of f is $\tilde{f}(x) = f(\mathbf{A}^{-1}x) + f(0) + \varepsilon_f$ at any point $x \in \mathbb{F}_2^n$ where $\varepsilon_f = 0$ if $wt(f) = 2^{n-1} - 2^{\frac{n}{2}-1}$ and 1 if $wt(f) = 2^{n-1} + 2^{\frac{n}{2}-1}$.*

Proof The necessary and sufficient condition for bentness of f is a well-known result ([15]). We now show that the dual of f can be explicitly computed. Indeed,

$$
\begin{aligned}
W_f(u) &= \sum_{x \in \mathbb{F}_2^n} (-1)^{f(x)+u \cdot x} \\
&= \sum_{x \in \mathbb{F}_2^n} (-1)^{f(x+\mathbf{A}^{-1}u)+u \cdot (x+\mathbf{A}^{-1}u)} \\
&= \sum_{x \in \mathbb{F}_2^n} (-1)^{f(x)+f(\mathbf{A}^{-1}u)+(\mathbf{A}\mathbf{A}^{-1}u) \cdot x + f(0) + u \cdot x + u \cdot \mathbf{A}^{-1}u} \\
&= \sum_{x \in \mathbb{F}_2^n} (-1)^{f(x)+f(\mathbf{A}^{-1}u)+u \cdot \mathbf{A}^{-1}u + f(0)} \quad \text{(since } (\mathbf{A}\mathbf{A}^{-1}u) \cdot x = u \cdot x \text{)} \\
&= (-1)^{f(\mathbf{A}^{-1}u)+u \cdot \mathbf{A}^{-1}u + f(0)} \sum_{x \in \mathbb{F}_2^n} (-1)^{f(x)} \\
&= (-1)^{f(\mathbf{A}^{-1}u)+u \cdot \mathbf{A}^{-1}u + f(0)} \widehat{\chi_f}(0) \\
&= (-1)^{(\mathbf{A}^{-1}u) \cdot (\mathbf{M}\mathbf{A}^{-1}u)+b \cdot (\mathbf{A}^{-1}u)+(\mathbf{A}\mathbf{A}^{-1}u) \cdot \mathbf{A}^{-1}u} \times 2^{\frac{n}{2}} (-1)^{\varepsilon_f} \\
&= 2^{\frac{n}{2}} (-1)^{(\mathbf{A}^{-1}u) \cdot ((\mathbf{M}+\mathbf{A})\mathbf{A}^{-1}u)+b \cdot (\mathbf{A}^{-1}u)+\varepsilon_f} \\
&= 2^{\frac{n}{2}} (-1)^{(\mathbf{A}^{-1}u) \cdot (\mathbf{M}^\star \mathbf{A}^{-1}u)+b \cdot (\mathbf{A}^{-1}u)+\varepsilon_f} \\
&= 2^{\frac{n}{2}} (-1)^{(\mathbf{M}\mathbf{A}^{-1}u) \cdot (\mathbf{A}^{-1}u)+b \cdot (\mathbf{A}^{-1}u)+\varepsilon_f} \\
&= 2^{\frac{n}{2}} (-1)^{f(\mathbf{A}^{-1}u)+f(0)+\varepsilon_f}. \qquad \square
\end{aligned}
$$

Note that one can associate likewise the symmetric square matrix $\mathbf{I} + \mathbf{J}$ of size n to the quadratic function s_2 where $\mathbf{I}$ is the identity matrix of size n and $\mathbf{J}$ the square matrix of size n whose all entries are equal to 1. The polar form of s_2 is then $x \cdot ((\mathbf{I} + \mathbf{J})y)$. Then one has

Theorem 8 *([15]) f is bent–negabent if and only if $\mathbf{A}$ and $\mathbf{A} + \mathbf{I} + \mathbf{J}$ are both of maximal rank.*

5.2 Secondary Constructions of Bent and Negabent Functions

5.2.1 Symplectic Forms

Let V be a symplectic vector space over a field F. A mapping σ from $V \times V$ to F is said to be a symplectic form if it is

1 symmetric: $\sigma(x, y) = -\sigma(y, x)$ for any $(x, y) \in V \times V$ (in characteristic two, skew symmetry and symmetry coincides);
2 totally isotropic: $\sigma(x, x) = 0$ for any $x \in V$;
3 non-degenerate: if $\sigma(u, v) = 0$ for any $v \in V$ then $u = 0$.

Then, (V, σ) denotes the vector space V equipped with a symplectic form. Let δ_{ij} be the Kronecker index: $\delta_{ij} = 0$ if $i \neq j$ and $\delta_{ii} = 1$. Suppose that $\dim(V) = 2n$.

Definition 2 A *symplectic basis* for (V, σ) is a basis $v_1, \cdots, v_n, w_1, \ldots, w_n$ such that

$$\sigma(v_i, w_j) = \delta_{ij}, \sigma(v_i, v_j) = \sigma(w_i, w_j) = 0$$

for any $1 \leq i, j \leq r$ (where $\delta_{ij} = 1$ if $i = j$ and 0 otherwise).

5.2.2 Secondary Constructions

A Boolean function f is said to be quadratic if and only if

$$\phi(x, y) = f(x + y) + f(x) + f(y) + f(0)$$

is bilinear, symmetric, and symplectic. The bilinear map ϕ is called the polar form of f. Write f as (5). Observe that

$$\begin{aligned} \phi(x, y) &= x \cdot (\mathbf{M}y) + (\mathbf{M}x) \cdot y & (6) \\ &= x \cdot (\mathbf{M}y) + x \cdot (\mathbf{M}^*y) \\ &= x \cdot (\mathbf{A}y). \end{aligned}$$

The dual of a quadratic bent function is again a quadratic bent function (see Proposition 1). On the other hand, notice that the polar form at point (a, b) coincides with the second-order derivative $D_a D_b f$. Then, Theorem 6 is rewritten as

Corollary 3 *Let f from $\mathbb{F}_2^n$ to $\mathbb{F}_2$ be a quadratic bent function. Denote $\tilde{\phi}$ the polar form of the quadratic part of the dual of f. Let $\beta_1, \ldots, \beta_r$ be points of $\mathbb{F}_2^n$ such that $\tilde{\phi}(\beta_i, \beta_j) = 0$ for $1 \leq i < j \leq r$. Let F be a Boolean function from $\mathbb{F}_2^r$ to $\mathbb{F}_2$. Then, the Boolean function h from $\mathbb{F}_2^n$ to $\mathbb{F}_2$ defined at any point $x \in \mathbb{F}_2^n$ as*

$$h(x) = f(x) + F(\beta_1 \cdot x, \ldots, \beta_r \cdot x)$$

is bent.

Now, according to Proposition 1, the polar form associated to the dual of f is

$$\tilde{\phi}(x, y) = \phi(\mathbf{A}^{-1}x, \mathbf{A}^{-1}y) = (\mathbf{A}^{-1}x) \cdot y = x \cdot (\mathbf{A}^{-1}y). \tag{7}$$

Therefore,

Corollary 4 *Let f from $\mathbb{F}_2^n$ to $\mathbb{F}_2$ be a quadratic bent function of the form (5). Let $\beta_1, \ldots, \beta_r$ be points of $\mathbb{F}_2^n$ such that $\beta_i \cdot (\mathbf{A}^{-1})\beta_j = 0$ for $1 \leq i < j \leq r$. Let F be a Boolean function from $\mathbb{F}_2^r$ to $\mathbb{F}_2$. Then, the Boolean function h from $\mathbb{F}_2^n$ to $\mathbb{F}_2$ defined at any point $x \in \mathbb{F}_2^n$ as*

$$h(x) = f(x) + F(\beta_1 \cdot x, \ldots, \beta_r \cdot x)$$

is bent.

Remark 1 Let $n = 2k$. Observe that ϕ is a symplectic form over $\mathbb{F}_2^n$. Thus, if $\{e_1, \ldots, e_k, f_1, \ldots, f_k\}$ is a symplectic basis of $(\mathbb{F}_2^n, \phi)$ then one can take $\{\beta_1, \ldots, \beta_r\} = \{\mathbf{A}e_i, i \in I\} \cup \{\mathbf{A}f_j, j \in J\}$ with $I \cap J = \emptyset$ and $I \cup J \subset \{1, \ldots, k\}$. The so-constructed bent function is then of algebraic degree r.

Next, observe that the polar form associated to $f + s_2$ is

$$\psi(x, y) = x \cdot ((\mathbf{A} + \mathbf{I} + \mathbf{J})y) \tag{8}$$

and thus, by the same calculation as for f, we get that the polar form of its dual is

$$\tilde{\psi}(x, y) = x \cdot ((\mathbf{A} + \mathbf{I} + \mathbf{J})^{-1}y). \tag{9}$$

Therefore,

Corollary 5 *Let f from $\mathbb{F}_2^n$ to $\mathbb{F}_2$ be a quadratic negabent function of the form (5). Let $\gamma_1, \ldots, \gamma_r$ be points of $\mathbb{F}_2^n$ such that $\gamma_i \cdot ((\mathbf{A} + \mathbf{I} + \mathbf{J})^{-1}\gamma_j) = 0$ for $1 \leq i < j \leq r$. Let F be a Boolean function from $\mathbb{F}_2^r$ to $\mathbb{F}_2$. Then, the Boolean function h from $\mathbb{F}_2^n$ to $\mathbb{F}_2$ defined at any point $x \in \mathbb{F}_2^n$ as*

$$h(x) = f(x) + F(\gamma_1 \cdot x, \ldots, \gamma_r \cdot x)$$

is negabent.

Remark 2 Like in Remark 1, one can deduce from a symplectic basis of $(\mathbb{F}_2^n, \psi)$ a set $\{\gamma_1, \ldots, \gamma_r\}$ which satisfies the condition of the above corollary.

6 A Characterization of Bent–Negabent Functions Through Their Second-Order Derivatives

A useful tool to study a Boolean function $f(x)$ is derivative. The derivatives play an important role in cryptography, related to the differential attack. They are also naturally involved in the definition of the strict avalanche criterion and the propagation criterion. These criteria evaluate some kind of diffusion of the function. Carlet and Prouff [5] gave a characterization of bent functions via their second-order derivatives as follows.

Lemma 5 *([5])A Boolean function $f(x)$ defined on $\mathbb{F}_2^n$ is bent if and only if*

$$\forall x \in \mathbb{F}_2^n, \sum_{a,b \in \mathbb{F}_2^n} (-1)^{D_a D_b f(x)} = 2^n.$$

Inspired by the work of [10], we present a characterization of bent–negabent functions, which is related to the second-order derivatives in the following.

Theorem 9 *Let $f(x)$ be n-variable bent function (n even). Then $f(x)$ is bent–negabent if and only if for all $b \in \mathbb{F}_2^n$*

$$\sum_{a \in \mathbb{F}_2^n : a \cdot b = 0} (-1)^{D_a D_b f(x)} = 2^n, \qquad \sum_{a \in \mathbb{F}_2^n : a \cdot b = 1} (-1)^{D_a D_b f(x)} = 0$$

when $wt(b)$ is even, and

$$\sum_{a \in \mathbb{F}_2^n : a \cdot \bar{b} = 0} (-1)^{D_a D_b f(x)} = 2^n, \qquad \sum_{a \in \mathbb{F}_2^n : a \cdot \bar{b} = 1} (-1)^{D_a D_b f(x)} = 0$$

when $wt(b)$ is odd.

Proof By Lemma 2, $f(x)$ is bent–negabent if and only if $f(x)$ and $f(x) \oplus s_2(x)$ are both bent, i.e., for $\forall x \in \mathbb{F}_2^n$,

$$\sum_{a,b \in \mathbb{F}_2^n} (-1)^{D_a D_b f(x)} = 2^n \text{ and } \sum_{a,b \in \mathbb{F}_2^n} (-1)^{D_a D_b (f(x) \oplus s_2(x))} = 2^n. \qquad (10)$$

Since

$$D_a D_b \sigma_2(x) = s_2(x) \oplus s_2(x \oplus a) \oplus s_2(x \oplus b) \oplus s_2(x \oplus a \oplus b)$$

$$= \bigoplus_{1 \le i \le n} a_i \left(\bigoplus_{1 \le j \le n, j \ne i} b_j \right),$$

so

$$D_a D_b s_2(x) = \begin{cases} a \cdot b, & \text{if } wt(b) \text{ is even,} \\ a \cdot \bar{b}, & \text{if } wt(b) \text{ is odd.} \end{cases}$$

From the second part of (10), we get

$$\sum_{a,b \in \mathbb{F}_2^n} (-1)^{D_a D_b f(x)} (-1)^{D_a D_b s_2(x)} = 2^n.$$

If $wt(b)$ is even, then

$$\sum_{a\in\mathbb{F}_2^n:a\cdot b=0} (-1)^{D_a D_b f(x)} - \sum_{a\in\mathbb{F}_2^n:a\cdot b=1} (-1)^{D_a D_b f(x)} = 2^n. \tag{11}$$

If $wt(b)$ is odd, then

$$\sum_{a\in\mathbb{F}_2^n:a\cdot\bar{b}=0} (-1)^{D_a D_b f(x)} - \sum_{a\in\mathbb{F}_2^n:a\cdot\bar{b}=1} (-1)^{D_a D_b f(x)} = 2^n. \tag{12}$$

From the first part of (10), we obtain

$$\sum_{a\in\mathbb{F}_2^n:a\cdot b=0} (-1)^{D_a D_b f(x)} + \sum_{a\in\mathbb{F}_2^n:a\cdot b=1} (-1)^{D_a D_b f(x)} = 2^n, \tag{13}$$

for all $b \in \mathbb{F}_2^n$. By (11)–(13), we have

$$\sum_{a\in\mathbb{F}_2^n:a\cdot b=0} (-1)^{D_a D_b f(x)} = 2^n, \qquad \sum_{a\in\mathbb{F}_2^n:a\cdot b=1} (-1)^{D_a D_b f(x)} = 0$$

when $wt(b)$ is even, and

$$\sum_{a\in\mathbb{F}_2^n:a\cdot\bar{b}=0} (-1)^{D_a D_b f(x)} = 2^n, \qquad \sum_{a\in\mathbb{F}_2^n:a\cdot\bar{b}=1} (-1)^{D_a D_b f(x)} = 0$$

when $wt(b)$ is odd. This completes the proof. $\qquad\square$

7 An Upper Bound on the Sum-of-Squares Indicator $\sigma_{f,g}$

In order to find the upper bound on the sum-of-squares indicator $\sigma_{f,g}$ for a given two n-variable Boolean functions f and g, we study some properties of the cross-correlation function. We firstly give the sum-of-squares indicators σ_f of $s_2(x) = \bigoplus_{1\le i<j\le n} x_i x_j$ in the following.

Proposition 2 *Let $s_2(x) = \bigoplus_{1\le i<j\le n} x_i x_j$ be the elementary symmetric Boolean function in n variables of degree 2. Then*

$$C_{s_2}(u) = \begin{cases} \pm 2^n, & \text{if } wt(u) \text{ is even,} \\ 0, & \text{if } wt(u) \text{is odd} \end{cases}$$

and $\sigma_f = 2^{3n-1}$.

Proof Since

$$s_2(x) \oplus s_2(x \oplus u) = \bigoplus_{1 \leq i < j \leq n} x_i x_j \oplus \bigoplus_{1 \leq i < j \leq n} (x_i \oplus u_i)(x_j \oplus u_j)$$

$$= \bigoplus_{1 \leq i < j \leq n} (x_i u_j \oplus x_j u_i \oplus u_i u_j)$$

$$= \bigoplus_{1 \leq i < j \leq n} (x_i u_j \oplus x_j u_i) \oplus \bigoplus_{1 \leq i < j \leq n} u_i u_j$$

$$= \bigoplus_{1 \leq i \leq n} \left(x_i \bigoplus_{1 \leq j \leq n, j \neq i} u_j \right) \oplus s_2(u),$$

thus,

$$s_2(x) \oplus s_2(x \oplus u) = \begin{cases} u \cdot x \oplus s_2(u), & \text{if } wt(u) \text{ is even,} \\ \overline{u} \cdot x \oplus s_2(u), & \text{if } wt(u) \text{ is odd.} \end{cases}$$

According to the definitions of the nega-autocorrelation and sum-of-squares indicator, we have

$$C_{s_2}(u) = \begin{cases} \sum_{x \in \mathbb{F}_2^n} (-1)^{s_2(u)} = \pm 2^n, & \text{if } wt(u) \text{ is even,} \\ \sum_{x \in \mathbb{F}_2^n} (-1)^{1 \cdot x + s_2(u)} = 0, & \text{if } wt(u) \text{ is odd} \end{cases}$$

and

$$\sigma_f = \sum_{u \in \mathbb{F}_2^n : wt(u) \text{ even}} C_f^2(u) + \sum_{u \in \mathbb{F}_2^n : wt(u) \text{ odd}} C_f^2(u) = 2^{3n-1}.$$

This proves the result.   □

Lemma 6 ([28]) Let $f(x), g(x) \in \mathcal{B}_n$. Then

$$\sigma_{f,g} = \sum_{u \in \mathbb{F}_2^n} C_{f,g}^2(u) = \sum_{v \in \mathbb{F}_2^n} C_f(v) C_g(v). \tag{14}$$

Remark 3 If we use *Cauchy's inequality* $(\sum_i a_i b_i)^2 \leq \sum_i a_i^2 \sum_i b_i^2$ to the sum on the right-hand side of (8), we get

$$\sigma_{f,g} = \sum_{u \in \mathbb{F}_2^n} C_{f,g}^2(u) = \sum_{v \in \mathbb{F}_2^n} C_f(v) C_g(v)$$

$$\leq \left(\sum_{v \in \mathbb{F}_2^n} C_f^2(v) \right)^{\frac{1}{2}} \left(\sum_{v \in \mathbb{F}_2^n} C_g^2(v) \right)^{\frac{1}{2}}$$

$$= \sigma_f^{\frac{1}{2}} \sigma_g^{\frac{1}{2}} = \sqrt{\sigma_f \sigma_g},$$

i.e., $\sigma_{f,g} \leq \sqrt{\sigma_f \sigma_g}$. Furthermore, for n-variable negabent functions $f(x)$ and $g(x)$, $\sigma_{f,g} = 2^{2n}$.

In order to give the upper bound on $\sigma_{f,g}$, we need the following important results.

Lemma 7 *([22]) Let $f(x), g(x) \in \mathcal{B}_n$. Then*

$$C_{f,g}(v) = 2^{-n} i^{wt(v)} \sum_{u \in \mathbb{F}_2^n} N_f(u) \overline{N_g(u)} (-1)^{u \cdot v}.$$

Lemma 8 *Let $f(x), g(x) \in \mathcal{B}_n$. Then*

$$\sum_{u \in \mathbb{F}_2^n} |N_f(u)|^2 |N_g(u)|^2 = 2^n \sum_{v \in \mathbb{F}_2^n} C_{f,g}^2(v).$$

Proof By Lemma 7, we have

$$\overline{N_f(u)} N_g(u) = \sum_{v \in \mathbb{F}_2^n} C_{f,g}(v)(-1)^{u \cdot v} i^{wt(v)}$$

and

$$
\begin{aligned}
|N_f(u)|^2 |N_g(u)|^2 &= \left(\sum_{v \in \mathbb{F}_2^n} C_{f,g}(v)(-1)^{u \cdot v} i^{-wt(v)} \right) \cdot \left(\sum_{w \in \mathbb{F}_2^n} C_{f,g}(w)(-1)^{u \cdot w} i^{wt(w)} \right) \\
&= \sum_{v,w \in \mathbb{F}_2^n} C_{f,g}(v) C_{f,g}(w)(-1)^{u \cdot (v \oplus w)} i^{wt(w)-wt(v)} \\
&= \sum_{v \in \mathbb{F}_2^n} C_{f,g}^2(v) + \sum_{v,w \in \mathbb{F}_2^n : v \neq w} C_{f,g}(v) C_{f,g}(w)(-1)^{u \cdot (v \oplus w)} i^{wt(w)-wt(v)}.
\end{aligned}
$$

Thus

$$
\begin{aligned}
\sum_{u \in \mathbb{F}_2^n} |N_f(u)|^2 |N_g(u)|^2 &= \sum_{u \in \mathbb{F}_2^n} \sum_{v \in \mathbb{F}_2^n} C_{f,g}^2(v) \\
&\quad + \sum_{u \in \mathbb{F}_2^n} \sum_{v,w \in \mathbb{F}_2^n : v \neq w} C_{f,g}(v) C_{f,g}(w)(-1)^{u \cdot (v \oplus w)} i^{wt(w)-wt(v)} \\
&= 2^n \sum_{v \in \mathbb{F}_2^n} C_{f,g}^2(v) \\
&\quad + \sum_{v,w \in \mathbb{F}_2^n : v \neq w} C_{f,g}(v) C_{f,g}(w) \sum_{u \in \mathbb{F}_2^n} (-1)^{u \cdot (v \oplus w)} i^{wt(w)-wt(v)},
\end{aligned}
$$

since $v \neq w$, $\sum_{u \in \mathbb{F}_2^n} (-1)^{u \cdot (v \oplus w)} = 0$, thus

$$\sum_{u \in \mathbb{F}_2^n} |N_f(u)|^2 |N_g(u)|^2 = 2^n \sum_{v \in \mathbb{F}_2^n} C_{f,g}^2(v).$$

This proves the result. □

If we take $f(x) = g(x)$ in the previous lemma, then we have

$$\sum_{u \in \mathbb{F}_2^n} |N_f(u)|^4 = 2^n \sum_{v \in \mathbb{F}_2^n} C_f^2(v). \tag{15}$$

Theorem 10 *Let $f(x), g(x) \in \mathcal{B}_n$. Then $\sigma_{f,g} \leq 2^{3n}$, with equality if and only if there exists $u_0 \in \mathbb{F}_2^n$ such that $|N_f(u_0)| = |N_g(u_0)| = 2^n$.*

Proof By Lemma 8 and *Nega-Parseval's Identity* $\sum_{u \in \mathbb{F}_2^n} |N_f(u)|^2 = 2^{2n}$, we have

$$\sigma_{f,g} = \frac{1}{2^n} \sum_{u \in \mathbb{F}_2^n} |N_f(u)|^2 |N_g(u)|^2$$

$$\leq \frac{1}{2^n} \left[\sum_{u \in \mathbb{F}_2^n} |N_f(u)|^2 \right] \cdot \left[\sum_{u \in \mathbb{F}_2^n} |N_g(u)|^2 \right] = 2^{3n}.$$

We know $\sigma_{f,g} = 2^{3n}$ if and only if

$$\sum_{u \in \mathbb{F}_2^n} |N_f(u)|^2 |N_g(u)|^2 = \sum_{u \in \mathbb{F}_2^n} |N_f(u)|^2 \sum_{u \in \mathbb{F}_2^n} |N_g(u)|^2,$$

that is,

$$\sum_{u,v \in \mathbb{F}_2^n, u \neq v} |N_f(u)|^2 |N_g(v)|^2 = 0$$

if and only if $|N_f(u)|^2 |N_g(v)|^2 = 0$ for any $u \neq v$. There are three cases:

(i) If there does not exist $u_0 \in \mathbb{F}_2^n$ such that $|N_f(u_0)|^2 \neq 0$, then $|N_f(u)|^2 = 0$ for all $u \in \mathbb{F}_2^n$, which leads to a contradiction with *Nega-Parseval's Identity*.
(ii) If there exists only one $u_0 \in \mathbb{F}_2^n$ such that $|N_f(u_0)|^2 \neq 0$, then $|N_g(v)|^2 = 0$ for all $v \neq u_0$. According to *Nega-Parseval's Identity*, we have $|N_f(u_0)|^2 = 2^{2n}$, i.e., $|N_f(u_0)| = 2^n$. On the other hand, we have $|N_g(u_0)|^2 = 2^{2n}$, i.e., $|N_g(u_0)| = 2^n$.
(iii) If there exist only two $u_1, u_2 \in \mathbb{F}_2^n (u_1 \neq u_2)$ such that $|N_f(u_1)|^2 \neq 0$ and $|N_f(u_2)|^2 \neq 0$, then we have $|N_g(v)|^2 = 0$ for all $v \neq u_1$ and $|N_g(v)|^2 = 0$ for all $v \neq u_2$. It implies that $|N_g(v)|^2 = 0$ for all $v \in \mathbb{F}_2^n$, which is in contradiction with *Nega-Parseval's Identity*. By the same way, we know that there does not exist only $k(3 \leq k \leq 2^n)$ different elements $u_i \in \mathbb{F}_2^n (1 \leq i \leq k)$ such that $|N_f(u_0)|^2 \neq 0$. □

Based on Theorem 10, we give tight lower and upper bounds on σ_f.

Corollary 6 *Let $f(x) \in \mathcal{B}_n$. Then*

(1) $2^{2n} \leq \sigma_f \leq 2^{3n}$;
(2) $\sigma_f = 2^{2n}$ *if and only if f is a negabent function;*
(3) $\sigma_f = 2^{3n}$ *if and only if there exists $u_0 \in \mathbb{F}_2^n$ such that $|N_f(u_0)| = 2^n$.*

Remark 4 Let $\mathfrak{R}(N_f(u_0))$ be the *real part* and $\mathfrak{I}(N_f(u_0))$ be the *imaginary part* of $N_f(u_0)$. Then $\mathfrak{R}(N_f(u_0))$ or $\mathfrak{I}(N_f(u_0))$ must be integer and $|N_f(u_0)|^2 = 2^{2n}$ must be a sum of two squares. From *Jacobi's Two-Squares Theorem* we know that $(2^n)^2 + 0^2 = 2^{2n}$. Thus, $(|\mathfrak{R}(N_f(u_0))|, |\mathfrak{I}(N_f(u_0))|) = (2^n, 0)$ or $(0, 2^n)$, i.e., either $\mathfrak{R}(N_f(u_0))$ or $\mathfrak{I}(N_f(u_0))$ must be zero.

8 Conclusion

In this paper, we have pushed further the theory of the so-called negabent and bent–negabent functions and derived results, which included methods of secondary constructions and characterizations.

References

1. Calderbank R, Kantor WM (1986) The geometry of two-weight codes. Bull Lond Math Soc 18(2):97–122
2. Carlet C (2004) On the secondary constructions of resilient and bent functions. In: Coding, Cryptography and combinatorics (Progress in computer science and applied logic), 18 vol 23, Basel, Switzerland, Birkhäuser, Verlag, , pp 3–28
3. Carlet C (2010) Boolean functions for cryptography and error correcting codes. chapter of the monography. In: Crama Y and Hammer P (eds) Boolean models and methods in mathematics, computer science, and engineering. Cambridge University Press, pp 257–397
4. Carlet C, Mesnager S (2016) Four decades of research on bent Functions. J Des Codes Cryptogr 78(1):5–50
5. Carlet C, Prouff E (2003) On plateaued functions and their constructions. In: Proceedings of fast software encryption FSE 2003, Lecture Notes in Computer Science 2887, pp 54–73
6. Cusick TW, Stănică P (2009) Cryptographic Boolean functions and applications. Elsevier-Academic Press
7. Cohen G, Honkala I, Litsyn S, Lobstein A (1997) Covering codes, North Holland
8. Dillon JF (1972) A survey of bent functions. NSA Tech J Spec Issue 191–215
9. Dillon JF (1974) Elementary Hadamard difference sets. Ph.D. dissertation. University of Maryland
10. Mandal B, Singh B, Gangopadhyay S, Maitra S, Vetrivel V (2018) On non-existence of bent-negabent rotation symmetric Boolean functions. Discret Appl Math 236:1–6
11. Mesnager S (2016) Bent functions: fundamentals and results. Springer, Switzerland
12. Mesnager S, Linear codes from functions. A concise encyclopedia of coding theory. To appear
13. Olsen JD, Scholtz RA, Welch LR (1982) Bent-function sequences. IEEE Transform Inf Theory 28(6):858–864

14. Parker MG (2000) The constant properties of Goley-Devis-Jedwab sequences. In: International symposium on information theory, Sorrento, Italy.http://www.ii.uib.no/matthew/mattweb.html
15. Parker MG, Pott A (2007) On Boolean functions which are bent and negabent. SSC 2007, LNCS 4893. Springer, Heidelberg, pp 9–23
16. Pott A, Tan Y, Feng T (2010) Strongly regular graphs associated with ternary bent functions. J Comb Theory Ser A 117:668–682
17. Pott A, Tan Y, Feng T, Ling S (2011) Association schemes arising from bent functions. J. Des Codes Cryptogr 59:319–331
18. Riera C, Parker MG (2006) Generalized bent criteria for Boolean functions. IEEE Transform Inform Theory 52(9):4142–4159
19. Rothaus O (1976) On bent functions. J Comb Theory Ser A 20:300–305
20. Sarkar S (2012) Characterizing negabent Boolean functions over finite fields. SETA 2012, vol 7280, LNCS, Springer, Berlin, Heidelberg, 2, pp 77–88
21. Schmidt KU, Parker MG, Pott A (2008) Negabent functions in the Maiorana-McFarland Class. SETA 390–402
22. Stănică P, Gangopadhyay S, Chaturvedi A, Gangopadhyay AK, Maitra S (2012) Investigations on bent and negabent functions via the Nega-Hadamard transform. IEEE Transform Inf Theory 58(6):4064–4072
23. Stănică P, Mandal B, Maitra S (2019) The connection between quadratic bent-negabent functions and the Kerdock code. Appl Algebra Eng Commun Comput 30(5):387–401
24. Su W, Pott A, Tang X (2013) Investigations on bent and negabent functions via the nega-Hadamard transform. IEEE Transform Inf Theory 59(6):3387–3395
25. Tang C, Zhou Z, Qi Y, Zhang X, Fan C, Helleseth T (2017) Generic construction of bent functions and bent idempotents with any possible algebraic degrees. IEEE Trans Inf Theory 63(10):6149–6157
26. Zhang F, Wei Y, Pasalic E (2015) Constructions of bent-negabent functions and their relation to the completed Maiorana-McFarland class. IEEE Trans Inf Theory 61(3):1496–1506
27. Zhou Y, Qu L (2017) Constructions of negabent functions over finite fields. Cryptogr Commun 9:165–180
28. Zhuo Z, Chong J (2015) On negabent functions and nega-Hadamard transform. Math Problems Eng Article ID 959617. https://doi.org/10.1155/2015/959617

Generalization of Lattice-Based Cryptography on Hypercomplex Algebras

Sonika Singh, Sahadeo Padhye⬛, and Ankal Pal

1 Introduction

Quantum computing is not a far-fetched reality. The mathematical model of quantum computing was first proposed by Feynman [18], but the practical implementation has still engineering limitations pertaining to cryogenics. IBM has come up with its small quantum computers, which can solve hard optimization problems [20]. In the post-quantum era, computational capabilities would increase exponentially. By Shor's algorithm [17], the discrete logarithm problem (DLP) and factorization problems can be solved efficiently. It poses a direct threat to the security of the elliptic curve discrete logarithm problem (ECDLP) and RSA cryptosystems. The national institute of standards and technologies (NIST) has emphasized the efficacy of quantum-resistant algorithms to be used in the future. In 2019, NIST already announced the second round of candidates for post-quantum cryptography [21]. Lattice-based schemes are inherently quantum-resistant for higher dimensions ($n \geq$ 100). The recent implementation of the "NewHope" [19] software has shown that it is possible to have a hardware implementation of lattice-based protocols with memory and speed constraints. This provides us with new hope that similar implementations are possible for our proposed scheme, STRU cryptosystem, based on the shortest

S. Singh (✉)
Department of Mathematics, CMP Degree College, University of Allahabad, Pryagraj, India
e-mail: sonikasinghcool10@gmail.com

S. Padhye
Department of Mathematics, Motilal Nehru National Institute of
Technology Allahabad, Pryagraj, India
e-mail: sahadeomathrsu@gmail.com

A. Pal
Department of Mathematics, University of L'Aquila, L'Aquila, Italy
e-mail: ankanpal100@gmail.com

© The Author(s), under exclusive license to Springer Nature Singapore Pte Ltd. 2021
P. Stănică et al. (eds.), *Security and Privacy*, Lecture Notes in Electrical Engineering 744,
https://doi.org/10.1007/978-981-33-6781-4_6

vector problem (SVP) on sedenion algebra obtained through the Cayley–Dickson process.

A sequence of algebras was constructed by A. Cayley and L. E. Dickson over the field of real numbers by defining specific/compatible multiplication and conjugation rules in such a way that each algebra has twice the dimension of the previous algebra.

In this construction, we keep losing some important properties of the algebras at each step. The gradual loss of properties manifests in the depletion in the algebraic structure of the higher dimensional algebras. When we double $\mathbb{R}$, we get $\mathbb{C}$. The ordering property of $\mathbb{R}$ is lost. Similarly, when we construct quaternions ($\mathbb{H}$) (Dimension 4), the commutative property is lost. Continuing the CD process, we arrive at octonions ($\mathbb{O}$) from quaternions; the associative property is lost. Continuing this process, we proceed further and construct the sedenions $\mathbb{S}$, and we observe that it is non-alternative. We can continue this process and attain the concept of generalized 2^n-ions. The power associativity remains intact for 2^n-ions, which gives us the freedom to construct and manipulate polynomials [3, 14, 16].

The question is "Why should one use these algebras for Cryptography?" The pivotal motivation is that a set of hierarchies can be developed. Moreover, the algebras provide a way for using obfuscation techniques as the number of bases in the higher dimensional algebra are more. Hence, heuristically we can safely assume that it might provide more security and interesting application scenarios. During the instantiation of this type of framework, we define a new property "inverse associative property (IAP)" for the composition of the basis elements.

The remaining parts are given as follows: in Sect. 2, we discuss cryptographic hierarchies. In Sect. 3, we discuss the algebraic structure of the sedenion algebra for the proposed STRU scheme. In the next section, we present our desired as well as anticipated inverse associative property. We propose the STRU scheme and its decryption verification in Sect. efsec5. Consequently, we analyze the proposed scheme in the context of different attacks in Sect. 6. In Sect. 7, we provide a comparative analysis of the generalized structure. After that, we conclude the article in the last section.

2 Cryptographic Hierarchies

The aim of the cryptographic hierarchy is to create different security levels using the same protocol [10]. It is an attempt to vary the security levels by keeping the same encryption–decryption process but changing the base algebraic configuration.

As the SVP is implemented over the quaternions, we notice that although it is four times slower than NTRU [7], QTRU [11] is much more secure to lattice-based attacks than NTRU. Hence, one can easily compensate for speed loss by reducing the dimension of the three parameters (N, p, q) and still gaining the same level of security. Similar arguments can be made for the non-associative counterpart OTRU [2]. The way forward from OTRU needs a structured framework as they are no more division algebras. We have implemented SVP on sedenions, and we call it STRU cryptosystem. A detailed explanation of the proposed scheme is provided in Sect. 7.

Table 1 A general hierarchy

Cryptosystem	Underlying hard lattice problem	Dimension
GTRU (Power associative but other properties lost)	SVP (Shortest Vector Problem)	2^n ($n = 5, 6, \ldots$)
STRU (Non-alternative)	SVP	2^4
OTRU [12] (Non-associative)	SVP	2^3
QTRU [11] (Non-commutative)	SVP	2^2
G-NTRU [9] (Non-ordered)	SVP	2^1
NTRU [7]	SVP	2^0

3 Sedenion Algebra

As we have discussed earlier that if we apply the CD construction to the octonions (an eight-dimensional non-commutative and non-associative algebra over the reals) [1], then we can obtain a 16-dimensional non-commutative, non-associative, and non-alternative algebra over the reals. This algebra is called sedenion algebra. We denote the set of sedenions by $\mathbb{S}$. The addition and the subtraction of sedenions are coefficient-wise, and the multiplication of sedenions is non-commutative and non-associative. Sedenions are power associative and flexible. Since sedenions have zero divisors, they are not division algebra [8]. For more details for sedenion algebra, please refer to Imaeda's work [8] or [13].

Sedenions: The real sedenions denoted by $\mathbb{S}$ can be viewed as an algebra of dimension 16 over real number field $\mathbb{R}$. We define $\mathbb{S}$ by

$$\mathbb{S} = \{y_0 + \Sigma_{i=1}^{15} y_i k_i : y_0, \ldots, y_{15} \in \mathbb{R}\},$$

where y_i's are the real scalar values and the set $\{1, k_1, \ldots, k_{15}\}$ are the basis elements (unit sedenions, we are using $k_0 = 1$). For our implementation, we consider only integer coefficients because of the modularity restrictions.

We elaborate the structure of $\mathcal{A}$, $\mathcal{A}_p$, and $\mathcal{A}_q$ sets which contains the desired polynomials of integer coefficients. Considering the convolution polynomial rings $\mathcal{R} = \frac{Z[x]}{x^N - 1}$, $\mathcal{R}_p = \frac{Z_p[x]}{x^N - 1}$, and $\mathcal{R}_q = \frac{Z_q[x]}{x^N - 1}$, the structures of $\mathcal{A}$, $\mathcal{A}_p$, and $\mathcal{A}_q$ are given by

$$\mathcal{A} = \{a_0 + \Sigma_{i=1}^{15} a_i(x)k_i : a_0(x), ..., a_{15}(x) \in \mathcal{R}\},$$
$$\mathcal{A}_p = \{a_0 + \Sigma_{i=1}^{15} a_i(x)k_i : a_0(x), ..., a_{15}(x) \in \mathcal{R}_p\},$$
$$\mathcal{A}_q = \{a_0 + \Sigma_{i=1}^{15} a_i(x)k_i : a_0(x), ..., a_{15}(x) \in \mathcal{R}_q\}.$$

4 Inverse Associative Property in the Basis Elements of Sedenions

We assume that k_i are basis elements where $1 \leq i \leq 15$ and $i \in \mathbb{N}$ and $\circ$ denotes the sedenionic multiplication. We recall some properties of the basis elements which would be necessary to verify the inverse associativity property in the basis elements of $\mathbb{S}$:

Property-1 [8] **(Anti-Commutativity)**:

$$-k_i \circ k_j = k_j \circ k_i$$
$$k_i \circ (-k_j) = k_j \circ k_i.$$

Property-2 [8]:

$$k_i \circ k_i = -k_0.$$

The second property is a particularly nice property because from it we can deduce that

$$-k_i = k_i^{-1}.$$

Types of Inverse Associativity Property: We assume that $f, g, h \in \{k_i \mid 1 \leq i \leq 15\}$ and $f \neq k_0, g \neq k_0, h \neq k_0$. We did the computations and found out that there are two types of inverse associativity that is followed by the basis elements:

1. Elements which satisfy *Inverse Associativity-D (Desired)* (IAP-D): $f \circ ((g \circ f) \circ h) = (g \circ h)$.

2. Elements which satisfy *Inverse Associativity-A (Anticipated)* (IAP-A): $f \circ ((g \circ f) \circ h) = (h \circ g)$.

We elaborate some of the algebraic manipulations here to show that the above properties which are the results of the computations can have many forms. We start from the following assumptions and analyze how Property-1 and Property-2 can be used to do the manipulations. We assume the following:

$$f \circ ((f^{-1} \circ g) \circ h) = (f \circ f^{-1}) \circ (g \circ h) = (g \circ h).$$

By using Property-2, it can be rewritten as

$$f \circ ((f^{-1} \circ g) \circ h) = (f \circ f^{-1}) \circ (g \circ h) = k_0 \circ (g \circ h).$$

Again, using Property-1, we can rewrite it as

$$f \circ ((f^{-1} \circ g) \circ h) = (f \circ f^{-1}) \circ (g \circ h) = (h \circ g).$$

We again use Property-2 to deduce that $f^{-1} = -f$:

$$f \circ ((-f \circ g) \circ h) = (h \circ g).$$

We again use Property-1 to deduce that

$$f \circ ((g \circ f) \circ h) = (h \circ g) \ (InverseAssociativityProperty - A).$$

We also define (*Inverse Associativity Property-D*):

$$f \circ ((g \circ f) \circ h) = (g \circ h).$$

Interestingly, we see that actually all the basis elements satisfy either of the two properties.

Extending the Property to Polynomials: We impose a condition that this property to be checked while constructing $\mathcal{A}$. Every polynomial in $\mathbb{S}$ will have a form:

$$p(x) = \sum_{i=0}^{N-1} a_i x^i,$$

where $a_i's$ are the sedenionic coefficients. Every $a_i's$ can be written in the form of the basis elements as

$$a_i = \sum_{j=0}^{15} y_{ij} k_j$$

, i.e., our $p(x)$ will be of the form:

$$p(x) = \sum_{i=0}^{N-1} (\sum_{j=0}^{15} y_{ij} k_j) x^i.$$

Hence, we need to multiply the basis elements and then do an iterative process. In this way, all the elements of $\mathcal{A}$ will follow either of the two properties. This is an additional computational task which needs to be performed for sedenions.

5   Proposed Scheme: STRU

There is an article, namely, "STRU: A Non-Alternative and Multi-dimensional Public
Key Cryptosystem" given by Thakur and Tripathi in 2017 [15]. They proposed an
STRU cryptosystem based on sedenions, but in the decryption process, they used
associativity directly. Since we know that sedenions are non-associative, we cannot
use associativity directly, as Thakur et al. did. So, their scheme does not follow the
sedenionic requirements.

Here, we propose a cryptographic scheme based on sedenion algebra and overcome the flaw of Thakur et al. scheme. We use the inverse associative property in
the decryption phase of the system. In our proposed scheme, the elements of $\mathcal{A}$ are
taken and called sedenion polynomial for brevity. The encryption and decryption
in STRU are done in a multi-dimensional space as in OTRU cryptosystem [12].
This cryptosystem has parameters (N, p, q) and four subsets L_f, L_g, L_ϕ, and L_m
of $\mathcal{A}$. N, p, q, d_f, d_g, d_ϕ all are constant parameters and perform a similar role as in
NTRU. The scheme of STRU cryptosystem is as follows.

Key-Generation: For generating key pairs, two random sedenion polynomials $F \in$
L_f and $G \in L_g$ are generated, where

$$F = f_0(x) + f_1(x)k_1 + \cdots + f_{15}(x)k_{15} : f_0, f_1, \ldots, f_{15} \in L_f,$$
$$G = g_0(x) + g_1(x)k_1 + \cdots + g_{15}(x)k_{15} : g_0, g_1, \ldots, g_{15} \in L_g.$$

The sedenion polynomial F should have an inverse over $\mathcal{A}_q$ and $\mathcal{A}_p$. If the inverses
do not exist, then a new sedenion polynomial F will be generated. The inverse of F
over $\mathcal{A}_p$ is denoted by F_p^{-1} and over $\mathcal{A}_q$ is by F_q^{-1}. Then, a new sedenion polynomial
H is computed by

$$H = F_q^{-1} \circ G \in \mathcal{A}_q.$$

This sedenion polynomial H acts as the public key, and the sedenion polynomial pair
(F, F_p^{-1}) is kept secret. When the same parameters are used in both cryptosystems,
then the key-creation process in STRU is 256 times slower in comparison to NTRU.

Encryption: For the encryption process, firstly, a random sedenion polynomial $\phi \in$
L_ϕ is generated. The message M, which is to be encrypted, is first expressed in terms
of a sedenion polynomial. Consequently, the ciphertext E is obtained by

$$E = pH \circ \phi + M \in \mathcal{A}_q,$$

where, $\phi = \phi_0(x) + \phi_1(x)k_1 + \cdots + \phi_{15}(x)k_{15} : \phi_0, \phi_1, \ldots, \phi_{15} \in L_\phi$ and $M =$
$m_0(x) + m_1(x)k_1 + \cdots + m_{15}(x)k_{15} : m_0, m_1, \cdots, m_{15} \in L_m$.
The encryption requires one sedenionic multiplication involving 256 convolution
multiplications and 16 polynomial additions having complexity $O(N^2)$ and $O(N)$,

respectively. Each encryption round takes a total of 16 data vectors.

Decryption: For decryption, we compute

$$B = (F \circ E) \bmod q = F \circ (pH \circ \phi + M) \bmod q$$
$$= pF \circ (H \circ \phi) + F \circ M \bmod q$$
$$= pF \circ ((F_q^{-1} \circ G) \circ \phi) + F \circ M \bmod q.$$

Now we use IAP-D to get

$$B = pG \circ \phi + F \circ M \ \bmod q.$$

If we select advisable parameters, the coefficients of the 16 polynomials in $pG \circ \phi + F \circ M \in \mathcal{A}_q$ will fall into the range $(-q/2, +q/2]$ so that the last reduction modulo q will not be required. So, we can proceed to the next step. $B \in \mathcal{A}_q$ should be analyzed with its corresponding candidate in $(-q/2, +q/2]$ and all coefficients in 16 polynomials should be reduced mod p. Thus, we get $(B \bmod p) = F \circ M \in \mathcal{A}_p$. To obtain the actual plaintext M, we multiply B on the left by F_p^{-1}.

The encryption and decryption algorithms in this cryptosystem are about 16 and 32 times slower than NTRU for similar dimension N. However, in STRU, we can deal with a lesser dimension N, without compromising security of the cryptosystem. Also, as in NTRU, the efficiency of STRU encryption/decryption may be optimized using various optimization methods [6] under appropriate assumptions. Additionally, a message of size $16N$ can be encrypted/decrypted in a single encryption/decryption process, whereas in NTRU the message of size $16N$ can be encrypted/decrypted using 16 times of encryption/decryption process.

5.1 Successful Decryption

We calculated the successful decryption probability in STRU cryptosystem as like as in the NTRU cryptosystem and by taking similar assumptions as in the standard version [9]. The decryption will be successful in STRU if all coefficients of $pG \circ \phi + F \circ M$ lie in $(\frac{-q+1}{2}, \frac{+q-1}{2})$. So, we have

$$B = F \circ E = F \circ (pH \circ \phi) + F \circ M = r_0 + \Sigma_{i=1}^{15} r_i(y) k_i,$$

where, for instance, r_0, a degree N polynomial is computed as

$$r_0 = [r_{0,0}, r_{0,1}, ..., r_{0,N-1}],$$
$$r_1 = [r_{1,0}, r_{1,1}, ..., r_{1,N-1}],$$
$$...$$
$$...$$
$$...$$
$$r_{15} = [r_{15,0}, r_{15,1}, ..., r_{15,N-1}].$$

If we consider all NTRU assumptions, then one can easily estimate the expected values for all coefficients of $r_0, r_1, ..., r_{15}$ in B will remain zero and their variances are 16 tuples. We assume that the coefficients of f_i, g_i, and ϕ_i are random independent variables and take one of the values from $\{1, 0, -1\}$. Then we can easily deduce

$$f_i = [f_{i,0}, f_{i,1}, ..., f_{i,N-1}], i = 0, 1, ..., 15,$$
$$g_i = [g_{i,0}, g_{i,1}, ..., g_{i,N-1}], i = 0, 1, ..., 15,$$
$$\phi_0 = [\phi_{i,0}, \phi_{i,1}, ..., \phi_{i,N-1}], i = 0, 1, ..., 15.$$

$\Pr(f_{i,j} = 1) = \frac{d_f}{N}$, $\Pr(f_{i,j} = -1) = \frac{d_f-1}{N} \approx \frac{d_f}{N}$, $\Pr(f_{i,j} = 0) = \frac{N-2d_f}{N}$,
$\Pr(g_{i,j} = 1) = \frac{d_g}{N}$, $\Pr(g_{i,j} = -1) = \frac{d_g}{N}$, $\Pr(g_{i,j} = 0) = \frac{N-2d_g}{N}$,
$\Pr(\phi_{i,j} = 1) = \frac{d_\phi}{N}$, $\Pr(\phi_{i,j} = -1) = \frac{d_\phi}{N}$, $\Pr(\phi_{i,j} = 0) = \frac{N-2d_\phi}{N}$,
$\Pr(m_{i,j} = j) = \frac{1}{p}$ where $i = 0, 1, ..., 15$ and $j = \frac{-(p-1)}{2}, ..., \frac{-(p+1)}{2}$.

Considering the above assumptions, expected values are $E(f_{i,j}) \approx 0$, $E(g_{i,j}) = 0$, $E(r_{i,j}) = 0$, and $E(m_{i,j}) = 0$. Thus, $E(r_{i,j}) = 0, i = 0, 1, ..., 15$.

The variances are calculated as in NTRU, i.e., $Var[g_{i,l}\phi_{j,t}] = \frac{4d_g d_\phi}{N^2}, i, l = 0, 1, ..., 15, j, t = 0, 1, ..., N - 1,$
$Var[f_{i,l}m_{j,t}] = \frac{d_f(p-1)(p+1)}{6N}$, $i, l = 0, 1, ..., 15, j, t = 0, 1, ..., N - 1$.

Therefore,
$Var[r_{0,l}] = Var[\Sigma_{i+j=l \bmod N}(p.g_{0,i}\phi_{0,j} - p.g_{1,i}\phi_{1,j} - p.g_{2,i}\phi_{2,j} - p.g_{3,i}\phi_{3,j} - p.g_{4,i}\phi_{4,j} - p.g_{5,i}\phi_{5,j} - p.g_{6,i}\phi_{6,j} - p.g_{7,i}\phi_{7,j} - p.g_{8,i}\phi_{8,j} - p.g_{9,i}\phi_{9,j} - p.g_{10,i}\phi_{10,j} - p.g_{11,i}\phi_{11,j} - p.g_{12,i}\phi_{12,j} - p.g_{13,i}\phi_{13,j} - p.g_{14,i}\phi_{14,j} - p.g_{15,i}\phi_{15,j} + f_{0,i}m_{0,j} - f_{1,i}m_{1,j} - f_{2,i}m_{2,j} - f_{3,i}m_{3,j} - f_{4,i}m_{4,j} - f_{5,i}m5, j - f_{6,i}m_{6,j} - f_{7,i}m_{7,j} - f_{8,i}m_{8,j} - f_{9,i}m_{9,j} - f10, im_{10,j} - f_{11,i}m_{11,j} - f_{12,i}m_{12,j} - f_{13,i}m_{13,j} - f_{14,i}m_{14,j} - f_{15,i}m_{15,j})].$

Putting the values of $Var[g_{i,l}\phi_{j,t}]$ and $Var[f_{i,l}m_{j,t}]$, we get
$Var[r_{0,l}] = \frac{1024p^2 d_g d_\phi}{N} + \frac{128d_f(p-1)(p+1)}{3}.$

In same manner, we have
$Var[r_{1,l}] = Var[r_{2,l}] = ... = Var[r_{15,l}] = \frac{1024p^2 d_g d_\phi}{N} + \frac{128d_f(p-1)(p+1)}{3}.$

It is required to compute the probability that $r_{i,l}$ lies between $\frac{-(q-1)}{2}$ to $\frac{q-1}{2}$ which would result in a successful decryption. Considering that $r_{i,l}$ have normal distribution having mean zero and the variance obtained as above, we have

$$\Pr\left(|r_{i,l}| \leq \frac{q-1}{2}\right) = \Pr\left(\frac{-q+1)}{2} \leq |r_{i,l}| \leq \frac{q-1}{2}\right) = 2\Phi\left(\frac{q-1}{2\sigma}\right) - 1,$$

where Φ denotes the distribution of the standard normal variable and

$$\sigma = \sqrt{\frac{1024 p^2 d_g d_\phi}{N} + \frac{128 d_f (p-1)(p+1)}{3}}.$$

According to the above observations, the probability that STRU has successful decryption can be obtained from the two investigated points:

1. Each of the messages $m_0, m_1, ..., m_{15}$ to be correctly decrypted has the probability

$$\left(2\Phi\left(\frac{q-1}{2\sigma}\right) - 1\right)^N.$$

2. All of the messages $m_0, m_1, ..., m_{15}$ to be correctly decrypted has the probability

$$\left(2\Phi\left(\frac{q-1}{2\sigma}\right) - 1\right)^{16N}.$$

6 Cryptanalysis of STRU

6.1 Brute Force Attack

An attacker tries each possible sedenion polynomial in L_f to find a short key for decryption for mounting a brute force attack. The size of the search space L_f will be

$$|L_f| = \binom{N}{d_f}^{16} \binom{N - d_f}{d_f - 1}^{16}, \text{ where } \binom{n}{k} = \frac{n!}{k!(n-k)!}.$$

Similar to NTRU, F along with all its rotations $y^i F$ can be taken as the decryption key. Hence, search space to find the key is $\frac{|L_f|}{N}$. Similarly, if an attacker wants to find the plaintext directly, then he has to search on $\frac{|L_g|}{N}$ possibilities where

$$|L_g| = \binom{N}{d_g}^{16} \binom{N - d_g}{d_g}^{16}.$$

6.2 Meet-in-the-Middle (MITM) Attacks

If sufficient memory is available, then for attacking with MITM attack [5], an attacker requires search spaces $\sqrt{\frac{|L_f|}{N}}$ and $\sqrt{\frac{|L_g|}{N}}$ for finding the key and plaintext, respectively, i.e., meet-in-the-middle attack shortens the search space by the order of the square root.

6.3 Message Expansion Scheme

For obtaining encryption speed, there is an important factor, namely, message expansion, which cannot be ignored. Message expansion is the ratio of the sizes of ciphertext search space and plaintext search space and given as $\frac{\log |C|}{\log |P|}$ where P is the plaintext space and C is the ciphertext search space. In STRU cryptosystem:

$$\text{messageexpansion} = \frac{\log |C|}{\log |P|} = \frac{\log q^{16N}}{\log p^{16N}} = \frac{\log q}{\log p}.$$

As this ratio involves with q and p, q should be chosen in such a manner that will give the smaller decryption failure.

6.4 Lattice Attacks

Lattice attacks [4] are prevalent in lattice-based cryptographic protocols. The key idea is to find an element having a small norm, satisfying the relations as per the protocol to construct a lattice, and then use lattice reduction schemes to find the secret key. In STRU, finding a sedenion polynomial having a small norm that satisfies the relation $F \circ H = G \pmod{q}$ is difficult. Also, it is exigent for attacker to build a sedenionic lattice on which lattice reduction schemes can be applied to render the protocol insecure. The sole strategy for applying the lattice attack on the STRU cryptosystem and to find a suitable decryption key is to analyze the relation $F \circ H = G \pmod{q}$ in the following way:

$$f_0 h_0 - f_1 h_1 - f_2 h_2 - f_3 h_3 - f_4 h_4 - f_5 h_5 - f_6 h_6 - f_7 h_7 - f_8 h_8 - f_9 h_9 - f_{10}$$
$$h_{10} - f_{11} h_{11} - f_{12} h_{12} - f_{13} h_{13} - f_{14} h_{14} - f_{15} h_{15} = g_0 + q u_0,$$

$$f_0 h_1 + f_1 h_0 + f_2 h_3 - f_3 h_2 + f_4 h_5 - f_5 h_4 - f_6 h_7 + f_7 h_6 + f_8 h_9 - f_9 h_8 - f_{10}$$
$$h_{11} + f_{11} h_{10} - f_{12} g_{13} + f_{13} h_{12} + f_{14} h_{15} - f_{15} g_{14} == g_1 + q u_1,$$

$$\cdot$$
$$\cdot$$

$$f_0 h_{15} + f_1 h_{14} - f_2 h_{13} - f_3 h_{12} + f_4 h_{11} + f_5 h_{10} - f_6 h_9 + f_7 h_8 - f_8 h_7 + f_9$$
$$h_6 - f_{10} h_5 - f_{11} h_4 + f_{12} h_3 + f_{13} h_2 - f_{14} h_1 + f_{15} h_0 = g_{15} + q u_{15}.$$

Let $M_{N \times N}$ be the linear representation of the polynomials $h_0, h_1, ..., h_{15}$:

$$M_{N \times N} = \begin{bmatrix} h_{i,0} & h_{i,1} & h_{i,2} \ ... \ h_{i,N-1} \\ h_{i,N-1} & h_{i,0} & h_{i,1} \ ... \ h_{i,N-2} \\ h_{i,N-2} & h_{i,N-1} & h_{i,0} \ ... \ h_{i,N-3} \\ ... & ... & ... \ ... \ ... \\ ... & ... & ... \ ... \ ... \\ h_{i,2} & h_{i,3} & h_{i,4} \ ... \ h_{i,1} \\ h_{i,1} & h_{i,2} & h_{i,3} \ ... \ h_{i,0} \end{bmatrix}$$

We can construct a $32N$-dimensional STRU lattice (L_{STRU}) generated by the rows of the matrix M defined above. It can be observed from the above equations that the vector $\langle f_0, f_1, ..., f_{15}, g_0, g_1, ..., g_{15} \rangle_{1 \times 32N}$ is contained in STRU lattice. In this lattice, a short vector may be used as our key as we do in the NTRU lattice (L_{NTRU}) [7]. For the STRU lattice, we have

1. $\text{Det}(L_{STRU}) = q^{16N}$.
2. $\|\langle f_0, f_1, ..., f_{15}, g_0, g_1, ..., g_{15} \rangle\| = \sqrt{64d} \approx 4.62378\sqrt{N}$ (we are assuming $d_f = d_g = d_\phi = d = N/3$).
3. The expected length of the shortest non-zero vector (by Gaussian heuristic) in the L_{STRU} is

$$\lambda_0 = \sqrt{\frac{n}{2\pi e}} Det(L)^{1/n} = \sqrt{\frac{32N}{2\pi e}} Det(q^{16N})^{1/32N} = \sqrt{\frac{16Nq}{\pi e}} \approx 1.368752\sqrt{Nq}.$$

4. $c = \frac{\|f_0, f_1, ..., f_{15}, g_0, g_1, ..., g_{15}\|}{\lambda_0} = \frac{4.62378\sqrt{N}}{1.368752\sqrt{Nq}} \equiv \frac{3.3780}{\sqrt{q}}.$

The target vectors in L_{STRU} are about $O(\sqrt{q})$ shorter than the expected shortest vector given by Gaussian heuristic. We can say that the STRU lattice has the same structure as NTRU lattice with the only difference that STRU lattice is not fully circular. When we choose the same parameter N in both the cryptosystems NTRU and STRU, the dimension of L_{STRU} is 16 times than L_{NTRU}. Hence, STRU lattice possesses all the properties of NTRU lattice.

All advantages of taking non-associative algebra [16] are same here as in OTRU cryptosystem [12].

7 Comparative Analysis

If we compare the speed of encryption and decryption processes of the STRU cryptosystem with the NTRU cryptosystem with equal dimensions, these are almost 16 times and 32 times slower, respectively. If we reduce N with the power of two, then it will affect the computation speed, given that the complexity of the convolution multiplication is $O(N^2)$. Consequently, NTRU with a size of $16N$ is almost 256 times slower than an NTRU with a dimension of N and also, naturally, much slower than an STRU. Therefore, we argue that higher security can be achieved by reducing N within reasonable limit, but then one can meet a claim about reducing the STRU speed. It could also be argued that the length of the parameter q in STRU is longer and should not be prime at an insignificant cost. Our proposed scheme, STRU cryptosystem, is efficient, fast, and cost-effective as the NTRU public key cryptosystem because of the nature of its underlying algebraic structure (having basic operations).

8 Conclusion

A public key cryptosystem, STRU, based on sedenion algebra (non-associative and non-alternative) containing all strengths and strong points of NTRU cryptosystem is introduced. It encrypts 16 data vectors at each encryption round. A new property "inverse associative property," which is required for successful decryption is also introduced. To attack STRU cryptosystem with the lattice threats is a very massive task than NTRU. The speed of STRU cryptosystem can be increased even higher than that of NTRU by reducing the size of the underlying convolution polynomial ring.

References

1. Feynman RP (1982) Simulating physics with computers. Int J Theor Phys 21(6/7)
2. Online Resource (2019). https://www.research.ibm.com/ibm-q/
3. Shor PW (1994) Algorithms for quantum computation: discrete logarithms and factoring. In: Goldwasser S (ed) Proceedings of the 35th annual symposium on foundations of computer science. IEEE Computer Society Press
4. Online Resource (2019). https://quantumcomputingreport.com/news/nist-to-announce-round-2-pqc-candidates-on-january-10-2019/
5. Alkim E, Ducas L, Poppelmann T, Schwabe P (2016) Post-quantum key exchange—A new hope. In: USENIX security symposium
6. Carmody K (1988) Circular and hyperbolic quaternions, octonions, and sedenions. Appl Math Comput 28(1):47–72
7. Tian Y (2000) Similarity and consimilarity over real cayley dickson algebra. arxiv: math-ph/0003031
8. Wonenburger MJ, Schafer RD (1969) An introduction to nonassociative algebras. Bull Am Math Soc 75(4):7–12

9. Kutyłowski M (2004) Anonymity and rapid mixing in cryptographic protocols. In: The 4th central European conference on cryptology, Wartacrypt

10. Malekian E, Zakerolhosseini A (2010) A non-associative lattice-based public key cryptosystem. Secur Commun Netw 5:145–163

11. Malekian E, Zakerolhosseini A, Mashatan A (2011) QTRU: quaternionic version of the NTRU public-key cryptosystems. ISC Int J Inf Secur 3(1):29–42

12. Kouzmenko R (2006) Generalizations of the NTRU cryptosystem

13. Hoffstein J, Pipher J, Silverman JH (1998) NTRU: A ring based public key cryptosystem. In: Proceedings of the ANTS, LNCS, vol 1423. Springer, pp 267–288

14. Bagheri K, Sadeghi MR. A new non-associative cryptosystem based on NTRU public key cryptosystem and octonions algebra. ACM Commun Comput Algebra 49(1)

15. Baez JC (2002) The octonions. Bull Am Math Soci 39:145–205

16. Imaeda K, Imaeda M (2000) Sedenions: algebra and analysis. Appl Math Comput 115:77–88

17. Schafer RD (1996) An introduction to non associative algebras. Dover Publications Inc., New York, corrected reprint of the 1966 original

18. Thakur K, Tripathi BP (2017) STRU: a non alternative and multidimensional public key cryptosystem. Glob J Pure Appl Math 13(5):1447–1464

19. Hoffstein J, Silverman J (2000) Optimizations for NTRU. In: Public key cryptography and computational number theory, pp 11–15

20. Graham NH, Silverman NH, Whyte W (2003) A meet-in-the-middle attack on an NTRU private key, NTRU Technical Report-004

21. Coppersmith D, Shamir A (1997) Lattice attacks on NTRU. In: proceeding of EUROCRYPT 1997, vol 1233. LNCS, Springer, pp 52-61

Health Monitoring of Hydraulic System Using Feature-based Multivariate Time-series Classification Model

Ananda Shivani Medishetty, Navya Sahithi Muthavarapu, Sai Goutham Goli, B Sirisha, and B Sandhya

1 Introduction

Time-series data classification is an active research area for the past decade [1]. Time series is a set of data points taken consecutively through time. It is mathematically denoted as

$$D_e(f); [e = 1, 2, \ldots, g; f = 1, 2, \ldots, t];\tag{1}$$

e = index of various measurement at each point of time—f,
t = number of observed variables, and
g = number of observations.

   In time-series data analysis, we have one variable called time. We can scrutinize this time-series data with the objective to extract meaningful statistics and other characteristics. The main goal of this time-series data is to predict the subsequent values on the basis of previous observation values. If the data has one variable, i.e., $g = 1$, it is referred as uni-variate. Uni-variate analysis is a very simplest form of statistical analysis. It is essentially the descriptive analysis of a single variable used

A. S. Medishetty (✉) · N. S. Muthavarapu · S. G. Goli · B. Sirisha · B. Sandhya
MVSR Engineering College, Hyderabad, India
e-mail: shivanigupta3797@gmail.com

N. S. Muthavarapu
e-mail: sahithimuthavarapu@gmail.com

S. G. Goli
e-mail: saigouthamgoli111@gmail.com

B. Sirisha
e-mail: sirishavamsi@gmail.com

B. Sandhya
e-mail: sandhyab16@gmail.com

© The Author(s), under exclusive license to Springer Nature Singapore Pte Ltd. 2021
P. Stănică et al. (eds.), *Security and Privacy*, Lecture Notes in Electrical Engineering 744,
https://doi.org/10.1007/978-981-33-6781-4_7

81

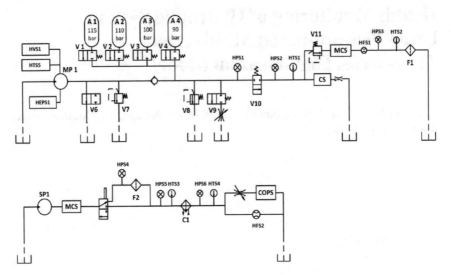

Fig. 1 Physical model of a hydraulic system used to collect training data

to describe characteristics of a sample. It is used to get the picture of how the sample looks like rather than examining their relationships and causes. If the data has one variable, i.e., $g > 1$, it is referred as multivariate.

Hydraulic systems must be contained at any rate for essential segments. There should be a compartment that stores oil and liquids, a pump that impels the liquids through the system, a valve to control the pressure and flow of the liquids inside the system, and a cylinder to change over the development of liquids into actual work. There are different segments in the middle, yet all systems must have these four [2]. Figure 1 illustrates a physical model of hydraulic test rig. The test system is outfitted with a few sensors measuring process values such as flow (HFS1, HFS2), electrical power (HEPS1), pressure (HPS1–HPS6), vibration (HVS1), and temperature (HTS1–HTS5) with standard industrial 20 mA current loop interfaces connected to a data acquisition system. Sampling rates range from 1 Hz (flow sensor) to 100 Hz (electric power/pressure) to contingent upon the dynamics of the underlying physical values.

Figure 2 illustrates an example of multivariate time series and is a hydraulic test rig data, where numerous parameters such as pressure sensors, hydraulic-(HPS1–3), motor power sensor-HEPS1, and volume flow sensor-HFS, are continually measured and stored by test rig in real time. The test rig system then executed various thousand working cycles during which distinct fault conditions were simulated in all combinations. Figure 2 shows hydraulic test rig multivariate time-series data consisting of five parameters [2].

Multivariate data classification is devised as a supervised machine learning problem mainly intended for labeling data of varying length. Each parameter is a time series, sequence of pairs (timestamp, value) [1]. Hydraulic system consists of a set of

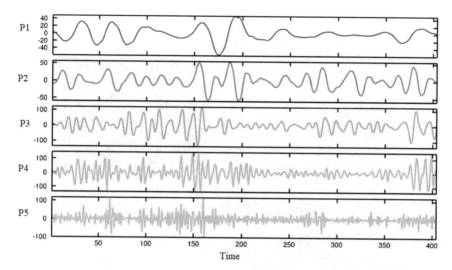

Fig. 2 A hydraulic test rig multivariate time-series data consisting of five parameters (pressure sensors hydraulic-(HPS1–3), motor power sensor-HEPS1, and volume flow sensor-HFS

parameters like HPS1–3, HEPS1, and HFS1, i.e., a multivariate time series (MTS). This system requires to be classified as Healthy or Unhealthy, in accordance with the values of the parameters [3, 4]. The time-series classification is divided into two broad categories: [1] conventional or weak classification [3] and contemporary or strong classification. Figure 3 shows weak classification, in which each succession is affiliated with only one class label and the entire succession is available to a classifier in prior to the classification. Figure 3 shows strong classification, in which each set of time-series data is organized into a different succession of classes.

The major contributions of this paper are as follows:

- In feature extraction phase, statistical features are explored. The features are extracted using a single-window approach as well as the segmented-window approach from raw sensor data with a given state of health.
- For classification phase, we come up with a window-feature-based classifier which takes the window feature of the current window into account.

The rest of the paper is catalogued as follows: Sect. 2, presents related work of multivariate classification. In Sect. 3, we introduce the proposed feature extraction and classification model. Section 4 presents the experimental results of the proposed approach and Sect. 5 concludes the work.

Weak Classification

Time	P1	P2	P3	Health
t1	1	2	1	
t2	1.1	2.13	0.85	
t3	1.2	2.15	0.67	
t4	1.4	2.1	0.5	
t5	1.3	2	0.7	Healthy
T6	1.2	2.1	0.6	
t7	1.3	2.2	0.9	
t8	1.32	2.1	0.96	

Time	P1	P2	P3	Health
t1	1	2	1	
t2	1.1	2.13	0.85	
t3	1.2	2.15	0.67	
t4	0.9	2.1	0.5	
t5	0.5	2	0.7	Unhealthy
T6	0.6	1.9	1.1	
t7	1.3	2	1	
t8	1.1	2	1.4	

Strong Classification

Time	P1	P2	P3	Health
t1	1	2	1	Healthy
t2	0.5	0.6	2.1	
t3	0.9	0.7	2.4	
t4	1.2	0.8	2.6	
t5	1.5	1.5	2.9	Unhealthy
t6	2.5	1.8	0.9	
t7	1.2	0.9	2	Healthy
t8	1.6	0.8	2.2	

Fig. 3 Example of weak and strong classification

2 Related work

Multivariate classification problem falls under two major categories: [1] distance/instance-based approach [3] and a feature-based approach. In instance-based approach, the distance between two time-series data is computed. There is an extensive survey on categories of distance measure employed for time-series classification. On the other side, feature-based approach mainly aims to represent data using a set of features or acquired properties and thus the temporal time-series problem is transformed to a static problem. For example, if we represent a time-series data using its maximum, minimum, variance, and mean, thus transforming varied length data into short length vectors which encapsulate the above four properties. Feature-based classification is most widely employed across various domains including science. This approach is mainly applied to longer time-series data like medical, electrical, mechanical, or recordings of speech signals than a short time-series pattern. Table 1 shows the list of features extracted in multivariate classification and Table 2 shows the list of algorithms used in various conditional monitoring systems. Nikolai Helwig detected sensor faults using feature-based approach and linear discriminant analysis using hydraulic dataset. A. D. Bykov applied machine learning classification approach for hydraulic system using gradient boosting, K-nearest neighbor, and SVM using hydraulic dataset. Frank L monitored health for gas turbine engine with artificial neural networks and rule-based algorithms. The data is collected by TEDANN. Yu Chen detected and diagnosed the fault of HVDC systems using extreme learning machines and bagged trees. Pallanti Srinivasa Rao et al. detected and diagnosed health of aircraft engine using ANN method. Mustagime monitored the health of aircraft engine (gas turbine) using multiple regression analysis.

3   Feature-Based Time-Series Classification Model

The modeling of the proposed framework involves two key phases: [1] feature extraction and [3] feature classification. Each of the phases is performed in two approaches: [1] single-window approach and [3] segment-window approach. **Feature Extraction:** In the current section, we explore the extraction of various statistical features from time-series data and their use in health monitoring (classification). Classification is accomplished on the basis of features extracted for each time series and not on real values. The extraction and selection of suitable features have been accepted as a significant problem. Obviously, the number of features required and nature of the feature (global or local) depend on their discriminating quality. The prime characteristics required for identified features are ease of computation, invariant to noise, and transformations. For multivariate data, and more especially for hydraulic systems data, we propose the use of statistical features, which are commonly used in systems health monitoring.

Algorithm 1 shows the window-feature-based classifier model. The first step in feature extraction is to divide the original noise-free multivariate time-series data T_o into a set of smaller sized window segments $W_i = W_1, W_2, W_3, \ldots, W_n$. The entire duration is divided into 14 windows of dissimilar size. For each current window W_i extract eight statistical features—sum, median, mean, length, standard deviation, variance, maximum, and minimum values from five given input parameters—HEPS1, HFS, HPS1, HPS2, and HPS3. In our paper, we have explored the window label $W F_i$ and it is added as feature value. Hence, for each window W_i nine features are extracted, and this is repeated for 14 windows, for 5 parameters.

Each parameter has 6000 samples and 2205 instances, and these 6000 samples are divided into 14 windows. For each window, we generate $2205 \times (8$ statistical features + 1 window feature + 1 label$) = 2205 \times 42$ feature map. Since we have 14 windows and 2205 instance for each window ($14 \times 2205 = 30870$), the training data size is 30870×42. The test data given to the model is noise-induced test data (high-level, medium-level, and low-level noise). In the traditional model, the features are extracted from the entire duration and hence we treat this to be single-window feature extraction. In this research paper, we compare our approach through the traditional approach which uses single-window feature extraction. Window-feature-based classifier is very simple, they improve classification accuracy and consistent across all three noise levels. Decision tree classification technique is used to classify the time-series data.

Table 1 Review of features extracted in multivariate classification

Year	Author	Extracted features	Datasets
2001	Nanopoulos et al. [5]	Mean (M), skewness (SK), kurtosis (K) and standard deviation (SD)	CCP data
2003	Morchen et al. [6]	Wavelets and Fourier features	Energy preservation tests
2006	Wang et al. [7]	non-linearity, skewness, periodicity, kurtosis, self-similarity, seasonality, serial correlation, chaos, and measures of trend	Benchmark time-series datasets
2009	Ye and Keogh et al. [8]	Shapelets are time-series succession which are in some sense, maximally representative of a class	Benchmark time-series datasets
2013	Deng et al. [9]	Mean (M), trend (T), and spread (S) in local data intervals	Benchmark time-series datasets
2014	Fulcher et al. [10]	Gaussianity, auto-mutual information, spread, outlier properties, auto-correlation, location, entropy, power spectrum features, Lyapunov exponent estimates, sliding window measures, surrogate data analysis prediction errors, the dimensions of correlation	Trace dataset, Wafer dataset from UCR time series
2014	Esmael et al. [11]	Discrete Fourier transform, piece-wise linear approximation, Discrete wavelet transform, piece-wise aggregate approximation, symbolic aggregate approximation, adaptive piece-wise constant approximation, and singular value decomposition	Benchmark time-series datasets
2015	Helwig et al. [12]	signal shape (position of max value, slope of linear fit) and distribution density characteristics (skewness, variance, kurtosis, and median)	Hydraulic dataset
2015	Helwig et al. [4]	Statistical moments median (Me), variance (V), skewness (Sk) and kurtosis (K) and signal shape parameters (fit of slope, the position of max value)	Hydraulic dataset
2015	Helwig et al. [2]	Skewness, Max features for oil aeration monitoring: variance, median	Hydraulic dataset
2017	Adams et al. [13]	Deep feature extraction using auto-encoder, mean, standard deviation, skewness, and kurtosis	Hydraulic dataset
2019	Chawathe et al.	Mean, variance, skewness, and kurtosis	Hydraulic dataset

Table 2 Review of algorithms used in conditional monitoring

Author	Title	Algorithm used	Dataset
Helwig et al. [12]	Detecting and compensating sensor faults in a hydraulic condition monitoring system	Statistical feature extraction, linear discriminant analysis feature selection	Hydraulic dataset
Bykov et al. [14]	Machine learning methods applying for hydraulic systems states classification	Gradient boosting, K-nearest neighbor, support vector machine	Hydraulic dataset
Greitzer et al. [15]	Gas turbine engine health monitoring and prognostics	Artificial neural networks, rule-based algorithm	Data collection by TEDANN (Turbine Engine Diagnostics using Artificial Neural Networks)
Chen [16]	Fault diagnosis of HVDC systems using machine-learning-based methods	Extreme learning machine, bagged trees	Data from high-voltage direct current
Rao et al. [17]	AI-based on-board diagnostic and prognostic health management system	Artificial neural networks	Fighter aircraft
Yildirim et al. [18]	Aircraft gas turbine engine health monitoring system by real flight data	Multiple regression analysis (MRA), ANN	Real flight data
Lovrec et al. [19]	Online condition monitoring systems for hydraulic machines	Expert system	Hydraulic machine

4 Experimental Results

This section details the process of inducing noise and its characterization. Classifier performance on an original and noise-injected multivariate time-series data will be compared under this section.

4.1 Dataset

Nikolai Helwig et al. created test data, which was experimentally acquired with hydraulic system test rig. This rig has both cooling-filter circuit and hydraulic working connected through the oil tank [2]. The hydraulic system repeats constantly with

Input : Original Multivariate Time-series (T_o), Noisy Multivariate Time-series (T_n) of
        length m; **Variables**-W_i- Input Window, I-Current Iteration
Output: Succession of predicted class labels.
while $(T_o{=}t_1)$ **do**
    Divide the Original Multivariate data (T_o), Noisy data (T_n) into set of W smaller sized
    window segments. (where $W_i = W_1, W_2, W_3, \ldots, W_n$);
    For Each W_i segment;
    Do ;
    1. Extract Statistical features for the current segment W_i.;
    2. Get the window feature $W F_i$ of the current window segment W_i.;
    3. Generate a Feature Vector F_m by concatenating the window feature $W F_i$ of the current
    window segment to W_i extracted from step:1.;
    End For;
    For Test T_j where j = 1, 2, 3;
    Do ;
    1.Call the prediction model **predict**(W_i, $W F_i$) which returns the status of the test class.;
    End For
end

Algorithm 1: Window-Feature-Based Multivariate Time-series Classification Model

Table 3 Dataset parameter description

Sensor	Sampling rate (Hz)	Samples per sensor (one sensor)
Motor power sensor (HEPS)	100	6000
Volume flow sensors (HFS)	10	600
Pressure sensors (HPS1–3)	100	6000

load cycles for the duration of 60 s and measures sensor values such as temperatures, pressures, and volume flows while the condition of three vital hydraulic components (valve, pump, and accumulator) differed significantly. The total number of instances are 2205. Table 3 shows the sensor attributes or samples recorded with varied sampling rates.

4.2 Noise Characterization

Singh et al. [20, 21] and Jim et al. [22] have reported that inducing controlled noise amounts to the original data improves the performance of the model. In our study, random noise data was produced using MATLAB. Random noise (RN) array is first produced between Max(maximum) and Min(minimum) value of the parameter, at that particular instance of time. The total number of instances are 2205, out of which 1449 instances are in stable condition and 756 instances are unstable. In this research work, we have induced 600 samples (attributes) of noise data in 100 instances for each parameter (HEPS1, HFS, HPS1, HPS2, and HPS3). The noise is categorized into three levels—high-level, medium-level, and low-level noise injection. Table 4 depicts

Table 4 Noise characterization: high-level noise

Param	Samp (Hz)	W_1	W_2	W_3	W_4	W_5	W_6	W_7	W_8	W_9	W_{10}	W_{11}	W_{12}	W_{13}	W_{14}
HEPS	100				0.12 RN	0.12 RN	0.12 RN	0.12 RN	0.12 RN	0.12 RN					
HFS	10	0.12 RN	0.12 RN	0.12 RN									0.12 RN	0.12 RN	0.12 RN
HPS1	100	0.12 RN	0.12 RN	0.12 RN									0.12 RN	0.12 RN	0.12 RN
HPS2	100		0.12 RN		0.12 RN	0.12 RN	0.12 RN	0.12 RN							
HPS3	100				0.12 RN	0.12 RN	0.12 RN	0.12 RN	0.12 RN						

the details of percentile of noise injected within each window for each parameter. Low-level noise represents a single parameter affected by random noise. Medium-level noise represents three parameters affected by random noise. High-level noise represents all five parameters affected by random noise.

4.3 Classifier Performance

Training data and test data are created for overall instance feature extraction and window-based feature extraction as per algorithm. Following that, decision tree is used to train and test the classifier using a tenfold cross-validation technique for both traditional approach and proposed approach. To examine the effect of noise on feature extraction and feature-level classification of multivariate data prediction. We evaluated and analyzed the working model performance on noise-free data, high-level, mid-level, and low-level noise-induced multivariate data. Three major observations are made from the experimental results.

- The classifier accuracy is >90% for both traditional- and window-feature-based classification model. Out of eight statistical features—median, standard deviation, and variance feature values are robust and correlate with fault characteristics.
- In case of low-level noise, the classifier accuracy drops down to 93% for the traditional model and 83.43% for the window-feature-based classification model, where a single parameter out of five affected by random noise.
- In case of medium-level noise, the classifier accuracy drops down to 93% for the traditional model and 80.34% for the window-feature-based classification model, where three parameters out of five are affected by random noise.
- In case of high-level noise, the classifier accuracy drops further down to 65% for the traditional model and 78.4% for the window-feature-based classification model, where all five parameters are affected by random noise (Tables 5 and 6).

Table 5 FP rate, TP rate, recall, and precision for window-feature-based classification model

Mode	Traditional model				Window-based classification model			
	FP rate	TP rate	Recall	Precision	TP rate	FP rate	Precision	Recall
Noise free	0.053	0.964	0.964	0.964	0.923	0.104	0.923	0.923
Low level	0.099	0.934	0.934	0.934	0.834	0.201	0.835	0.834
Mid-level	0.1	0.933	0.933	0.933	0.803	0.233	0.805	0.803
High level	0.658	0.655	0.655	0.431	0.784	0.263	0.784	0.784

Table 6 Classification accuracy of window-feature-based classification model

Mode	Traditional model			Window-based classification model		
	ROC area	F-measure	Accuracy	ROC area	F-measure	Accuracy
Noise free	0.965	0.964	**96.4**	0.925	0.923	**92.3**
Low-level noise	0.898	0.934	**93.4**	0.823	0.834	**83.4**
Mid-level noise	0.896	0.932	**93.2**	0.788	0.804	**80.3**
High-level noise	0.507	0.507	**65.4**	0.737	0.784	**78.4**

5 Conclusion

The impact of induced noise on multivariate time-series data prediction is very significant to quantify for precise prediction. This paper examines the effect of noise on feature extraction and classification model. It is observed that for noise-free data the decision tree classifier accuracy is >90% for both traditional and window-feature-based classification model. When all the five parameters are affected by random noise, the decision tree classifier accuracy decreases to 65% for the traditional model and 78.4% for the window-feature-based classification model. Though the window-based classifier is simple, it improves the classification accuracy significantly in the presence of noise. The results show that the enhancement in decision tree classification accuracy is about 13% compared to a traditional classifier.

References

1. Kadous MW et al (2005) Classification of multivariate time series and structured data using constructive induction. Mach Learn 58:179–216
2. Helwiga N et al (2015) Identification and quantification of hydraulic system faults based on multivariate statistics using spectral vibration features. In: ZeMA , Germany
3. Liu X et al (2012) Study on knowledge-based intelligent fault diagnosis of hydraulic system. TELKOMNIKA 10:2041–2046
4. Helwig N. et al (2015) Condition monitoring of a complex hydraulic system using multivariate statistics. In: Proceedings of the I2MTC
5. Nanopoulos A et al (2001) Feature-based classification of time-series data. Int J Comput Res 10:49–61
6. Morchen F et al (2003) Time series feature extraction for data mining using DWT and DFT
7. Wang X et al (2006) Characteristic-based clustering for time series data. Data Mining Knowl Discov 13:335–364
8. Ye L et al (2011) Time series shapelets: a novel technique that allows accurate, interpretable and fast classification. Data Mining Knowl. Discov 22:149–182
9. Deng H et al (2013) A time series forest for classification and feature extraction. Inf Sci 239:142–153

10. Fulcher BD et al (2014) Highly comparative feature-based time-series classification. IEEE Trans Knowl Data Eng 3026–3037
11. Esmael B et al (2012) Multivariate time series classification by combining trend-based and value-based approximations. Comput Sci Appl—ICCSA
12. Helwig N et al (2015) Detecting and compensating sensor faults in a hydraulic condition monitoring system. In: Proceedings of the sensor
13. Adams S et al (2017) A comparison of feature selection and feature extraction techniques for condition monitoring of a hydraulic actuator
14. Bykov AD, Voronov VI et al, Machine learning methods applying for hydraulic system states classification. In: 2019 systems of signals generating and processing in the field of on board communications
15. Greitzer FL et al, Gas turbine engine health monitoring and prognostics. In: International society of logistics (SOLE) 1999 symposium
16. Chen Y (2019) Fault diagnosis of HVDC systems using machine learning based methods. The University of Wisconsin-Milwaukee
17. Rao SP et al (2015) AI based on-board diagnostic and prognostic health management system. In: Annual conference of the prognostics and health management society
18. Yildirim MT, Kurt B, Aircraft gas turbine engine health monitoring system by real flight data. Int J Aerosp Eng 2018:12, Article ID 9570873
19. Lovrec D, Ti V (2012) On-line condition monitoring systems for hydraulic machines. Facta Univ Mech Eng 10(1):81–89
20. Singh S et al (1998) Effect of noise on generalisation in Massively Parallel Fuzzy Systems. Pattern Recogn 31(11):25–33
21. Singh S et al (1999) Noise impact on time-series forecasting using an intelligent pattern matching technique. Pattern Recognit 32(8):1389–1398
22. Jim K et al (1995) Effects of noise on convergence and generalisation in recurrent networks. MIT Press, p 649

Image Security Using Hyperchaos and Multidimensional Playfair Cipher

Krishnaraj Bhat, Dindayal Mahto, Dilip Kumar Yadav, and Chandrashekhar Azad

1 Introduction

Communicating the plain secret image over the open network is prone to attacks causing to loose its confidentiality. Therefore, the secret image has to be made unintelligible while transmission over the network. Even for the standard ciphers such as AES, 3DES, and RSA exist, their efficiency and security with respect to the encryption of images are not sufficient [23, 24]. This leads to the need for a novel image encryption method.

In 1854, Charles Wheatstone proposed the Playfair cipher which could encrypt 26 English alphabets treating I and J as the same. Then some improved versions of the Playfair cipher were proposed among which only a few supported image encryption. Chakravarthy et al. [11] proposed methods in which the frequency domain of the images is being applied by a spatial domain algorithm for encryption. By modifying one pixel value in the plain image, only respective two side-by-side pixel values in the cipher image are modified leading to low resistance against differential attacks. Bhat et al. [8, 9] proposed two variations of Playfair cipher where the dimension of the key matrix varies from 1 to 8 for encrypting any kind of information by treating

K. Bhat (✉)
Department of Computer Science and Engineering, NMAM Institute of Technology,
Nitte 574110, India
e-mail: krrishvaradha08@gmail.com

D. Mahto
Department of Information Technology, School of Computing, SASTRA Deemed
to be University, Thanjavur 613401, India
e-mail: dindayal.mahto@gmail.com

D. K. Yadav · C. Azad
Department of Computer Applications, National Institute of Technology Jamshedpur,
Jamshedpur 831014, India

P. Stănică et al. (eds.), *Security and Privacy*, Lecture Notes in Electrical Engineering 744,
https://doi.org/10.1007/978-981-33-6781-4_8

93

them in terms of bytes, and these two variations have more resistance against brute force attack in comparison to the AES-256 [6, 10].

The security provided by an encryption scheme can be ameliorated by applying to the permutation in image encryption procedure on grounds of a chaotic system [15, 27]. Chen et al. [12] proposed a method in which the shuffling of the positions and gray values of image pixels is done by using 3D cat map and the confusion of the affinity between the plain image and the cipher image is achieved by using another chaotic map. Ren et al. [22] proposed a chaotic system in which the actualization of the sequence image encryption uses two types of means on the encryption for the same image which is, respectively, from the alternative operating on image pixel grayscale value and the confusion of the pixel location in the particular operation method done on the grounds of logistic generation and transformation. Albahrani and Alshekly [3] proposed a chaotic substitution and permutation method for image encryption on grounds of fusion between block cipher with a block size of 500 bytes, hyperchaotic map, and 1D Bernoulli map. It does not propose what has to be done when the last block in the image contains less than 500 bytes. Iqbal et al. [14] proposed a RGB image block cipher applying chaotic tent map, intertwining logistic map, 15-puzzle artificial intelligence problem, SHA-256 hash function, and DNA computing. Liu et al. [18] proposed a color image encryption algorithm in which dynamic DNA mechanism on grounds of 4D memristive hyperchaos is carried out on the processes of confusion, diffusion, and encoding. Belazi et al. [5] proposed a chaos-based encryption scheme for medical images on grounds of compounding of logistic-Chebyshev map, sine-Chebyshev map, and DNA computing under two encryption iterations, premised by a key generation using SHA-256 hash function, and espouses the permutation–substitution–diffusion organization. Luo et al. [19] proposed an image encryption method on grounds of the elliptic curve Elgamal cryptography, paired logistic-tent map, paired tent-sine map, and SHA-512 hash function for generating initial values of chaotic system. Zhang et al. [28] proposed an image encryption method on grounds of secure hash algorithm 3, piece-wise linear chaotic map, Rossler chaotic systems, Hilbert curve, and H-fractal for the key generation, scrambling, confusion, and diffusion processes. Liu et al. [16] proposed a color image encryption algorithm that carries out simultaneous scrambling and diffusion on grounds of hopfield chaotic neural network. Liu and Liu [17] proposed a color image encryption algorithm on grounds of Arnold algorithm, DNA coding, double-chaos system framed with Lorenz chaotic mapping with variable parameters, and fourth-order Rossler hyperchaotic mapping. Malik et al. [20] proposed a color image encryption algorithm on grounds of DNA computing and hyperchaotic dynamical system designed with eminent plain-text sensitivity. Abdelfatah [1] proposed a scheme for real-time and secure image transmission in which block-based elliptic curve public key encryption is utilized for key distribution, and Sine, Ten, and Henon maps are merged to enhance the security against brute force attacks. Also, after the two levels of encryption, the encrypted image is digitally signed by an effective method to attain authentication, integrity, and non-repudiation. Niu and Zhang [21] proposed a plain-text-related image encryption scheme based on Josephus traversing, piece-wise linear chaotic map, and hyperchaotic Chen system for achieving confusion and diffusion. In this, if size of the image is not divisible by 4, then how pixel permutation has to be done is not specified. Herbadji et al. [13] proposed an enhanced quadratic map for color image encryption based on the permutation–diffusion process. Albahrani et al. [4] proposed a method that produces 16×16 Playfair matrix as a key by using two cross-chaotic maps. Then the image is divided into a certain number of blocks where every block has got 16×16 bytes and every block is ciphered by a distinct Playfair matrix. Following limitations exist in the methods briefed so far:

1. Only ability to encrypt 24-bit pixel images [13, 14, 16–18, 20].
2. Cipher image size is greater than plain image size [4, 9].
3. Low resistance against differential attacks [9, 11, 12].
4. Correlation coefficient is high between cipher images obtained using same plain image but with one pixel difference [9, 11, 12].
5. Restriction on size of the secret image for using the encryption method [1, 3, 12, 14, 21].
6. As a unique key will be generated for each different secret image, there is an overhead of sharing secret key every time among participants [5, 18, 19, 28].

The proposed method overcomes all the abovementioned limitations in the existing image encryption methods. The proposed method has been analyzed in respect of the parameters: correlation coefficient, encryption quality, diffusion characteristics, histogram analysis, key and search space analysis, and computational complexity. The results of these analysis indicate that the proposed method is efficient for image encryption. This article is formatted as follows: Sect. 2 highlights on preliminaries, Sect. 3 describes the proposed method, Sect. 4 provides the statistical analysis and experimental results, and Sect. 5 provides the conclusion.

2 Preliminaries

2.1 Multidimensional Playfair Cipher

Bhat et al. [7] proposed the generalization for multidimensional Playfair cipher in which it is shown that maximum dimension for a Playfair cipher variant depends on the number of elements supported by that variant. If Z is the number of elements supported by a Playfair cipher variant then its maximum dimension can be the number of prime factors in the factorized form of Z. If K is the dimension of a Playfair cipher variant, then each element in the key matrix of that variant is represented by using K coordinates $(C_1, C_2, ...C_{K-1}, C_K)$.

During encryption, a group having K elements is considered at once. If $(L_0, L_1, ... L_{K-1})$ are the elements in the group according to the order they appear, then each element L_i where $0 \leq i \leq K - 1$ is substituted by the element with the coordinates: $(L_{(i+2) \bmod K}.C_1, \quad L_{(i+3) \bmod K}.C_2, \quad ... \quad L_{(i+K-2) \bmod K}.C_{K-3}, \quad L_{(i+K-1) \bmod K}.C_{K-2},$

$L_i.C_{K-1}$, $L_{(i+1) \mod K}.C_K$). Here, $L_i.C_j$ represents the C_j coordinate value for the element L_i where $1 \le j \le K$.

During decryption, each element L_i in the group is substituted by the element with the coordinates: $(L_{(i+K-2) \mod K}.C_1, L_{(i+K-3) \mod K}.C_2, ... L_{(i+2) \mod K}.C_{K-3}, L_{(i+1) \mod K}.C_{K-2}, L_i.C_{K-1}, L_{(i+K-1) \mod K}.C_K)$. For details on illustration, refer [7].

2.2 Five-dimensional Shimizu–Morioka System (5D-SMS)

5D-SMS is a hyperchaotic system [25] defined as in (1):

$$
\begin{aligned}
p_{i+1} &= q_i \\
q_{i+1} &= -q_i + cp_i + dp_i^3 + ep_i t_i \\
r_{i+1} &= s_i \\
s_{i+1} &= -s_i + fr_i + gr_i^3 + hr_i t_i \\
t_{i+1} &= jt_i + kp_i^2 + lr_i^2
\end{aligned}
\tag{1}
$$

where c, d, e, f, g, h, j, and l are the constant parameters and p_i, q_i, r_i, s_i, and t_i are the state variables of the 5D-SMS. For $(c, d, e, f, g, h, j, l) = (4, -1, -1, 7, -1, -1, 0.1, 5, 0.01)$, 5D-SMS will be in hyperchaotic state [25].

3 Proposed Method

The proposed method combines 5D-SMS and multidimensional Playfair cipher for encrypting an image. The encryption and decryption procedures are described below.

3.1 Encryption

The encryption procedure takes a secret image SI and key tuple $\langle p_0, q_0, r_0, s_0, t_0 \rangle$ as input and produces the cipher image CI. There are mainly five phases in the encryption procedure:

1. Secret image permutation.
2. XORed image formation.
3. XORed image permutation.
4. Multidimensional Playfair encryption.
5. Encrypted image permutation.

Here, 1st, 3rd, and 5th phases induce diffusion, and 2nd and 4th phases induce confusion. Each of these phases are described in detail below.

3.1.1 Secret Image Permutation

The steps in this phase are as follows:

1. Use p_0, q_0, r_0, s_0, and t_0 as initial values of p_k, q_k, r_k, s_k, and t_k.
2. Assign the variable values p_k, q_k, r_k, s_k, and t_k to $o1_i, o2_i, o3_i, o4_i$, and $o5_i$, respectively, where $k \geq 0$.
3. Generate new values $o1_{i+1}, o2_{i+1}, o3_{i+1}, o4_{i+1}$, and $o5_{i+1}$ in the range 1 to I_S from $o1_i, o2_i, o3_i, o4_i$, and $o5_i$ by using (2).

$$o1_{i+1} = \lfloor |(o1_i(o2_i + o3_i + o4_i + o5_i)10^{16}) + (S_{OP})| \rceil \bmod I_S + 1$$
$$o2_{i+1} = \lfloor |(o2_i(o1_i + o3_i + o4_i + o5_i)10^{16}) + (S_{OP})| \rceil \bmod I_S + 1$$
$$o3_{i+1} = \lfloor |(o3_i(o1_i + o2_i + o4_i + o5_i)10^{16}) + (S_{OP})| \rceil \bmod I_S + 1 \quad (2)$$
$$o4_{i+1} = \lfloor |(o4_i(o1_i + o2_i + o3_i + o5_i)10^{16}) + (S_{OP})| \rceil \bmod I_S + 1$$
$$o5_{i+1} = \lfloor |(o5_i(o1_i + o2_i + o3_i + o4_i)10^{16}) + (S_{OP})| \rceil \bmod I_S + 1$$

where $\lfloor x \rceil$ gives the round value of x, $|y|$ gives the absolute value of y, S_{OP} is the sum of values of SI's pixels, and I_S is the number of pixel values in SI.
4. Append the non-repetitive values from $o1_{i+1}, o2_{i+1}, o3_{i+1}, o4_{i+1}$, and $o5_{i+1}$ to the pixel position array P_{PA}. If any value is repeated then find the next free pixel position and add it to P_{PA}.
5. Assign the values of $o1_i, o2_i, o3_i, o4_i$, and $o5_i$ to p_i, q_i, r_i, s_i, and t_i, respectively, to generate the next state variable values p_k, q_k, r_k, s_k, and t_k by using (1).
6. Repeat steps 2 to 5 unless all pixel positions in the range 1 to I_S are added to P_{PA}.
7. Form the permuted secret image PSI by permuting the pixels of SI based on the location values in P_{PA}.

3.1.2 XORed Image Formation

The steps in this phase are as follows:

1. Use p_0, q_0, r_0, s_0, and t_0 as initial values of p_k, q_k, r_k, s_k, and t_k.
2. Assign the variable values p_k, q_k, r_k, s_k, and t_k to $m1_i, m2_i, m3_i, m4_i$, and $m5_i$, respectively, where $k \geq 0$.
3. Generate new values $m1_{i+1}, m2_{i+1}, m3_{i+1}, m4_{i+1}$, and $m5_{i+1}$ in the range 0 to 255 from $m1_i, m2_i, m3_i, m4_i$, and $m5_i$ by using (3).

$$m1_{i+1} = \lfloor |m1_i(m2_i + m3_i + m4_i + m5_i)10^{16}| \rceil \bmod 256$$
$$m2_{i+1} = \lfloor |m2_i(m1_i + m3_i + m4_i + m5_i)10^{16}| \rceil \bmod 256$$
$$m3_{i+1} = \lfloor |m3_i(m1_i + m2_i + m4_i + m5_i)10^{16}| \rceil \bmod 256 \qquad (3)$$
$$m4_{i+1} = \lfloor |m4_i(m1_i + m2_i + m3_i + m5_i)10^{16}| \rceil \bmod 256$$
$$m5_{i+1} = \lfloor |m5_i(m1_i + m2_i + m3_i + m4_i)10^{16}| \rceil \bmod 256$$

4. Append the values $m1_{i+1}, m2_{i+1}, m3_{i+1}, m4_{i+1}$, and $m5_{i+1}$ as pixel values to a random image RI.
5. Assign the values of $m1_i, m2_i, m3_i, m4_i$, and $m5_i$ to p_i, q_i, r_i, s_i, and t_i, respectively, to generate the next state variable values p_k, q_k, r_k, s_k, and t_k by using (1).
6. Repeat steps 2 to 5 unless RI size has become equal to PSI size.
7. Form the XORed image XI by XORing RI with PSI.

3.1.3 XORed Image Permutation

This phase is same as 1st phase. But, it uses XI in place of SI to produce the permuted XORed image PXI and S_{OP} is the sum of values of XI's pixels.

3.1.4 Multidimensional Playfair Encryption

The steps in this phase are as follows:

1. Use p_0, q_0, r_0, s_0, and t_0 as initial values of p_k, q_k, r_k, s_k, and t_k.
2. Assign the variable values p_k, q_k, r_k, s_k, and t_k to $m1_i, m2_i, m3_i, m4_i$, and $m5_i$, respectively, where $k \geq 0$.
3. Generate new values $m1_{i+1}, m2_{i+1}, m3_{i+1}, m4_{i+1}$, and $m5_{i+1}$ in the range 0 to 255 from $m1_i, m2_i, m3_i, m4_i$, and $m5_i$ by using (3).
4. Append the non-repetitive values from $m1_{i+1}, m2_{i+1}, m3_{i+1}, m4_{i+1}$, and $m5_{i+1}$ as elements to the key matrix KM of the Multidimensional Playfair cipher. If any value is repeated then find the next unrepeated value in the range 0 to 255 and add it to KM.
5. Assign the values of $m1_i, m2_i, m3_i, m4_i$, and $m5_i$ to p_i, q_i, r_i, s_i, and t_i, respectively, to generate the next state variable values p_k, q_k, r_k, s_k, and t_k by using (1).
6. Repeat steps 2–5 unless all values in the range 0–255 are added to KM.
7. Form groups of eight non-overlapping pixels from PXI and encrypt each group by using eight-dimensional Playfair encryption as described in [7] by using KM as the key matrix. If the last group contains n elements where $n = 2, 3, ...7$, then encrypt this group by using the n-dimensional Playfair encryption as described in [8]. Else if the last group contains 1 element, then substitute that element by

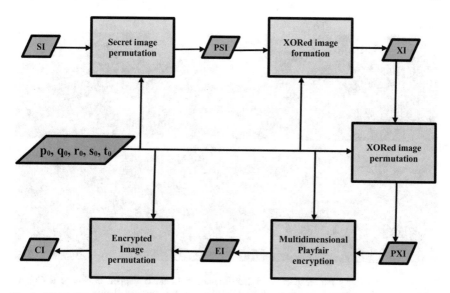

Fig. 1 Block diagram of the proposed encryption procedure

the element to its right in KM in circular fashion. The resultant image so formed is the encrypted image EI.

3.1.5 Encrypted Image Permutation

This phase is same as 1st phase. But it uses S_{OP} as the sum of values of EI's pixels and it uses EI in place of SI to produce the permuted encrypted image CI which is the net cipher image. Figure 1 displays the block diagram of the proposed encryption procedure.

3.2 Decryption

The decryption procedure takes the cipher image CI and key tuple $\langle p_0, q_0, r_0, s_0, t_0 \rangle$ as input and produces the secret image SI. There are mainly five phases in the decryption procedure:

1. Reverse encrypted image permutation.
2. Multidimensional Playfair decryption.
3. Reverse XORed image permutation.
4. Reverse XORed image formation.
5. Reverse secret image permutation.

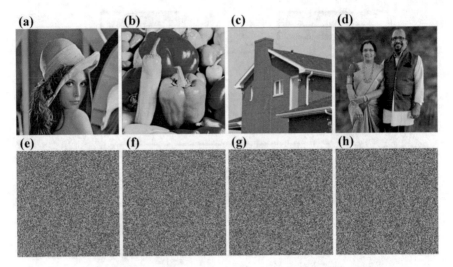

Fig. 2 Secret images and respective cipher images. **a** Lena. **b** Pepper. **c** House. **d** Couple.
e Encrypted Lena. **f** Encrypted Pepper. **g** Encrypted house. **h** Encrypted couple

These five phases are the reverse operations of the corresponding phases in the encryption procedure. As they are straightforward, they are not detailed here.

4 Statistical Analysis and Experimental Results

The experiment platform is GNU Octave 5.2.0. For the experimental purpose, four color images each of size $256 \times 256 \times 3$ (height $\times$ width $\times$ planes) are taken as secret images. Figure 2 displays the secret images and respective cipher images obtained by applying the proposed encryption procedure. All the respective deciphered images are as same as displayed in Fig. 2a–d.

This section provides the analysis details of the proposed method in respect of the following parameters: correlation coefficient, encryption quality, diffusion characteristics, histogram analysis, key and search space analysis, and computational complexity.

4.1 Correlation Coefficient (CC)

CC is utilized to judge the encryption quality of an image encryption cipher [2]. The values of CC between equal images, complement images, and entirely distinct images are 1, -1, and ≈ 0, respectively. It can be noticed from Table 1 that the CC values between secret images and respective cipher images are ≈ 0, and it can

Table 1 CC between secret images and respective cipher images

Image	Lena	Pepper	House	Couple
CC	−0.0009	0.0006	0.0028	0.0018

Table 2 CC between two diagonally, vertically, and horizontally adjacent pixels in images

Image	Horizontal	Vertical	Diagonal	Image	Horizontal	Vertical	Diagonal
Lena	0.9651	0.9812	0.9517	Encrypted Lena	−0.0012	−0.0017	−0.0010
Pepper	0.9649	0.9694	0.9451	Encrypted Pepper	0.0022	0.0009	−0.0010
House	0.9555	0.9101	0.8819	Encrypted house	0.0034	0.0015	−0.0002
Couple	0.9568	0.9757	0.9371	Encrypted couple	0.0007	0.0001	−0.0033

Table 3 Deviation from uniform histogram, maximum deviation, and PSNR values between secret images and respective cipher images

Image	D_{UH}	M_D	PSNR
Lena	0.4691	91,765	8.6376
Pepper	0.3940	75,772.5	8.0962
House	0.7791	152,593	8.8109
Couple	0.6847	133,729.5	8.7162

be noticed from Table 2 that the CC values between two diagonally, vertically, and horizontally adjacent pixels in secret images and cipher images are ≈ 1 and ≈ 0, respectively. The formula to compute the correlation coefficient is referred from [2].

4.2 Encryption Quality

To measure the encryption quality of an image encryption method, maximum deviation (M_D), deviation from uniform histogram D_{UH}, and peak signal-to-noise ratio (PSNR) between secret images and respective cipher images are computed. For an efficient image encryption method, M_D value should be high, D_{UH} value should be low, and PSNR value should be low. It can be observed from Table 3 that the proposed method meets this encryption quality criteria. The formulas to compute M_D, D_{UH}, and PSNR are referred from [2].

Table 4 UACI, NPCR, and MSE results for 1-bit change in key and plain image

Image	Key			Image		
	MSE	NPCR (%)	UACI (%)	MSE	NPCR (%)	UACI (%)
Lena	10,927.5353	99.603	33.511	10,963.7429	99.635	33.551
Pepper	10,966.6451	99.604	33.557	10,924.7284	99.593	33.470
House	10,935.1042	99.607	33.498	10,941.3289	99.595	33.503
Couple	10,894.4755	99.625	33.418	10,964.1375	99.582	33.540

4.3 Diffusion Characteristics

Diffusion characteristics of an image encryption method specifies that the cipher image pixels should rely on the plain image pixels in a very complicated manner. A small modification in plain image or key should give rise to significant modification in the respective cipher image which is known as avalanche effect. To test the avalanche effect, mean square error (MSE) is utilized and it is defined as the cumulative squared error between two images. Higher the value of MSE, higher is the avalanche effect. Unified average change intensity (UACI) and number of pixel change rate (NPCR) are utilized to measure the effect of 1- bit modification in plain image and 1-bit modification in key on the overall cipher image. The expected values of UACI and NPCR randomness tests for image encryption are 33.4635% and 99.6094%, respectively [26]. From Table 4, it can be noticed that MSE values are high, and UACI and NPCR values are close to standard values. Thus, the proposed method is repellent against known plain message, known cipher message, chosen plain message, chosen cipher message, and differential attacks. The formulas to compute MSE, UACI, and NPCR are referred from [2].

4.4 Histogram Analysis

A histogram ex-cogitates the statistics of all the pixels values in an image. Figure 3 displays the histograms of secret images and the respective cipher images. In secret images, the dispersion of pixel values is comparatively centralized showing certain statistical features. However, the dispersion of pixel values in the cipher images is invariant, so this dispersion does not possess any statistical features. It is hard for attackers to decipher the secret image by utilizing the corresponding cipher image. Thus, the proposed method is repellent against statistical analysis attacks.

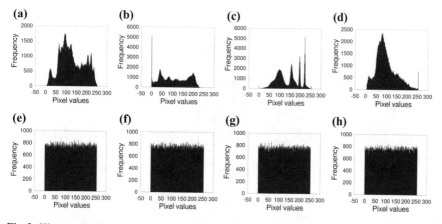

Fig. 3 Histograms of secret and cipher images. **a–d** Histograms of Lena, Pepper, house, and couple, respectively. **e–h** Histograms of encrypted Lena, encrypted pepper, encrypted house, and encrypted couple, respectively

4.5 Key and Search Space Analysis

If the key space is large enough then an encryption method is considered secure. Brute force attack is made infeasible with a large key space. The minimum key space to be secure against brute force attack is 2^{128} [2]. If 16 decimal places after the decimal point are considered in the proposed method, then the possible number of keys with the key tuple $\langle p_0, q_0, r_0, s_0, t_0 \rangle$ is $(10^{16})^5 \approx 2^{266}$. Table 5 displays the comparison of key space value of the proposed method with some of the existing chaos-based image encryption methods. Key space value of the proposed method is greater than that of the methods in [3, 4, 12, 28].

Search space is the number of groups of elements the attacker has to look up with the objective of solving the relation between a given group of pixel values using the Playfair encryption. For the proposed method, since the maximum number of elements in a group considered during multidimensional Playfair encryption is 8, the search space is $256^8 = 18,446,744,073,709,551,616$. Table 6 displays the comparison of search space value of the proposed method with that of Playfair variants in [4, 8, 9, 11]. It can be noticed that the proposed method has got the highest search space value.

4.6 Computational Complexity

If P is the count of an image's pixel values, then computational complexities for three permutation phases, one XORing phase, and one multidimensional Playfair encryption phase are $O(P\sqrt{P})$, $O(P)$, and $O(P)$, respectively. Thus, $O(P\sqrt{P})$

Table 5 Comparison of key space values

Method	Chen et al. [12]	Albahrani et al. [3]	Iqbal et al. [14]	Liu et al. [18]	Belazi et al. [5]	Luo et al. [19]	Zhang et al. [28]	Liu et al. [16]	Liu and Liu [17]	Malik et al. [20]	Abdelfatah [1]	Herbadji et al. [13]	Iqubal et al. [4]	Proposed
Value	2^{128}	2^{213}	2^{359}	2^{373}	2^{716}	2^{564}	2^{261}	2^{374}	2^{798}	2^{715}	2^{772}	2^{449}	2^{213}	2^{266}

Table 6 Comparison of search space values

Method	Chakravarthy et al. [11]	Bhat et al. [9]	Bhat et al. [8]	Albahrani et al. [4]	Proposed
Value	256^2	$256^{3.1964}$	256^8	256^2	256^8

Table 7 Comparison of computational complexity

Method	Belazi et al. [5]	Liu et al. [16]	Liu and Liu [17]	Albahrani et al. [4]	Proposed
Value	$O(P)$	$O(P)$	$O(P)$	$O(P\sqrt{P})$	$O(P\sqrt{P})$

is the total computational complexity of the proposed encryption method. Table 7 displays the comparison of computational complexity of the proposed method with the variants in [4, 5, 16, 17]. It can be noticed that the proposed method has got the same computational complexity as that in [4].

5 Conclusion

The encryption of grayscale and color images can be done by applying the proposed method. The cipher image size is equal to secret image size and there is no confinement on the secret image size. Also, there is no overhead of sharing secret key among participants for every secret image encryption. From the statistical analysis results, it is observed that the proposed method is immune to different differential and statistical attacks. Due to its high potency, the proposed method can be utilized for safe image communication.

References

1. Abdelfatah RI (2020) Secure image transmission using chaotic-enhanced elliptic curve cryptography. IEEE Access 8:3875–3890
2. Ahmad J, Ahmed F (2012) Efficiency analysis and security evaluation of image encryption schemes. Int J Video Image Process Netw Secur 12(4):18–31
3. Albahrani EA, Alshekly TK (2017) New chaotic substation and permutation method for image encryption. Int J Appl Inf Syst 12(4):34–39
4. Albahrani EA, Maryoosh AA, Lafta SH (2020) Block image encryption based on modified playfair and chaotic system. J Inf Secur Appl 51:1–9
5. Belazi A, Talha M, Kharbech S, Xiang W (2019) Novel medical image encryption scheme based on chaos and DNA encoding. IEEE Access 7:36667–36681
6. Bhat K, Mahto D, Yadav DK (2017) Comparison analysis of AES-256, RSA-2048 and four dimensional playfair cipher fused with linear feedback shift register. Int J Adv Res Comput Sci 8(3):420–422

7. Bhat K, Mahto D, Yadav DK (2017) Generalization for multidimensional playfair cipher. Int J Adv Res Comput Sci 8(3):379–381

8. Bhat K, Mahto D, Yadav DK (2017) Information security using adaptive multidimensional playfair cipher. Int J Adv Res Comput Sci 8(5):372–380

9. Bhat K, Mahto D, Yadav DK (2017) A novel approach to information security using four dimensional (4d) playfair cipher fused with linear feedback shift register. Indian J Comput Sci Eng 8(1):15–32

10. Bhat K, Mahto D, Yadav DK (2017) Vantages of adaptive multidimensional playfair cipher over AES-256 and RSA-2048. Int J Adv Res Comput Sci 8(5):498–500

11. Chakravarthy S, Venkatesan SP, Anand JM, Ranjani JJ (2016) Enhanced playfair cipher for image encryption using integer wavelet transform. Indian J Sci Technol 9(39):1–12

12. Chen G, Mao Y, Chui CK (2004) Cryptanalysis of a chaotic image encryption method. Chaos Solitons Fractals 21:749–761

13. Herbadji D, Belmeguenai A, Derouiche N, Liu H (2020) Colour image encryption scheme based on enhanced quadratic chaotic map. IET Image Process 14:40–52

14. Iqbal N, Abbas S, Khan MA, Alyas T, Fatima A, Ahmad A (2019) An RGB image cipher using chaotic systems, 15-puzzle problem and DNA computing. IEEE Access 7:174051–174071

15. Li S, Zheng X (2002) Cryptanalysis of a chaotic image encryption method. In: IEEE international symposium on circuits and systems, vol 2, pp 708–711

16. Liu L, Zhang L, Jiang D, Guan Y, Zhang Z (2019) A simultaneous scrambling and diffusion color image encryption algorithm based on hopfield chaotic neural network. IEEE Access 7:185796–185810

17. Liu Q, Liu L (2020) Color image encryption algorithm based on DNA coding and double chaos system. IEEE Access 8:83596–83610

18. Liu Z, Wu C, Wang J, Hu Y (2019) A color image encryption using dynamic DNA and 4-d memristive hyper-chaos. IEEE Access 7:78367–78378

19. Luo Y, Ouyang X, Liu J, Cao L (2019) An image encryption method based on elliptic curve elgamal encryption and chaotic systems. IEEE Access 7:38507–38522

20. Malik MGA, Bashir Z, Iqbal N, Imtiaz MA (2020) Color image encryption algorithm based on hyper-chaos and DNA computing. IEEE Access 8:88093–88107

21. Niu Y, Zhang X (2020) A novel plaintext-related image encryption scheme based on chaotic system and pixel permutation. IEEE Access 8:22082–22093

22. Ren H, Dai L, Zhang J (2013) Image encryption algorithm based on chaos mapping and the sequence transformation. Res J Appl Sci Eng Technol 5(22):5308–5313

23. Silva-García V, Flores-Carapia R, López-Yáñez I, Rentería-Márquez C (2012) Image encryption based on the modified triple-des cryptosystem. Int Math Forum 7(59):2929–2942

24. Singh G (2013) A study of encryption algorithms (RSA, DES, 3DES and AES) for information security. Int J Comput Appl 67(19):33–38

25. Wang H, Li X (2018) A novel hyperchaotic system with infinitely many heteroclinic orbits coined. Chaos Solitons Fractals 106:5–15

26. Wu Y, Noonan JP, Agaian S (2011) NPCR and UACI randomness tests for image encryption. Cyber J: Multidiscip J Sci Technol J Sel Areas Telecommun 1:31–38

27. Yen JC, Guo JI (2000) A new chaotic key-based design for image encryption and decryption. In: IEEE international symposium on circuits and systems, vol 4, pp 49–52

28. Zhang X, Wang L, Zhou Z, Niu Y (2019) A chaos-based image encryption technique utilizing hilbert curves and h-fractals. IEEE Access 7:74734–74746

Iris Recognition Using Improved Xor-Sum Code

Neeru Bala, Ritesh Vyas, Rashmi Gupta, and Anil Kumar

1 Introduction

Biometric authentication had been used in personal identification frameworks since decades. The automated identification of persons relying upon behavioral and physical features is termed as biometric authentication [1]. Embracing innovative methods to furnish greater accuracy, extra security, and promptness, biometric authentication system has grown as a novel arena to be explored. Biometric authentication framework can be driven in two manners, i.e., identification and verification mode. DNA, ear, face, fingerprint, palmprint, iris, keystrokes, odor, retinal scan, signature, periocular, gait, ECG, EEG, palm vein, finger vein, hand geometry, and voice are some physical and behavioral traits which can be used in human authentication [2]. Biometric system is expedient in terms of validation, secrecy or data concealment, access control, and non-abandonment. The most persistent trait in biometrics is iris [3]. Iris is the shaded circle around the pupil which controls the entering of light in eye [4].

One of the most encouraging fields in biometrics is iris recognition as the attributes of iris are essentially distinctive which can be perceived even from certain distance. The false acceptance/rejection rates are perceptibly lower than the other traits that is why forgery and spoofing are a very perplexing chore in case of iris. The key stages of an iris recognition system comprise of image acquirement, pre-processing of image,

N. Bala
Amity School of Engineering and Technology, Amity University, Gurugram, India

R. Vyas (✉)
Lancaster University, Lancaster, UK
e-mail: ritesh.vyas157@gmail.com

R. Gupta
East Campus, Netaji Subhas University of Technology (NSUT), Delhi, India

A. Kumar
Amity School of Engineering and Technology, Amity University, Gurugram, India

© The Author(s), under exclusive license to Springer Nature Singapore Pte Ltd. 2021
P. Stănică et al. (eds.), *Security and Privacy*, Lecture Notes in Electrical Engineering 744,
https://doi.org/10.1007/978-981-33-6781-4_9

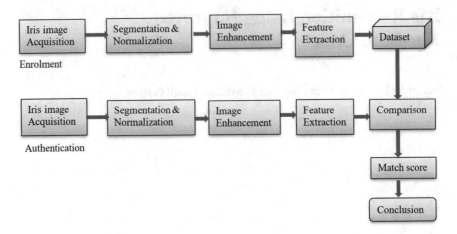

Fig. 1 A common iris recognition system

feature extraction, and classification. A general block diagram of iris recognition framework is depicted in Fig. 1.

Following are the various indispensable pluses of iris recognition system:

1. Precision: Iris is the extraordinary modality as compared to other biometric modalities regarding precision. FAR and FRR are perceptibly lesser in iris recognition system, which certifies the greater precision.
2. Adaptability: This technique is profoundly adaptable and can be utilized in both huge and little scope programs. That is why it has been deployed in many person authentication systems as well as in various governments' authentication systems.
3. Permanence: The texture of iris designs stays invariant all through a person's life.
4. Accessible: Iris recognition system is modest to utilize related to other biometric traits. The only requirement is to stand facing camera for image acquisition.
5. Contactless: Authentication: The acquisition system in iris recognition acquires the image without having any substantial contact of individual with the machine and hence this method is sterile.

2 Related Work

Firstly, Flom and Safir [5] anticipated the idea of an iris recognition system based on inimitable characteristics of iris and pupil. Subsequently, Daugman [6] developed an iris recognition system which applies Gabor filters for texture feature extraction of iris and encrypts iris data into series of 2D Gabor wavelet coefficients and then for recognition it applies Hamming distance method. Successively many outstanding research works based on iris recognition were proposed. Zhao et al. [7] proposed negative iris recognition system that was solely focused on the security of confidentiality of iris database, irrespective of augmenting the accuracy of segmentation or the efficiency of recognition. Shifting and masking strategies were applied for efficient matching in addition to matching rule. Dhage et al. [8] extracted features employing Discrete Wavelet Transform (DWT) and Discrete Cosine Transform (DCT) and swarm optimization for selecting features.

Chen et al. [9] introduced a novel iris recognition system for identification and matching of iris crypts automatically regardless of their sizes. To manage the possible topological variations in the extraction of identical crypt in dissimilar images, Earth Mover's Distance matching model has been used. Hofbauer et al. [10] proposed an experimental analysis to check the effect of segmentation and feature extraction techniques on recognition rate of the system and proved that decision for selecting segmentation and feature extraction technique must be done together as these are interdependent.

Nalla and Kumar [11] developed a novel algorithm based on Markov random field model to enhance the iris recognition rate and an EDA-NBNN-based classification structure for matching of cross-domain images. The efficacy of the proposed framework has been evaluated on two public datasets. Ahmadi and Akbarizadeh [12] introduced an effective and robust iris recognition system that uses MLPNN and PSO for classification of images. For feature extraction, it employs 2D Gabor kernel algorithm and results are validated on publicly available datasets.

Chen et al. [13] presented an innovative technique for efficiently extracting distinctive feature vectors of iris. Amalgamation of T-Center loss and traditional softmax loss functions augmented the discerning capability of CNN-based deep features. Nguyen et al. [14] suggested a novel approach on the basis of artificial intelligence. Their experimental outcomes demonstrate that even though the network was primarily trained with features of general things, it performs well in representation of iris images, and validation of proposed approach has been done on two publicly available datasets. Daugman and Downing [15] investigated the correlation of texture features amid radially scattered bits of iris codes acquired form iris images instead of correlation between raw pixels. Two-dimensional wavelet is employed to obtain iris codes. Vyas et al. [16] introduced a novel feature extractor, derived through sub-bands of curvelet transform, for better iris recognition.

Liu et al. [17] applied collaborative representation method for feature detection and categorization of iris images. Ahmadi et al. [18] suggested amalgamation of step filter, polynomial filter, and 2D Gabor filter, for extracting features of iris images and employed combination of Radial Basis Function Neural Network (RBFNN) and Genetic Algorithm (GA) for classification of images, which results in efficient iris recognition system. Sahu et al. [19] introduced a novel feature reduction technique for Phase Intensive Local Pattern (PILP) by employing Density-Based Clustering Technique (DBSCAN), which results in feature vector of five times lesser dimensionality with same recognition accuracy.

Barpanda et al. [20] proposed wavelet mel-cepstrum for extracting features of iris images and employed MFCC for classification of iris patterns. They also compared the outcome of their suggested approach with another existent approaches and proved that proposed system beats the others. Galdi and Dugelay [21] amalgamated color and texture features and proposed a novel approach for smartphones with lesser computational power. Oktiana et al. [22] employed homomorphic filters for conquering the reflection and phase-based classifier for categorizing images in order to design a cross-spectral iris recognition system with augmented recognition accuracy.

In this paper, the existing Xor-sum code is modified by including the curvature information in the 2D Gabor filters. This curvature information aids to the uniqueness of the extracted iris features, which in turn leads to the performance improvement of the overall recognition system. Further, inclusion of curvature information may prove to be effective with images acquired under visible wavelength illumination, which are otherwise more challenging to represent. Hence, this paper provides a comprehensive evaluation of iris recognition system. Rest of the paper is organized in the following manner: introduction and related works are discussed in Sects. 1 and 2, respectively. Whereas the proposed approach through curvature Gabor filter is elucidated in Sect. 3. Subsequently, discussions of database, performance metrics, and obtained results are completed in Sect. 4. Lastly, Sect. 5 concludes the paper along with specifying few future directions of work.

3 Proposed Approach

This paper presents an Improved Version of Xor-Sum Code (IXSC) [23], making it more suitable to iris recognition application both in Visible Wavelength (VW) and Near-Infrared (NIR) spectrum. As was apparent from the original approach [23] that the use of two-dimensional (2D) Gabor filters could facilitate the task of iris recognition in an effective manner. This efficacy could be attributed to the ability of Gabor filters to model the receptive fields of a simple cell in the primary visual cortex [24]. It is due to this property only that the Gabor filter could yield unprecedented performance by highlighting the micro-textures present in the normalized iris templates.

However, after carrying out the outperforming legacy of the aforementioned approach [23] into the datasets acquired through modern-era devices, we have observed that the approach could not deliver to the fullest of its capabilities. This may be happening because of the extended challenges in case of visible wavelength iris images (which are very popular in more recent datasets). Some of the common challenges are huge reflections, illumination variations, blur, and off-focus. All these challenges make it hard for the conventional Gabor filters to perform in an epochal way. Hence, there has been a need to have an efficient feature descriptor that can perform well for both NIR and VW images.

The conventional Gabor filter has been effectively used to capture the orientation of micro-textural regions present in the iris template. However, if the curvature of these regions can also be taken into account, then the recognition accuracy can be enhanced to a considerable extent. These small curvatures present in the textural edges can aid to the distinctiveness of Xor-sum code features, hence making it a more suitable descriptor for VW images as well.

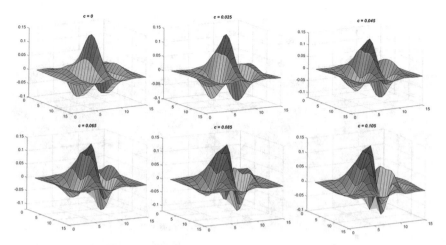

Fig. 2 Effect of curvature control parameter ("c")

3.1 Curvature Gabor Filter (CGF)

CGF is a modified form of the traditional 2D Gabor filter, where a curvature parameter gets included in the mathematical expression itself [25], as shown in the equation below:

$$\xi\,(x, y, \sigma, v, \phi, c) = \frac{1}{\sqrt{2\pi\sigma^2}} \exp\left\{-\frac{x^2+y^2}{2\sigma^2}\right\}$$
$$\times \exp\left\{2\pi i\left(v\,(x\cos(\phi)+y\sin(\phi))+c\sqrt{x^2+y^2}\right)\right\}. \quad (1)$$

In addition to the known parameters from [23], above equation is equipped with a curvature control parameter, "c," which usually defines the degree of curvature in the filter responses. Figure 2 illustrates the varying curvature with different values of "c," where smaller "c" tends to a smaller degree of curvature and vice versa. Notably, if curvature control parameter ("c") becomes zero, the filter turns into a conventional Gabor filter (i.e., with no curvature information). Whereas Fig. 3 illustrates the 2D surface plots of CGF, where the curvature degrees can be easily visualized.

4 Results and discussion

In this paper, two challenging databases, namely, IITD [26, 27] and CrossEyed iris databases [28, 29], are employed for the purpose of experimentation. Out of these two databases, the IITD iris database consists of eye images acquired in NIR wavelength. Furthermore, the images of this database were acquired in a constrained environment, i.e., with minimal illumination variations and nominal challenges like

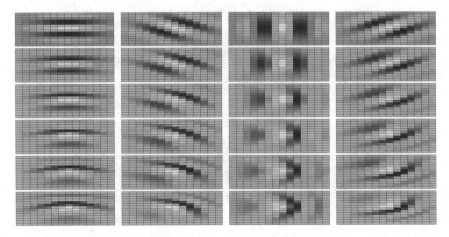

Fig. 3 2D surface plots of CGF; (rows) "c" = [0, 0.025, 0.045, 0.065, 0.085, 0.105]; (columns) orientations (in degrees) = [0, 45, 90, 135]

specular reflections and/or blur. Further, this database provides 2240 eye images from 224 subjects, with 5 images from each eye of the subject. On the other hand, the second employed database, the CrossEyed database is a more contemporary one, providing eye images in both NIR and VW wavelengths, that too possessing pixel-to-pixel correspondence among different wavelength images. The images in this database suffer from more real-life challenges, such as larger reflections and off-focus error. Moreover, this database consists of 960 iris images captured in NIR and VW wavelengths from both the left and right eyes of 120 subjects, respectively. However, current work employs only 500 images from 50 subjects from both the VW and NIR illuminations.

Notably, before the feature extraction stage, all the employed eye images are processed through the segmentation procedure followed by normalization of the iris regions into rectangular templates of dimensions 64×512. These constant dimensions of iris templates facilitate the invariable matching irrespective of the dilation and contraction of pupil. The sample eye images from both the employed databases and their corresponding normalized iris templates are shown in Fig. 4. Readers are advised to refer to [30] for details of the segmentation procedure. For comparison purpose, the famous performance metrics of the biometrics domain are utilized, especially the Equal Error Rate (EER), Genuine Acceptance Rate (GAR), False Acceptance Rate (FAR), and Decidability Index (DI). Notably, all the GARs are reported at FAR of 1%. The Receiver Operating Characteristics (ROC) curves are also exhibited for enhanced visualization of the recognition performance. Another vital metric is the Area Under the ROC Curve (AUC).

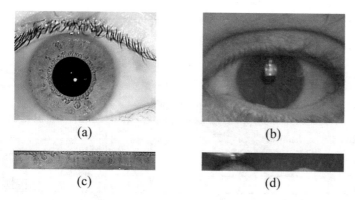

Fig. 4 Sample images; **a** eye image from IITD database, **b** Eye image from CrossEyed-VW database, **c** iris template corresponding to eye image in (**a**), (**d**) Iris template corresponding to eye image in (**b**)

4.1 IITD Iris Database

The investigations in this paper first consider the IITD iris database, where multiple values of curvature control parameters are explored to identify the best suited value. The obtained performance metrics and corresponding ROC curves are demonstrated in Table 1 and Fig. 5.

It is apparent from Table 1 that inclusion of curvature information into the Gabor filter has certainly led to improvements in all the performance metrics. However, for ascertaining the optimal degree of curvature, experiments are performed with five different values of parameter "c." However, larger values of "c" are not tested because of absence of huge curvatures in the iris texture. From the employed values, it can be noticed from the ROC curves that curvature of 0.065 proves to be suitable for the problem on hand. As is evident from Table 1, this optimal value of curvature yields approximately 37% improvement in EER when compared with that of original XSC. This huge improvement can be vital and decisive, looking at the large number

Table 1 Performance metrics for IITD database

Approach	EER (%)	DI	GAR (%)	AUC
Xor-sum code (XSC)	3.62	2.7427	95.48	0.9807
Improved XSC (c = 0.025)	2.55	2.5599	96.67	0.9907
Improved XSC (c = 0.045)	2.36	2.6882	97.00	0.9919
Improved XSC (c = 0.065)	**2.28**	**2.7326**	**97.38**	**0.9938**
Improved XSC (c = 0.085)	2.70	2.6541	96.48	0.9946
Improved XSC (c = 0.105)	2.43	2.6285	96.84	0.9945

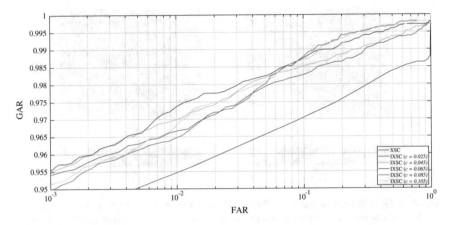

Fig. 5 ROC curves for IITD iris database using various curvature degrees

of classes of the IITD database. At the same time, incorporation of this curvature also enhances the GAR value from 95.48 to 97.38%, which is also quite significant.

In addition to EER and GAR, the other two performance metrics (DI and AUC) for CGF with "c" = 0.065 are reported as 2.7326 and 0.9938, respectively. This points toward improvement in AUC and almost similar DI, as compared to the original XSC. Furthermore, it is interesting to see that every degree of curvature, which is investigated in the current work, has contributed toward the improvement in almost all the performance metrics. This fact can be validated through the ROC curves shown in Fig. 5, where all the curves corresponding to the improved XSC (IXSC) lie above that of XSC. This clearly supports the hypothesis of gathering the curvature information about the textural edges of iris for improved performance.

4.2 CrossEyed Iris Database

This database has more challenging eye images, emerging from the visible wavelength as well. Moreover, this database comes up with registered NIR and VW images, which means that there is pixel-to-pixel correspondence within the NIR and VW versions of images for every eye. Hence, this database can be suitable for investigations on cross-spectral iris recognition. However, the current work is focused toward establishing the generalized capability of IXSC approach to both the NIR and VW matching scenarios individually, and not toward the cross-spectral matching framework. Hence, only individual VW results are reported here, which are subsequently reflected in the NIR counterpart as well.

After careful inspection of Table 2, it is observed that the CrossEyed database exhibits better performance with IXSC for the curvature control parameter value of 0.045, most of the other values also display improvements though. For this optimal

Table 2 Performance metrics for CrossEyed-VW database

Approach	EER (%)	DI	GAR (%)	**AUC**
Xor-sum code (XSC)	9.75	1.8581	83.16	0.9509
Improved XSC (c = 0.025)	11.79	1.5416	79.03	0.9353
Improved XSC (c = 0.045)	**7.96**	**2.0513**	**86.72**	**0.9654**
Improved XSC (c = 0.065)	8.48	2.2301	86.59	0.9619
Improved XSC (c = 0.085)	9.07	2.1900	86.08	0.9540
Improved XSC (c = 0.105)	8.82	2.3002	87.32	0.9514

curvature, the improvements in EER and GAR are counted to be approximately 18% and 4%, respectively. These improvements are clear indication of the discriminative capability of curvature Gabor filters. Concurrently, the other metrics, namely, DI and AUC also get improved substantially. Similar trends of improvements after incorporation curvature property are illustrated in the ROC curves shown in Fig. 6.

Just in order to evaluate the proposed IXSC approach on NIR images, we have conducted the experiments with the optimal value of "c" obtained from the experiments with VW images, i.e., 0.045. Notably, IXSC has outperformed XSC for NIR images as well. The corresponding performance metrics are tabulated in Table 3, where the IXSC has again produced better, though slightly, results as compared with XSC.

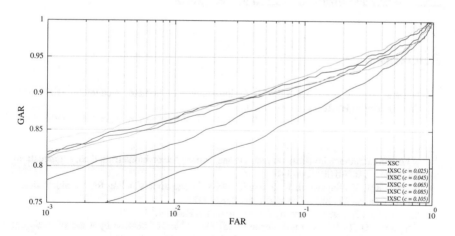

Fig. 6 ROC curves for CrossEyed-VW iris database using various curvature degrees

Table 3 Quick comparison of performance for CrossEyed NIR database

Approach	EER (%)	DI	GAR (%)	AUC
Xor-sum code (XSC)	8.74	2.2712	84.91	0.9504
Improved XSC (c = 0.045)	**8.58**	**2.3982**	**85.44**	**0.9611**

5 Conclusion

In this article, an improved Xor-sum code feature descriptor is proposed for the problem of iris recognition. Laid on the basis of original Xor-sum code, the proposed approach makes it inclusive of the curvature information along with the orientation information. Inclusion of curvature information leads to extraction of increased discriminatory features from the normalized iris templates. The proposed approach is hypothesized to work well for both types of iris images, acquired in near-infrared and visible wavelength. The same fact is validated through extensive experiments with two publicly available databases, namely, IITD and CrossEyed database. Huge improvements are reflected through the proposed approach in terms of common performance metrics, like EER, GAR, and AUC. The largest improvement achieved is in EER for IITD iris database, where the proposed approach exhibits an improvement of almost 37%. This proves the promising nature of the proposed IXSC approach. In future, the proposed approach can be tested for more challenging frameworks, like cross-spectral and smartphone-based iris recognition.

References

1. Jain AK, Ross A, Prabhakar S (2004) An introduction to biometric recognition. IEEE Trans Circuits Syst Video Technol 14(1):4–20
2. Jain AK, Nandakumar K, Ross A (2016) 50 years of biometric research: accomplishments, challenges, and opportunities. Pattern Recognit Lett 79:80–105
3. McGinn K, Tarin S, Bowyer KW (2013) Identity verification using iris images: Performance of human examiners. In: IEEE 6th international conference on biometrics: theory, applications and systems, BTAS 2013, pp 1–6
4. Bowyer KW, Hollingsworth K, Flynn PJ (2008) Image understanding for iris biometrics: a survey. Comput Vis Image Underst 110(2):281–307
5. Flom L, Safir A (1987) Iris recognition system. US Patent 4,641,349
6. Daugman JG (1993) High confidence visual recognition of persons by a test of statistical independence. IEEE Trans Pattern Anal Mach Intell 15(11):1148–1161
7. Zhao D, Luo W, Liu R, Yue L (2018) Negative iris recognition. IEEE Trans Dependable Secur Comput 15(1):112–125
8. Dhage SS, Hegde SS, Manikantan K, Ramachandran S (2015) DWT-based feature extraction and radon transform based contrast enhancement for improved iris recognition. Int Conf Adv Comput Technol Appl 45:256–265
9. Chen JX, Shen F, Chen DZ, Flynn PJ (2016) Iris recognition based on human-interpretable features. IEEE Trans Inform Forensics Secur 11(7):1476–1485

10. Hofbauer H, Alonso-Fernandez F, Bigun J, Uhl A (2016) Experimental analysis regarding the influence of iris segmentation on the recognition rate. IET Biom 5:200–211
11. Nalla PR, Kumar A (2017) Towards more accurate iris recognition using cross-spectral matching. IEEE Trans Image Process 26(1):208–221
12. Ahmadi N, Akbarizadeh G (2018) Hybrid robust iris recognition approach using iris image preprocessing, two-dimensional gabor features and multi-layer perceptron neural network/PSO. IET Biom 7(2):153–162
13. Chen Y, Wu C, Wang Y (2020) T-center: a novel feature extraction approach towards large-scale iris recognition. IEEE Access 8:32365–32375
14. Nguyen K, Fookes C, Ross A, Sridharan S (2017) Iris recognition with off-the-shelf CNN features: a deep learning perspective. IEEE Access 6:18848–18855
15. Daugman J, Downing C (2019) Radial correlations in iris patterns, and mutual information within IrisCodes. IET Biom 8(3):185–189
16. Vyas R, Kanumuri T, Sheoran G, Dubey P (2019) Efficient iris recognition through curvelet transform and polynomial fitting. Optik 185:859–867
17. Liu X, Bai Y, Luo Y, Yang Z, Liu Y (2019) Iris recognition in visible spectrum based on multi-layer analogous convolution and collaborative representation. Pattern Recognit Lett 117:66–73
18. Ahmadi N, Nilashi M, Samad S, Rashid TA, Ahmadi H (2019) An intelligent method for iris recognition using supervised machine learning techniques. Optics Laser Technol 120:105701
19. Sahu B, Kumar Sa P, Bakshi S, Sangaiah AK (2018) Reducing dense local feature key-points for faster iris recognition. Comput Electr Eng 70:939–949
20. Barpanda SS, Majhi B, Sa PK, Sangaiah AK, Bakshi S (2018) Iris feature extraction through wavelet mel-frequency cepstrum coefficients. Optics Laser Technol 110:13–23
21. Galdi C, Dugelay JL (2017) FIRE: fast iris recognition on mobile phones by combining colour and texture features. Pattern Recognit Lett 91:44–51
22. Oktiana M, Horiuchi T, Hirai K, Saddami K, Arnia F, Away Y, Munadi K (2020) Cross-spectral iris recognition using phase-based matching and homomorphic filtering. Heliyon 6(2):e03407
23. Vyas R, Kanumuri T, Sheoran G (2016) Iris recognition using 2-D Gabor filter and XOR-SUM code. In: 2016 1st India international conference on information processing (IICIP), pp 1–5
24. Kong WK, Zhang D, Li W (2003) Palmprint feature extraction using 2-D gabor filters. Pattern Recognit 36(10):2339–2347
25. Wang H, Du M, Zhou J, Tao L (2019) Weber local descriptors with variable curvature gabor filter for finger vein recognition. IEEE Access 7:108261–108277
26. Kumar A, Passi A (2010) Comparison and combination of iris matchers for reliable personal authentication. Pattern Recognit 43:1016–1026
27. IITD iris database. http://www4.comp.polyu.edu.hk/~csajaykr/IITD/Database_Iris.htm
28. Sequeira AF, Chen L, Ferryman J, Alonso-Fernandez F, Bigun J, Raja KB, Raghavendra R, Busch C, Wild P (2016) Cross-Eyed—Cross-spectral iris/periocular recognition database and competition. In: 5th international conference of the biometrics special interest group (BIOSIG 2016), pp 1–5. https://sites.google.com/site/crossspectrumcompetition/home
29. Sequeira AF, Chen L, Ferryman J, Wild P, Alonso-Fernandez F, Bigun J, Raja KB, Raghavendra R, Busch C, Pereira TDF, Marcel S, Behera SS, Gour M, Kanhangad V (2017) Cross-Eyed 2017: cross-spectral iris/periocular recognition competition. In: IEEE international joint conference on biometrics (IJCB), pp 725–732
30. Vyas R, Kanumuri T, Sheoran G, Dubey P (2019) Efficient features for smartphone-based iris recognition. Turkish J Electr Eng Comput Sci 27(3):1589–1602

Linear Complementary Dual Codes Over $\mathbb{Z}_2\mathbb{Z}_4$

Sanjit Bhowmick, Satya Bagchi, and Ramakrishna Bandi

1 Introduction

A $\mathbb{Z}_2\mathbb{Z}_4$-linear code, is an additive subgroup of $\mathbb{Z}_2^\alpha \times \mathbb{Z}_4^\beta$, which is a generalization of classical binary and quaternary linear codes, where $\alpha, \beta \in \mathbb{N}$ and β is odd. Some important classes of non-linear binary codes which are not $\mathbb{Z}_4$ codes can be seen as $\mathbb{Z}_2\mathbb{Z}_4$ linear codes. $\mathbb{Z}_2\mathbb{Z}_4$ linear codes have become significant due their interesting constructions with duality. The development of a general theory of $\mathbb{Z}_2\mathbb{Z}_4$ linear codes such as generator matrices, parity check matrices, duality, cyclic structure, etc are in done in recent time [1–3]

Let $\mathbb{Z}_2^\alpha \times \mathbb{Z}_4^\beta$ be an additive code in which a codeword consists its of first α coordinates are taken from $\mathbb{Z}_2$ and last β coordinates are taken from $\mathbb{Z}_4$. Suppose $\mathcal{C}$ denotes an additive subgroup of $\mathbb{Z}_2^\alpha \times \mathbb{Z}_4^\beta$ which is isomorphic to the $\mathbb{Z}_2^\gamma \times \mathbb{Z}_4^\delta$-additive linear code. So the type of the code $\mathcal{C}$ is $2^\gamma 4^\delta$, and it contains $2^{\gamma+2\delta}$ codewords and the number of two order codewords in $\mathcal{C}$ is $2^{\gamma+\delta}$. These two order codewords form a subcode $\mathcal{C}_1$ of $\mathcal{C}$ with dimension γ (say). Suppose κ is the maximal number of linearly independent codewords in $\mathcal{C}_1$. From above discussion we can say that $\mathcal{C}$ is a $\mathbb{Z}_2\mathbb{Z}_4$-linear code of length $n = \alpha + \beta$ and of type $(\alpha, \beta; \gamma, \delta; \kappa)$.

Suppose $\mathcal{C}$ is an additive code over $\mathbb{Z}_2\mathbb{Z}_4$ of type $(\alpha, \beta; \gamma, \delta; \kappa)$ then $\mathcal{C}$ is a permutation equivalent to a $\mathbb{Z}_2\mathbb{Z}_4$-additive code with the canonical generator matrix [2]

S. Bhowmick (✉) · S. Bagchi
Department of Mathematics, National Institute of Technology Durgapur,
Durgapur 713209, India
e-mail: sanjitbhowmick392@gmail.com

S. Bagchi
e-mail: satya.bagchi@maths.nitdgp.ac.in

R. Bandi
Department of Mathematics, International Institute of Information Technology,
Naya Raipur, India
e-mail: ramakrishna@iiitnr.edu.in

© The Author(s), under exclusive license to Springer Nature Singapore Pte Ltd. 2021
P. Stănică et al. (eds.), *Security and Privacy*, Lecture Notes in Electrical Engineering 744,
https://doi.org/10.1007/978-981-33-6781-4_10

of the form

$$G = \begin{bmatrix} I_\kappa & T_b & 2T_2 & \mathbf{0} & \mathbf{0} \\ \mathbf{0} & \mathbf{0} & 2T_1 & 2I_{\gamma-\kappa} & \mathbf{0} \\ \mathbf{0} & S_b & S_q & R & I_\delta \end{bmatrix},$$

where T_b, S_b are matrices over $\mathbb{Z}_2$; T_1, T_2, R are matrices over $\mathbb{Z}_4$ with all entries in $\{0, 1\} \subset \mathbb{Z}_4$; and S_q is a matrix over $\mathbb{Z}_4$.

A $\mathbb{Z}_2\mathbb{Z}_4$-additive code $\mathcal{C}$ is said to be separable if $\mathcal{C} = \mathcal{C}_X \times \mathcal{C}_Y$, where $\mathcal{C}_X$ be the set of $\mathbb{Z}_2$ (first α) coordinates and $\mathcal{C}_Y$ be the set of $\mathbb{Z}_4$ (last β) coordinates. Let $G^\top$ be the transpose of the matrix G. We can calculate the determinant of the square matrix $GG^\top$ over $\mathbb{Z}_4$ and is denoted by $\det(GG^\top)$. The standard product is denoted by $\langle u, v \rangle$ and defined [2] as

$$\langle u, v \rangle = \left(2 \left(\sum_{i=1}^{r} u_i v_i \right) + \sum_{i=r+1}^{r+s} u_i v_i \right) \in \mathbb{Z}_4,$$

where $u, v \in \mathbb{Z}_2^\alpha \times \mathbb{Z}_4^\beta$ and the computations are made considering the binary zeros and ones as quaternary zeros and ones, respectively. We include an example for better under stand the required inner product as follows:

Example 1 [2] Let $\mathcal{C}_2$ be a $\mathbb{Z}_2\mathbb{Z}_4$-additive linear code of type $(1, 3; 1, 2; 1)$ with a generator matrix

$$G = \begin{bmatrix} 1 & 2 & 2 & 2 \\ 0 & 1 & 1 & 0 \\ 1 & 1 & 2 & 3 \end{bmatrix}.$$

Let $U = (1|2, 2, 2)$ and $V = (1|1, 2, 3)$ be two elements, the the inner product of U and V, i.e., $\langle U, V \rangle = 2(1 \cdot 1) + (2 \cdot 1 + 2 \cdot 2 + 2 \cdot 3) = 2 \in \mathbb{Z}_4$.

The orthogonal complement of a code $\mathcal{C}$, denoted by $\mathcal{C}^\perp$, is defined as

$$\mathcal{C}^\perp = \{ v \in \mathbb{Z}_2^\alpha \times \mathbb{Z}_4^\beta \mid \langle u, v \rangle = 0 \text{ for all } u \in \mathcal{C} \}.$$

The additive linear code $\mathcal{C}^\perp$ is called the additive dual code of $\mathcal{C}$.

2 LCD Codes Over $\mathbb{Z}_2\mathbb{Z}_4$

Linear complementary dual (abbreviated as LCD) codes are one of the most important classes of codes. Due to its practical applications in data protection, it has become a topic of current interest in the field of coding theory over recent years. LCD code was first introduced by Massey in [6]. A linear code $\mathcal{C}$ is linear complementary dual if it has a trivial intersection with its dual, i.e., $\mathcal{C} \cap \mathcal{C}^\perp = \{0\}$. An application of LCD codes against side-channel attacks was shown by Carlet and Guilley [4].

Theorem 1 *Let $\mathcal{C}$ be a linear code of type $(\alpha, \beta; \gamma, \delta; \kappa)$ with $\gamma \neq \kappa$ over $\mathbb{Z}_2\mathbb{Z}_4$ generated by the canonical generator matrix G. Then $\det(GG^\top) = 0$.*

Proof Let $\mathcal{C}$ be a linear code of type $(\alpha, \beta; \gamma, \delta; \kappa)$ over $\mathbb{Z}_2\mathbb{Z}_4$, with

$$G = \begin{bmatrix} I_\kappa & T_b & 2T_2 & 0 & 0 \\ 0 & 0 & 2T_1 & 2I_{\gamma-\kappa} & 0 \\ 0 & S_b & S_q & R & I_\delta \end{bmatrix}.$$

Then

$$G^\top = \begin{bmatrix} I_\kappa & 0 & 0 \\ T_b^\top & 0 & S_b^\top \\ 2T_2^\top & 2T_1^\top & S_q^\top \\ 0 & 2I_{\gamma-\kappa} & R^\top \\ 0 & 0 & I_\delta \end{bmatrix} \quad \text{and}$$

$$GG^\top = \begin{bmatrix} 2I_{k_1} + 2T_b T_b^\top & 0 & 2T_b S_b^\top + 2T_2 S_q^\top \\ 0 & 0 & 2T_1 S_q^\top + 2R^\top \\ 2S_b T_b^\top + 2S_q T_2^\top & 2S_q T_1^\top + 2R & 2S_b S_b^\top + S_q S_q^\top + RR^\top + I_\delta \end{bmatrix},$$

a matrix of order $r = \gamma + \delta$ over $\mathbb{Z}_4$.

This implies that $\det(GG^\top) = 0$. $\qquad\square$

Theorem 2 *Suppose $\mathcal{C}$ is a $\mathbb{Z}_2\mathbb{Z}_4$-additive code with the canonical generator matrix G of type $(\alpha, \beta; \gamma, \delta; \kappa)$ with $\gamma \neq \kappa$ over $\mathbb{Z}_2\mathbb{Z}_4$. Then $\mathcal{C}$ is not an LCD code.*

Proof Let $\mathcal{C}$ be a linear code of type $(\alpha, \beta; \gamma, \delta; \kappa)$ over $\mathbb{Z}_2\mathbb{Z}_4$ with matrix

$$G = \begin{bmatrix} I_\kappa & T_b & 2T_2 & 0 & 0 \\ 0 & 0 & 2T_1 & 2I_{\gamma-\kappa} & 0 \\ 0 & S_b & S_q & R & I_\delta \end{bmatrix}.$$

Then

$$GG^\top = \begin{bmatrix} 2I_\kappa + 2T_b T_b^\top & 0 & 2T_b S_b^\top + 2T_2 S_q^\top \\ 0 & 0 & 2T_1 S_q^\top + 2R^\top \\ 2S_b T_b^\top + 2S_q T_2^\top & 2S_q T_1^\top + 2R & 2S_b S_b^\top + S_q S_q^\top + RR^\top + I_\delta \end{bmatrix}.$$

Let H be a parity-check matrix of the code C. Then for any $\mathbf{x} \in C \cap C^{\perp}$; there exist elements $\mathbf{u} \in \mathbb{Z}_2^{\gamma} \times \mathbb{Z}_4^{\delta}$ and $\mathbf{v} \in \mathbb{Z}_2^{\alpha-\gamma} \times \mathbb{Z}_4^{\beta-\delta}$ such that $\mathbf{x} = \mathbf{u}G = \mathbf{v}H$. Remaining part of the proof, considering $\mathbf{u} \in \mathbb{Z}_4^{\gamma+\delta}$ and $\mathbf{v} \in \mathbb{Z}_4^{\alpha+\beta-\gamma-\delta}$, we find some solutions, then we convert these solutions over $\mathbb{Z}_2\mathbb{Z}_4$ taking first γ positions in modulo 2.

Thus

$$\mathbf{u}G = \mathbf{v}H \Rightarrow G^{\top}\mathbf{u}^{\top} = H^{\top}\mathbf{v}^{\top} \Rightarrow GG^{\top}\mathbf{u}^{\top} = GH^{\top}\mathbf{v}^{\top}.$$

Since $GH^{\top} = \mathbf{0}$, we have $GG^{\top}\mathbf{u}^{\top} = \mathbf{0}$. Let $\mathbf{u} = (\mathbf{u}_1, \mathbf{u}_2, \mathbf{u}_3)$ and each $\mathbf{u}_i$ is a row vector over $\mathbb{Z}_4$, where $\mathbf{u}_1, \mathbf{u}_2, \mathbf{u}_3$'s are $\kappa, \gamma - \kappa, \delta$ tuples, respectively. So this implies that

$$GG^{\top}\mathbf{u}^{\top} = \begin{bmatrix} 2I_{\kappa} + 2T_b T_b^{\top} & \mathbf{0} & 2T_b S_b^{\top} + 2T_2 S_q^{\top} \\ \mathbf{0} & \mathbf{0} & 2T_1 S_q^{\top} + 2R^{\top} \\ 2S_b T_b^{\top} + 2S_q T_2^{\top} & 2S_q T_1^{\top} + 2R & 2S_b S_b^{\top} + S_q S_q^{\top} + RR^{\top} + I_{\delta} \end{bmatrix}$$

$$\times \begin{bmatrix} \mathbf{u}_1^{\top} \\ \mathbf{u}_2^{\top} \\ \mathbf{u}_3^{\top} \end{bmatrix} = \begin{bmatrix} \mathbf{0} \\ \mathbf{0} \\ \mathbf{0} \end{bmatrix}.$$

Since $\det(GG^{\top}) = 0$, above homogeneous equations provide a nonzero solution with $\mathbf{u}_3 \neq \mathbf{0}$. So we get a nozero vector $\mathbf{x}$ such that $\mathbf{x} \in C \cap C^{\perp}$. Hence, C is not LCD. □

Theorem 2 investigates that an additive code C of type $(\alpha, \beta; \gamma, \delta; \kappa)$ with $\gamma \neq \kappa$ cannot be LCD. Now, let us consider an additive code C of type $(\alpha, \beta; \gamma, \delta; \kappa)$ with $\gamma = \kappa$. Then the canonical generator matrix of C is denoted by G_d and defined as

$$G_d = \begin{bmatrix} I_{\gamma} & T_b & 2T_2 & \mathbf{0} \\ \mathbf{0} & S_b & S_q & I_{\delta} \end{bmatrix}.$$

Theorem 3 *Let C be an additive linear code over $\mathbb{Z}_2\mathbb{Z}_4$ of type $(\alpha, \beta; \gamma, \delta; \kappa = \gamma)$ generated by the canonical generator matrix G_d. Then $\det(G_d G_d^{\top})$ is a multiple of 2.*

Proof The canonical generator matrix of the code C is

$$G_d = \begin{bmatrix} I_{\gamma} & T_b & 2T_2 & \mathbf{0} \\ \mathbf{0} & S_b & S_q & I_{\delta} \end{bmatrix}.$$

Therefore,

$$G_d G_d^{\top} = \begin{bmatrix} 2I_{\gamma} + 2T_b T_b^{\top} & 2T_b S_b^{\top} + 2T_2 S_q^{\top} \\ 2S_b T_b^{\top} + 2S_q T_2^{\top} & 2S_b S_b^{\top} + S_q S_q^{\top} + I_{\delta} \end{bmatrix}.$$

One can easily check the determinant of $G_d G_d^{\top}$ is a multiple of 2. □

Let us denote

$$G_d G_d^\top = \left[\begin{array}{c|c} G_1 & G_2 \\ \hline G_2^T & G_3 \end{array} \right],$$

where $G_1 = 2I_\gamma + 2T_b T_b^\top$, $G_2 = 2T_b S_b^\top + 2T_2 S_q^\top$, $G_3 = 2S_b S_b^\top + S_q S_q^\top + I_\delta$.

Now the determinant of $G_d G_d^T$ may or may not be equal to 0. To show this we cite the following examples:

Example 2 [2] Let C_1 be a $\mathbb{Z}_2\mathbb{Z}_4$-additive linear code of type $(3, 4; 3, 1; 3)$ with the canonical generator matrix

$$G_d = \left[\begin{array}{ccc|cccc} 1 & 0 & 0 & 2 & 2 & 0 & 0 \\ 0 & 1 & 0 & 2 & 0 & 2 & 0 \\ 0 & 0 & 1 & 2 & 2 & 0 & 0 \\ \hline 0 & 0 & 0 & 1 & 1 & 1 & 1 \end{array} \right].$$

Now

$$G_d G_d^T = \left[\begin{array}{ccc|c} 2 & 0 & 0 & 0 \\ 0 & 2 & 0 & 0 \\ 0 & 0 & 2 & 0 \\ \hline 0 & 0 & 0 & 0 \end{array} \right] \in M_4(\mathbb{Z}_4).$$

We see that $\det(G_d G_d^T) = 0$.

Let $\mathbf{x} \in C \cap C^\perp$, there exist elements $\mathbf{u} \in \mathbb{Z}_2^3 \mathbb{Z}_4^1$ and $\mathbf{v} \in \mathbb{Z}_2^0 \mathbb{Z}_4^3$ such that $\mathbf{x} = \mathbf{u}G_d = \mathbf{v}H_d$. Thus

$$\mathbf{u}G_d = \mathbf{v}H_d \Rightarrow G_d^\top \mathbf{u}^\top = H_d^\top \mathbf{v}^\top \Rightarrow G_d G_d^\top \mathbf{u}^\top = G_d H_d^\top \mathbf{v}^\top.$$

Since $G_d H_d^\top = \mathbf{0}$, we have $G_d G_d^\top \mathbf{u}^\top = 0$, where $\mathbf{u} = (u_1, u_2, u_3, u_4)$ and now suppose each $u_i \in \mathbb{Z}_4$. So this implies that

$$G_d G_d^\top \mathbf{u}^T = \left[\begin{array}{ccc|c} 2 & 0 & 0 & 0 \\ 0 & 2 & 0 & 0 \\ 0 & 0 & 2 & 0 \\ \hline 0 & 0 & 0 & 0 \end{array} \right] \left[\begin{array}{c} u_1 \\ u_2 \\ u_3 \\ u_4 \end{array} \right] = \left[\begin{array}{c} 0 \\ 0 \\ 0 \\ 0 \end{array} \right]. \tag{1}$$

We can see that $\mathbf{u} = (0, 0, 0, 2)$ is a solution of the Eq. (1). This show that $(0, 0, 0 \,|\, 2, 2, 2, 2) \in C \cap C^\perp$. Therefore, C is not an LCD.

Example 3 [2] Let C_2 be a $\mathbb{Z}_2\mathbb{Z}_4$-additive linear code of type $(1, 3; 1, 2; 1)$ with a generator matrix

$$G_d = \begin{bmatrix} 1 & 2 & 2 & 2 \\ \hline 0 & 1 & 1 & 0 \\ 1 & 1 & 2 & 3 \end{bmatrix}.$$

Now

$$G_d G_d^T = \begin{bmatrix} 2 & 0 & 2 \\ \hline 0 & 2 & 3 \\ 2 & 3 & 2 \end{bmatrix}.$$

The determinant of $\det(G_d G_d^T) = 2$.

Let $\mathbf{x} \in C \cap C^{\perp}$, there exist elements $\mathbf{u} \in \mathbb{Z}_2^1 \mathbb{Z}_4^2$ and $\mathbf{v} \in \mathbb{Z}_2^0 \mathbb{Z}_4^1$ such that $\mathbf{x} = \mathbf{u}G_d = \mathbf{v}H_d$. Thus

$$\mathbf{u}G_d = \mathbf{v}H_d \Rightarrow G_d^{\top} \mathbf{u}^{\top} = H_d^{\top} \mathbf{v}^{\top} \Rightarrow G_d G_d^{\top} \mathbf{u}^{\top} = G_d H_d^{\top} \mathbf{v}^{\top}.$$

Since $G_d H_d^{\top} = \mathbf{0}$, we have $G_d G_d^{\top} \mathbf{u}^{\top} = \mathbf{0}$, $\mathbf{u} = (u_1, u_2, u_3)$. So this implies that

$$G_d G_d^{\top} \mathbf{u}^T = \begin{bmatrix} 2 & 0 & 2 \\ \hline 0 & 2 & 3 \\ 2 & 3 & 2 \end{bmatrix} \begin{bmatrix} u_1 \\ u_2 \\ u_3 \end{bmatrix} = \begin{bmatrix} 0 \\ 0 \\ 0 \end{bmatrix}$$

$$\Rightarrow \begin{bmatrix} 2 & 0 & 2 \\ \hline 2 & 3 & 2 \\ 0 & 2 & 3 \end{bmatrix} \begin{bmatrix} u_1 \\ u_2 \\ u_3 \end{bmatrix} = \begin{bmatrix} 0 \\ 0 \\ 0 \end{bmatrix}.$$

Therefore, we have the equations $2\alpha_1 + 2\alpha_3 = 0$; $2\alpha_2 + 3\alpha_3 = 0$; $2\alpha_1 + 3\alpha_2 + 2\alpha_3 = 0$.

There are only two solution exist $\mathbf{u} = (0, 0, 0)$ and $\mathbf{u} = (2, 0, 0)$. In either case $\mathbf{x} = (0, 0, 0)$ is the only vector in $C \cap C^{\perp}$. Therefore, C is LCD.

We see in above examples that if C is generated by G_d, then C may or may not be LCD. It is natural to ask that under what conditions, a linear code $C = < G_d >$ over $\mathbb{Z}_2 \mathbb{Z}_4$ is LCD. We answer this question below:

Theorem 4 *Let C be a code over $\mathbb{Z}_2 \mathbb{Z}_4$ with the canonical generator matrix G_d. If $G_d G_d^T$ is invertible, then C is an LCD code.*

Proof If possible suppose that C is not an LCD code. Then there exists a nozero $\mathbf{x} \in \mathbb{Z}_2^{\alpha} \times \mathbb{Z}_4^{\beta}$ such that $\mathbf{x} \in C \cap C^{\perp}$. Let H_d be a parity-check matrix of C. Then for any $\mathbf{x} \in C \cap C^{\perp}$, there exist elements $\mathbf{u} \in \mathbb{Z}_2^{\gamma} \times \mathbb{Z}_4^{\delta}$ and $\mathbf{v} \in \mathbb{Z}_2^{\alpha-\gamma} \times \mathbb{Z}_4^{\beta-\delta}$ such that $\mathbf{x} = \mathbf{u}G = \mathbf{v}H$. $GG^T \mathbf{u}^T = GH^T \mathbf{v}^T$. Since $GH^T = \mathbf{0}$, we have $GG^T \mathbf{u}^T = \mathbf{0}$. It follows that $\mathbf{u}^T = \mathbf{0}$ as GG^T is invertible. Therefore, $\mathbf{x} = \mathbf{0}$, a contradiction.

Theorem 5 *Let C be a linear code over $\mathbb{Z}_2\mathbb{Z}_4$ with the canonical generator matrix G_d and suppose that*

$$G_d G_d^\top = \left[\begin{array}{c|c} G_1 & G_2 \\ \hline G_2^T & G_3 \end{array}\right],$$

where $G_1 = 2I_k + 2T_b T_b^\top$, $G_2 = 2T_b S_b^\top + 2T_2 S_q^\top$, $G_3 = 2S_b S_b^\top + S_q S_q^\top + I_\delta$, and $\det(G_d G_d^\top) = 2$, then

1. *C is LCD, if $\det(G_1) = 2$,*
2. *C is not LCD if $\det(G_3) = 2$.*

Proof Let $\mathbf{x} \in C \cap C^\perp$; there exist elements $\mathbf{u} \in \mathbb{Z}_2^\gamma \times \mathbb{Z}_4^\delta$ and $\mathbf{v} \in \mathbb{Z}_2^{\alpha-\gamma} \times \mathbb{Z}_4^{\beta-\delta}$ such that $\mathbf{x} = \mathbf{u}G_d = \mathbf{v}H_d$. Thus $\mathbf{u}G_d = \mathbf{v}H_d$. This implies that $G_d^\top \mathbf{u}^\top = H_d^\top \mathbf{v}^\top$, which further implies that $G_d G_d^\top \mathbf{u}^\top = G_d H_d^\top \mathbf{v}^\top$.

Since $G_d H_d^\top = \mathbf{0}$, we have $G_d G_d^\top \mathbf{u}^\top = \mathbf{0}$. Let $\mathbf{u} = (\mathbf{u}_1, \mathbf{u}_2)$ and each $\mathbf{u}_i$ is a row vector. Then

$$G_d G_d^\top \mathbf{u}^\top = \left[\begin{array}{c|c} G_1 & G_2 \\ \hline G_2^T & G_3 \end{array}\right]\left[\begin{array}{c} \mathbf{u}_1^\top \\ \mathbf{u}_2^\top \end{array}\right] = \left[\begin{array}{c} \mathbf{0} \\ \mathbf{0} \end{array}\right]. \tag{2}$$

Since $G_d G_d^T$ is matrix over $\mathbb{Z}_4$ and $\mathbb{Z}_4$ is a local ring, there exists an invertible matrix P [5] such that $PG_d G_d^T = U$, where

$$U = \left[\begin{array}{c|c} U_1 & U_2 \\ \hline \mathbf{0} & U_3 \end{array}\right]$$

is an upper triangular matrix over $\mathbb{Z}_4$. Now from (2) $PG_d G_d^\top \mathbf{u}^\top = \mathbf{0}$ implies that

$$\left[\begin{array}{c|c} U_1 & U_2 \\ \hline \mathbf{0} & U_3 \end{array}\right]\left[\begin{array}{c} \mathbf{u}_1^\top \\ \mathbf{u}_2^\top \end{array}\right] = \left[\begin{array}{c} \mathbf{0} \\ \mathbf{0} \end{array}\right]. \tag{3}$$

Now $\det(G_d G_d^\top) = \det(U) = 2$.

1. Suppose $P_1, \ldots, P_m$ are the permutation matrices for corresponding row operations on G_1, therefore, $P_1 \cdots P_m G_1 = U_1$. We know that the invertible elements of $\mathbb{Z}_4$ are 1 and 3 so, $\det(P_i) = 1$ or 3 for $1 \le i \le m$. Since $\det(G_1) = 2$ thus $\det(U_1) = \det(P_1) \cdots \det(P_m)\det(G_1) = 2$. Notice that here we have used $1 \cdot 2 \equiv 2 \pmod 4$ and $3 \cdot 2 \equiv 2 \pmod 4$. Also we obtain $\det(U_3) = 1$ or 3. Therefore, from $U_3 \mathbf{u}_2^T = \mathbf{0}$ we have $\mathbf{u}_2 = \mathbf{0}$. Plug in $\mathbf{u}_2 = \mathbf{0}$ in equation $U_1 \mathbf{u}_1^T + U_2 \mathbf{u}_2^T = \mathbf{0}$, we have $U_1 \mathbf{u}_1^T = \mathbf{0}$. Without loss of generality, assume

$$U_1 \mathbf{u}_1^T = \begin{pmatrix} a_{11} & \cdots & a_{1\kappa} \\ \vdots & \ddots & \vdots \\ 0 & \cdots & a_{\kappa\kappa} \end{pmatrix} \cdot \begin{pmatrix} u_{11} \\ \vdots \\ u_{1\kappa} \end{pmatrix} = \begin{pmatrix} 0 \\ \vdots \\ 0 \end{pmatrix}.$$

Since $det(U_1) = a_{11}a_{22} \cdots a_{\kappa\kappa} = 2$, so one of diagonal entry of U_1, say $a_{ii} = 2$ and all other 1, for some $i \in \{1, \ldots, \kappa\}$. Without loss of generality, assume $a_{11} = 2$ and all other diagonal elements of U_1 is 1. Also we have $a_{\kappa\kappa}u_{1\kappa} = 0$, this implies that $u_{1\kappa} = 0$, as $a_{\kappa\kappa} = 1$. Also, putting $u_{1\kappa} = 0$ in $a_{\kappa-1\kappa-1}u_{1\kappa-1} + a_{\kappa-1\kappa}u_{1\kappa} = 0$, we obtain $u_{1\kappa-1} = 0$. Continuing this process, we have $u_{1\kappa} = \cdots = u_{12} = 0$ and $a_{11}u_{11} = 0$. Since $a_{11} = 2$, then $u_{11} = 0$ or 2. Then $\mathbf{u}_1 = \mathbf{0}$ or $(2, 0, \ldots, 0)$.

If $a_{jj} = 2$ and all other diagonal elements of U_1 is 1, for some $j \in \{1, \ldots, \kappa\}$, then similarly we have $u_1 = \mathbf{0}$ or $(\underbrace{2, 2, \ldots, 2}_{j \text{ times}}, 0, \ldots, 0)$.

Therefore, $\mathbf{u}_1 = \mathbf{0}$ or $(\underbrace{2, 2, \ldots, 2}_{j \text{ times}}, 0, \ldots, 0)$, for some $j \in \{1, \ldots, \kappa\}$. So $\mathbf{x} = \mathbf{u}G_d = \mathbf{0}$, row vector, is the only vector lie in $\mathcal{C} \cap \mathcal{C}^{\perp}$. Hence, $\mathcal{C}$ is an LCD.

2. Since $det(G_3) = 2$, $det(U_3) = 2$. Therefore, there exists a nonzero solution to the equation $U_3\mathbf{u}_2 = \mathbf{0}$. Therefore, $\mathbf{x} = \mathbf{u}G = (\mathbf{u}_1, \mathbf{u}_1 T_b + 2S_b, \mathbf{u}_2 T_2 + 2S_q, 0, \ldots, 0, 2)$ is a nonzero vector in $\mathcal{C} \cap \mathcal{C}^{\perp}$. Hence, $\mathcal{C}$ is not an LCD. $\square$

Theorem 6 *Let $\mathcal{C}$ be a linear code over $\mathbb{Z}_2\mathbb{Z}_4$ generated by G_d and*

$$G_d G_d^{\top} = \left[\begin{array}{c|c} G_1 & G_2 \\ \hline G_2^T & G_3 \end{array} \right],$$

where $G_1 = 2I_\kappa + 2T_bT_b^{\top}$, $G_2 = 2T_bS_b^{\top} + 2T_2S_q^{\top}$, $G_3 = 2S_bS_b^{\top} + S_qS_q^{\top} + I_\delta$. Suppose U_1 is the upper triangular matrix form of the block-matrix G_1 and $\det(G_d G_d^{\top}) = 0$. Then

1. *$\mathcal{C}$ is an LCD, if the block-matrix G_3 is invertible and U_1 does not contain 0 as a diagonal element,*
2. *$\mathcal{C}$ is not LCD if $\det(G_3) = 0$.*
3. *$\mathcal{C}$ is not LCD, if U_1 contains 0 as a diagonal element.*

Proof We have from (3) that $U_1\mathbf{u}_1 + U_2\mathbf{u}_2 = \mathbf{0}$ and $U_3\mathbf{u}_2 = \mathbf{0}$.

1. Since G_3 is invertible, U_3 is also invertible. Therefore, $\mathbf{u}_2 = \mathbf{0}$ from $U_3\mathbf{u}_2 = \mathbf{0}$. This implies that $U_1\mathbf{u}_1 = \mathbf{0}$. Since U_1 does not contain 0 as a diagonal element, then the coordinates of $\mathbf{u}_1$ are either $\mathbf{0}$ or a nonzero vector, whose nonzero elements are only 2. Therefore, $\mathbf{x} = \mathbf{u}G = \mathbf{0}$ is the only vector in $\mathcal{C} \cap \mathcal{C}^{\perp}$. Hence, $\mathcal{C}$ is LCD.
2. $\det(G_3) = 0$ implies that $\det(U_3) = 0$. Therefore, we have a nonzero solution to $U_3\mathbf{u}_2 = \mathbf{0}$, say $(0, \ldots, 0, 2)$. We can easily see that $\mathbf{x} = \mathbf{u}G$ is a nonzero in $\mathcal{C} \cap \mathcal{C}^{\perp}$. Hence, $\mathcal{C}$ is not LCD.
3. If G_3 is not invertible, then from (3), $\mathcal{C}$ is not LCD. If G_3 is invertible, then we have $\mathbf{u}_2 = \mathbf{0}$ as shown in (1). So we get $U_1\mathbf{u}_1 = \mathbf{0}$. Since U_1 contains 0 into diagonal, there exists a nonzero co-ordinate in $\mathbf{u}_1$. Therefore, $\mathbf{x} = \mathbf{u}G$ is nonzero in $\mathcal{C} \cap \mathcal{C}^{\perp}$. Hence, $\mathcal{C}$ is not LCD.

These complete the proof. $\square$

It is note that Theorem 3 says that $\det(G_d G_d^\top)$ is multiple of 2, so there is no matrix G_d such that $G_d G_d^\top$ is invertible. It is clear from the Example 1 the converse part of the Theorem 4 may not be true.

Now we consider two generators made from the matrix G_d. One is $G_{\mathbb{Z}_2}$ and other is $G_{\mathbb{Z}_4}$, defined by

$$G_{\mathbb{Z}_2} = \left[I_k \ T_b \big| 2T_2 \right], \quad \text{and} \quad G_{\mathbb{Z}_4} = \left[S_b \big| S_q \ I_\delta \right].$$

Theorem 7 *Let C be a linear code generated by $G_{\mathbb{Z}_4}$. Then C is an LCD code iff $G_{\mathbb{Z}_4} G_{\mathbb{Z}_4}^\top$ is invertible.*

Proof If possible suppose that C is not an LCD code. Then there exists a nonzero $\mathbf{x} \in \mathbb{Z}_4^n$ such that $\mathbf{x} \in C \cap C^\perp$. Let $H_{\mathbb{Z}_4}$ be a parity-check matrix of C. For $\mathbf{x} \in C \cap C^\perp$, there exist elements $\mathbf{u} \in \mathbb{Z}_4^\delta$ and $\mathbf{v} \in \mathbb{Z}_4^{n-\delta}$ such that $\mathbf{x} = \mathbf{u}G_{\mathbb{Z}_4} = \mathbf{v}H_{\mathbb{Z}_4}$. Thus $\mathbf{u}G_{\mathbb{Z}_4} = \mathbf{v}H_{\mathbb{Z}_4}$ implies that $G_{\mathbb{Z}_4} G_{\mathbb{Z}_4}^T \mathbf{u}^T = G_{\mathbb{Z}_4} H_{\mathbb{Z}_4}^T \mathbf{v}^T$. Since $G_{\mathbb{Z}_4} H_{\mathbb{Z}_4}^T = \mathbf{0}$, we have $G_{\mathbb{Z}_4} G_{\mathbb{Z}_4}^T \mathbf{u}^T = \mathbf{0}$. It follows that $\mathbf{u}^T = \mathbf{0}$ as $G_{\mathbb{Z}_4} G_{\mathbb{Z}_4}^T$ is invertible. Therefore, $\mathbf{x} = \mathbf{0}$, a contradiction.

On the other hand, suppose C is an LCD code over $\mathbb{Z}_4$. If possible let $G_{\mathbb{Z}_4} G_{\mathbb{Z}_4}^T$ be non-invertible. Then there exists a nonzero $\mathbf{v} \in \mathbb{Z}_4^\delta$ such that $\mathbf{v}G_{\mathbb{Z}_4} G_{\mathbb{Z}_4}^T = \mathbf{0}$. Since $G_{\mathbb{Z}_4}$ is a generator matrix for C, $\mathbf{u} = \mathbf{v}G_{\mathbb{Z}_4} \in C$. Also we have $\mathbf{u}G_{\mathbb{Z}_4}^T = \mathbf{0} = G_{\mathbb{Z}_4}\mathbf{u}^T$. This implies that $\mathbf{u} \in C^\perp$. Therefore, $C \cap C^\perp \neq \{\mathbf{0}\}$, a contradiction. $\square$

Example 4 Let us consider a generator matrix of a code C be

$$G_{\mathbb{Z}_4} = \begin{bmatrix} 1 & 0 & 0 & 1 & 2 & 1 & 0 & 0 \\ 0 & 1 & 0 & 1 & 2 & 0 & 1 & 0 \\ 0 & 0 & 1 & 1 & 2 & 0 & 0 & 1 \end{bmatrix}.$$

Then

$$G_{\mathbb{Z}_4} G_{\mathbb{Z}_4}^T = \begin{bmatrix} 0 & 2 & 0 \\ 2 & 0 & 3 \\ 0 & 3 & 0 \end{bmatrix}.$$

It is easy to see that $\det(G_{\mathbb{Z}_4} G_{\mathbb{Z}_4}^T) = 0$ and $00020200 \in C \cap C^\perp$.

Example 5 Let us consider a generator matrix of another code C be

$$G_{\mathbb{Z}_4} = \begin{bmatrix} 1 & 0 & 1 & 2 & 3 & 0 & 0 \\ 0 & 1 & 3 & 0 & 2 & 1 & 0 \end{bmatrix}.$$

Then

$$G_{\mathbb{Z}_4} G_{\mathbb{Z}_4}^T = \begin{bmatrix} 1 & 2 \\ 2 & 1 \end{bmatrix}.$$

It is easy to see that $\det(G_{\mathbb{Z}_4} G_{\mathbb{Z}_4}^T) \neq 0$ and $C \cap C^\perp = \{0\}$.

3   Application on Cryptography

Implementations of cryptographic algorithms are prone to fault attacks that aim at extracting the secret key when the algorithm is running over some device. Non-invasive attacks observe some leakage (such as electromagnetic emanations) or perturb internal data (for example with electromagnetic impulses), without damaging the system. They are a special concern insofar as they leave no evidence that they have been perpetrated. This type of attack is called fault injection attack (FIA). FIA consists of actively perturbing the computation so as to obtain exploitable differences at the output.

Now we present an application of LCD code over $K = \mathbb{Z}_2\mathbb{Z}_4$ of the length n against fault-injection attacks (FIA), which is shown in [4] over a finite field. But we modified this application in additive ring $K = \mathbb{Z}_2\mathbb{Z}_4$ also satisfying $C = \langle G \rangle$ is an LCD if and only if GG^T is invertible. We observed that a $k \times n$ generator matrix G of an LCD code C has a property that GG^T is non-singular. Certainly, the same holds for $n - k \times n$ parity-check matrix H of an LCD code C, meaning that HH^T is non-singular. Notice that $GH^T = 0$ and $C \oplus C^\perp = K^n$, as C is LCD. Now suppose that a sensitive data x with k information symbols, let $c = xG$, where G is a generator matrix of C. To protect x, $n - k$ random information symbols are required, which are denoted by y. Let $d = yH$. Denote $z = c + d$, where $c = xG$ is called the coded sensitive data and $d = yH$ is called the mask. In fact, $x \in K^k$ and $y \in K^{n-k}$.

The question is how to recover x from the state z. Also, we have

$$z = xG + yH.$$

Hence, the sensitive x and random y are recovered from z as follows:

$$x = zG^T(GG^T)^{-1},$$

$$y = zH^T(HH^T)^{-1}.$$

Given a FIA, the state z may be modified into $z + \epsilon$. We similarly have

$$\epsilon = eG + fH,$$

where $e \in K^k$ and $f \in K^{n-k}$. Thus we have

$$z + \epsilon = (x + e)G + (y + f)H.$$

Then,

$$(z + \epsilon)H^T(HH^T)^{-1} = y + f.$$

Notice that

$$(z + \epsilon)H^\top(HH^\top)^{-1} = y.$$

It is clear that the equality holds if and only if $f = 0$, i.e., $\epsilon \in C$. If weight of ϵ, i.e., $wt(\epsilon) < d$, where d is the minimum distance of C. Thus, the fault is detected. This is the most importance application of LCD codes in cryptography.

4 Conclusion

We have shown that a linear code C over $\mathbb{Z}_2\mathbb{Z}_4$ of type $(\alpha, \beta; \gamma, \delta; \kappa)$ with $\gamma \neq \kappa$ is not LCD. We have also obtained few conditions on G for which C is LCD or not. It is interesting to see cyclic LCD codes over $\mathbb{Z}_2\mathbb{Z}_4$ in future research.

References

1. Abualrub T, Siap I, Aydin N (2014) $\mathbb{Z}_2\mathbb{Z}_4-$ additive cyclic codes. IEEE Trans Inform Theory 60:1508–1518
2. Borges J, Córdoba CF, Rifa J, Villanueva M (2010) $\mathbb{Z}_2\mathbb{Z}_4$ linear codes: generator matrices and duality. Des Codes Cryptogr 54:167–179
3. Borges J, Córdoba CF, Ten-Valls R (2016) $\mathbb{Z}_2\mathbb{Z}_4-$ additive cyclic codes, generator polynomials, and dual codes. IEEE Trans Inf Theory 62:6348–6354
4. Carlet C, Guilley S (2016) Complementary dual codes for counter-measures to side-channel attacks. In: Pinto ER et al (eds) Coding theory and applications, CIM series in mathematical sciences, vol 3. Springer, pp 97–105; J Adv Math Comm 10(1):131–150
5. McDonald BR (1972) Diagonal equivalence of matrices over a finite local ring. J Comb Theory 13(A):100–104
6. Massey JL (1992) Linear codes with complementary duals. A collection of contributions in honour of Jack van Lint. Discret Math 106(107):337–342

Low c-Differential Uniformity for the Gold Function Modified on a Subfield

Pantelimon Stănică

1 Introduction and Basic Definitions

In [10], we defined a multiplier differential and difference distribution table (in any characteristic). There seems to be quite a bit of interest in this new notion, as it opens the possibility for a modification of the differential attack. Using this concept, we extended the notion of the Boomerang Connectivity Table in [22]. In this paper, we investigate the c-differential uniformity for the Gold function, modified on a subfield.

As customary, n is a positive integer, p is a prime number, $\mathbb{F}_{p^n}$ is the finite field with p^n elements, and $\mathbb{F}_{p^n}^* = \mathbb{F}_{p^n} \setminus \{0\}$ is the multiplicative group (for $a \neq 0$, $\frac{1}{a}$ means the inverse of a in the multiplicative group of the corresponding finite field). We let $\mathbb{F}_p^n$ be the n-dimensional vector space over $\mathbb{F}_p$. We use $\#S$ to denote the cardinality of a set S and $\bar{z}$, for the complex conjugate. We call a function from $\mathbb{F}_{p^n}$ (or $\mathbb{F}_p^n$) to $\mathbb{F}_p$ a *p-ary function* on n variables. For positive integers n and m, any map $F : \mathbb{F}_{p^n} \to \mathbb{F}_{p^m}$ (or $\mathbb{F}_p^n \to \mathbb{F}_p^m$) is called a *vectorial p-ary function*, or (n, m)-*function*. When $m = n$, F can be uniquely represented as a univariate polynomial over $\mathbb{F}_{p^n}$ (using some identification, via a basis, of the finite field with the vector space) of the form $F(x) = \sum_{i=0}^{p^n-1} a_i x^i$, $a_i \in \mathbb{F}_{p^n}$, whose *algebraic degree* is then the largest Hamming weight of the exponents i with $a_i \neq 0$.

Given a p-ary function f, the derivative of f with respect to $a \in \mathbb{F}_{p^n}$ is the p-ary function $D_a f(x) = f(x + a) - f(x)$, for all $x \in \mathbb{F}_{p^n}$, which can be naturally extended to vectorial p-ary functions.

The next concept can be defined for general (n, m)-functions, though in this paper we only consider $m = n$. For an (n, n)-function F, and $a, b \in \mathbb{F}_{p^n}$, we let $\Delta_F(a, b) = \#\{x \in \mathbb{F}_{p^n} : F(x + a) - F(x) = b\}$. We call the quantity $\delta_F = \max\{\Delta_F(a, b) : a, b \in \mathbb{F}_{p^n}, a \neq 0\}$ the *differential uniformity* of F. If $\delta_F = \delta$, then

P. Stănică (✉)
Applied Mathematics Department, Naval Postgraduate School, Monterey, USA
e-mail: pstanica@nps.edu

© The Author(s), under exclusive license to Springer Nature Singapore Pte Ltd. 2021
P. Stănică et al. (eds.), *Security and Privacy*, Lecture Notes in Electrical Engineering 744,
https://doi.org/10.1007/978-981-33-6781-4_11

we say that F is differentially δ-uniform. If $\delta = 1$, then F is called a *perfect nonlinear (PN) function*, or *planar function*. If $\delta = 2$, then F is called an *almost perfect nonlinear (APN) function*. It is well known that PN functions do not exist if $p = 2$.

For a p-ary (n, m)-function $F : \mathbb{F}_{p^n} \to \mathbb{F}_{p^m}$ and $c \in \mathbb{F}_{p^m}$; the *(multiplicative) c-derivative* of F with respect to $a \in \mathbb{F}_{p^n}$ is the function

$$_cD_aF(x) = F(x + a) - cF(x), \text{ for all } x \in \mathbb{F}_{p^n}.$$

For an (n, n)-function F, and $a, b \in \mathbb{F}_{p^n}$, we let the entries of the c-Difference Distribution Table (c-DDT) be defined by $_c\Delta_F(a, b) = \#\{x \in \mathbb{F}_{p^n} : F(x + a) - cF(x) = b\}$. We call the quantity

$$\delta_{F,c} = \max\left\{_c\Delta_F(a, b) \,|\, a, b \in \mathbb{F}_{p^n}, \text{ and } a \neq 0 \text{ if } c = 1\right\}$$

the *c-differential uniformity* of F (see [2] for a particular case). If $\delta_{F,c} = \delta$, then we say that F is differentially (c, δ)-uniform (or that F has c-uniformity δ, or for short, F is δ-uniform c-DDT). If $\delta = 1$, then F is called a *perfect c-nonlinear (PcN)* function (certainly, for $c = 1$, they only exist for odd characteristic p; however, as proven in [10], there exist PcN functions for $p = 2$, for all $c \neq 1$). If $\delta = 2$, then F is called an *almost perfect c-nonlinear (APcN)* function. It is easy to see that if F is an (n, n)-function, that is, $F : \mathbb{F}_{p^n} \to \mathbb{F}_{p^n}$, then F is PcN if and only if $_cD_aF$ is a permutation polynomial.

This concept has been picked up quickly by the community and a flurry of papers started appearing [1, 17, 21–24, 27–29]. It is the purpose of this paper to investigate the c-differential uniformity for a subfield-modified (concept defined below) Gold function in the binary case. These affine modifications are occurring in many papers (see [12–14, 18–20, 26, 30], to cite just a few works).

The reader can consult [4–6, 8, 16, 25] for more on Boolean and p-ary (p is an odd prime) functions beyond what we have introduce here.

We will only consider the $p = 2$ case in this note. Given $F : \mathbb{F}_{2^n} \to \mathbb{F}_{2^n}$, and a divisor of n, say $s \mid n$, a fixed $t \in \mathbb{F}_{2^s}$, we let G be the $\mathbb{F}_{2^s}$-modification of F defined by

$$G(x) = F(x) + t\left(x^{2^s} + x\right)^{2^n - 1} + t = \begin{cases} F(x) + t & \text{if } x \in \mathbb{F}_{2^s} \\ F(x) & \text{if } x \notin \mathbb{F}_{2^s}. \end{cases}$$

In this paper, we consider the $\mathbb{F}_{2^s}$-modification of the Gold function only, so, $G(x) = x^{2^k+1} + t\left(x^{2^s} + x\right)^{2^n - 1} + t$, $1 \leq k < n$, $\gcd(k, n) = 1$, $s \mid n$, $t \in \mathbb{F}_{2^s}$.

2 The c-Differential Uniformity of the Subfield Modified Gold Function

We will now state and prove our result for the c-differential uniformity of the binary $\mathbb{F}_{2^s}$-modification of the Gold function $F(x) = x^{2^k+1}$, $\gcd(n, k) = 1$, which is known to be APN under $\gcd(n, k) = 1$ (it is differentially 4-uniformity when $n \equiv 2 \pmod 4$ and $\gcd(n, k) = 2$).

Theorem *Let $G(x) = x^{2^k+1} + t\left(x^{2^s} + x\right)^{2^n-1} + t$ be the $\mathbb{F}_{2^s}$-modification of the Gold function, $1 \le k < n$, $\gcd(k, n) = 1$, $s \mid n, t \in \mathbb{F}_{2^s}$. Then, for $c \ne 1$, the c-differential uniformity of G is $\delta_{G,c} \le 3$.* $\qquad\square$

Proof There is no need to consider $c = 0$ for the c-differential uniformity, since we can easily show that G is a permutation, and we argue that below. We assume that $G(x_1) = G(x_2)$, for some $x_1, x_2 \in \mathbb{F}_{2^n}$. If both $x_1, x_2 \notin \mathbb{F}_{2^s}$, then we get $x_1^{2^k+1} + t = x_2^{2^k+1} + t$, implying that $x_1 = x_2$ from the invertibility of F. If $x_1 \in \mathbb{F}_{2^s}, x_2 \in \mathbb{F}_{2^n}$, then $x_2^{2^k+1} = x_1^{2^k+1} + t \in \mathbb{F}_{2^s}$, implying that $x_2 \in \mathbb{F}_{2^s}$, as well, which is a contradiction. If none of x_1, x_2 are in $\mathbb{F}_{2^s}$, then again $x_1^{2^k+1} = x_2^{2^k+1}$, implying that $x_1 = x_2$.

From here on, we assume that $c \ne 0, 1$. The c-differential equation $G(x + a) - cG(x) = b$ of G at $a, b \in \mathbb{F}_{2^n}$ is

$$(x+a)^{2^k+1} + t\left((x+a)^{2^s} + (x+a)\right)^{2^n-1} + t + cx^{2^k+1} + ct\left(x^{2^s} + x\right)^{2^n-1} + ct = b,$$

which is equivalent to

$$(1+c)x^{2^k+1} + ax^{2^k} + a^{2^k}x + t\left(x^{2^s} + x + a^{2^s} + a\right)^{2^n-1} + ct\left(x^{2^s} + x\right)^{2^n-1}$$
$$+ a^{2^k+1} + t(1+c) + b = 0.$$

Case 1. Let $a \in \mathbb{F}_{2^s}, x \in \mathbb{F}_{2^s}$. By expanding the first term, the above equation transforms into

$$(1+c)x^{2^k+1} + x^{2^k}a + a^{2^k}x + a^{2^k+1} + t(1+c)\left(x^{2^s} + x\right)^{2^n-1} + t(1+c) + b = 0.$$

Since $x \in \mathbb{F}_{2^s}$, the equation becomes (when divided by a^{2^k+1} and by relabeling $\frac{x}{a} \mapsto x$)

$$x^{2^k+1} + \frac{1}{1+c}x^{2^k} + \frac{1}{1+c}x + d = 0, \tag{1}$$

where $d = \frac{a^{2^k+1}+t(1+c)+b}{(1+c)a^{2^k+1}}$. If $d = 0$, then $x = 0$ is a solution. The cofactor, with the relabeling $\frac{1}{x} \mapsto x$, becomes

$$x^{2^k} + x + (c+1) = 0.$$

We now need to investigate the number of solutions of this linearized polynomial. We rewrite (simplifying some parameters) a result from [7, 15]. Let $f(z) = z^{p^k} - Az - B$ in $\mathbb{F}_{p^n}$, $g = \gcd(n, k)$, $m = n/\gcd(n, k)$, and $\mathrm{Tr}_{\mathbb{F}_{p^n}/\mathbb{F}_{p^g}}$ be the relative trace from $\mathbb{F}_{p^n}$ to $\mathbb{F}_{p^g}$. For $0 \le i \le m - 1$, we define $t_i = \frac{p^{nm} - p^{n(i+1)}}{p^n - 1}$, $\alpha_0 = A$, $\beta_0 = B$. If $m > 1$, then, for $1 \le r \le m - 1$, we let $\alpha_r = A^{\frac{p^{k(r+1)}-1}{p^k-1}}$ and $\beta_r = \sum_{i=0}^{r} A^{s_i} B^{p^{ki}}$, where $s_i = \frac{p^{k(r+1)} - p^{k(i+1)}}{p^k - 1}$, for $0 \le i \le r - 1$ and $s_r = 0$. The trinomial f has no roots in $\mathbb{F}_{p^n}$ if and only if $\alpha_{m-1} = 1$ and $\beta_{m-1} \ne 0$. If $\alpha_{m-1} \ne 1$, then it has a unique root, namely $x = \beta_{m-1}/(1 - \alpha_{m-1})$, and, if $\alpha_{m-1} = 1$, $\beta_{m-1} = 0$, it has p^g roots in $\mathbb{F}_{p^n}$ given by $x + \delta\tau$, where $\delta \in \mathbb{F}_{p^g}$, τ is fixed in $\mathbb{F}_{p^n}$ with $\tau^{p^k-1} = a$ (that is, a $(p^k - 1)$-root of a), and, for any $e \in \mathbb{F}_{p^n}^*$ with $\mathrm{Tr}_g(e) \ne 0$,

$$\text{then } x = \frac{1}{\mathrm{Tr}_{\mathbb{F}_{p^n}/\mathbb{F}_{p^g}}(e)} \sum_{i=0}^{m-1} \left(\sum_{j=0}^{i} e^{p^{kj}} \right) A^{t_i} B^{p^{ki}}.$$

For our prior case, $p = 2$, $A = 1$, $B = c + 1$, $m = n$, $g = 1$, and so, $\alpha_{n-1} = 1$, $\beta_{n-1} = \sum_{i=0}^{n-1} (c+1)^{2^{ki}}$. Thus, if $\beta_{n-1} \ne 0$, we have no roots, and if $\beta_{n-1} = 0$, we have 3 roots (we added the previous 0 root to the count). We make the observation that these roots can belong to $\mathbb{F}_{2^s}$ if we force $c \in \mathbb{F}_{2^s}$, and we take $e \in \mathbb{F}_{2^s}$ in the formula above.

If $d \ne 0$, taking $y = x + (c + 1)^{-1}$ we obtain

$$y^{2^k+1} + \frac{1}{1+c}\left(1 + \frac{1}{(1+c)^{2^k-1}}\right) y + d + \frac{1}{(c+1)^2} = 0.$$

Now, let $y = \alpha z$, where $\alpha = \left(\frac{1}{1+c} + \frac{1}{(1+c)^{2^k}} \right)^{2^{-k}} = 1 + \frac{1}{(1+c)^{2^{-k}}}$ (the 2^k-root exists since $\gcd(2^k, 2^n - 1) = 1$). The previous equation becomes

$$z^{2^k+1} + z + \beta = 0, \tag{2}$$

where $\beta = \frac{d(1+c)^2 + 1}{\alpha^{2^k+1}(1+c)^2} = \frac{ca^{2^k+1} + t(1+c)^2 + b(1+c)}{a^{2^k+1}\alpha^{2^k+1}(1+c)^2}$. Assuming $\beta \ne 0$, we will be using some results of [11] (see also [3, 9]), under $\gcd(n, k) = 1$. By [11] [Theorem 1], we know that Eq. (2) has either none, one or three solutions in $\mathbb{F}_{2^n}$. In fact, the distribution of these cases for n odd (respectively, n even) is (denoting by M_ℓ the amount of equations of type (2) with ℓ solutions)

$$M_0 = \frac{2^n + 1}{3}, \ M_1 = 2^{n-1} - 1, \ M_3 = \frac{2^{n-1} - 1}{3}, \text{ for } n \text{ odd,}$$

$$M_0 = \frac{2^n - 1}{3}, \ M_1 = 2^{n-1}, \ M_3 = \frac{2^{n-1} - 2}{3}, \text{ for } n \text{ even.}$$

Then, for $n \geq 3$, $c \neq 0, 1$, and $\gcd(n, k) = 1$, and since β is linear on b, this implies that, for any β and any a, c, we can find b such that $\beta = \dfrac{ca^{2^k+1} + b(1-c)}{\alpha^{2^k+1}(1-c)^2}$, so the maximum (attainable, if they happen to be in $\mathbb{F}_{2^s}$) number of solutions for (1) in this case is 3.

Case 2. Let $a \in \mathbb{F}_{2^s}$, $x \notin \mathbb{F}_{2^s}$. Then our equation becomes (when divided by a^{2^k+1} and relabeling $\frac{x}{a} \mapsto x$)

$$x^{2^k+1} + \frac{1}{1+c}x^{2^k} + \frac{1}{1+c}x + \frac{a^{2^k+1}+b}{(1+c)a^{2^k+1}} = 0. \tag{3}$$

Arguing as above we get that the maximum number of solutions is, yet again, 3, if $b \neq a^{2^k+1}$.

Case 3. Let $a \notin \mathbb{F}_{2^s}$, $x \in \mathbb{F}_{2^s}$. As in the first case, by expanding the first term, the above equation transforms into

$$(1+c)x^{2^k+1} + ax^{2^k} + a^{2^k}x + a^{2^k+1} + tc + b = 0,$$

which, as before, is equivalent to

$$x^{2^k+1} + \frac{1}{1+c}x^{2^k} + \frac{1}{1+c}x + d = 0,$$

with $d = \frac{a^{2^k+1}+tc+b}{(c+1)a^{2^k+1}}$. A similar analysis as in the prior case renders a maximum of 3 solutions.

Case 4. Let $a \notin \mathbb{F}_{2^s}$, $x \notin \mathbb{F}_{2^s}$, and $x + a \in \mathbb{F}_{2^s}$. The c-differential equation of G becomes

$$(1+c)x^{2^k+1} + ax^{2^k} + a^{2^k}x + a^{2^k+1} + t + b = 0,$$

which resembles the prior equations, and so, by appropriate substitutions and arguing similarly, we infer that it has a maximum of 3 solutions.

Case 5. Let $a \notin \mathbb{F}_{2^s}$, $x \notin \mathbb{F}_{2^s}$, and $x + a \notin \mathbb{F}_{2^s}$. The relevant equation is then

$$(1+c)x^{2^k+1} + ax^{2^k} + a^{2^k}x + a^{2^k+1} + b = 0,$$

which, as we got used by now, renders a maximum of 3 solutions. The theorem is shown. $\qquad\Box$

3 Concluding Remarks

In this paper, we find the c-differential uniformity of the $\mathbb{F}_{2^s}$-modification of the Gold function on $\mathbb{F}_{2^n}$, $s \mid n$, and show that its c-differential uniformity is less than or equal to 3. As we saw already, investigating questions on c-differential uniformity by this method is not a simple matter, mostly because the obtained equations need to be solved over finite fields and not many techniques have been developed for that purpose. In spite of that, it would be interesting to find other classical PN/APN functions and study their properties through the new differential. It will also be worthwhile to check into the general p-ary versions of the results from this paper, as well as other modifications of the Gold, the inverse, or other PN/APN functions.

References

1. Bartoli D, Calderini M, On construction and (non)existence of c-(almost) perfect nonlinear functions. https://arxiv.org/abs/2008.03953
2. Bartoli D, Timpanella M (2020) On a generalization of planar functions. J. Algebr Comb 52:187–213
3. Bluher AW (2004) On $x^{q+1} + ax + b$. Finite Fields Appl 10(3):285–305
4. Budaghyan L (2014) Construction and analysis of cryptographic functions. Springer
5. Carlet C (2010) Boolean functions for cryptography and error correcting codes. In: Crama Y, Hammer P (eds) Boolean methods and models. Cambridge University Press, Cambridge, pp 257–397
6. Carlet C (2010) Vectorial Boolean functions for cryptography. In: Crama Y, Hammer P (eds) Boolean methods and models. Cambridge University Press, Cambridge, pp 398–472
7. Coulter RS, Henderson M (2004) A note on the roots of trinomials over a finite field. Bull Austral Math Soc 69:429–432
8. Cusick TW, Stănică P (2017) Cryptographic Boolean functions and applications, 2nd edn. Academic Press, San Diego, CA
9. Dobbertin H, Felke P, Helleseth T, Rosendahl P (2006) Niho type cross-correlation functions via Dickson polynomials and Kloosterman sums. IEEE Trans Inf Theory 52(2):613–627
10. Ellingsen P, Felke P, Stănică CRP, Tkachenko A (2020) C-differentials, multiplicative uniformity and (almost) perfect c-nonlinearity. IEEE Trans Inf Theory 66(9):5781–5789
11. Helleseth T, Kholosha A (2008) On the equation $x^{2^\ell+1} + x + a = 0$ over $GF(2^k)$. Finite Fields Appl 14:159–176
12. Kaleyski NS (2019) Changing APN functions at two points. Cryptogr Commun 11(6):1165–1184
13. Li K, Qu L, Sun B, Li C (2019) New results about the boomerang uniformity of permutation polynomials. IEEE Trans Inf Theory 65(11):7542–7553
14. Li Y, Wang M, Yu Y, Constructing differentially 4-uniform permutations over $GF(2^{2k})$ from the inverse function revisited. https://eprint.iacr.org/2013/731
15. Liang J (1978) On the solutions of trinomial equations over finite fields. Bull Cal Math Soc 70:379–382
16. Mesnager S (2016) Bent functions: fundamentals and results. Springer
17. Mesnager S, Riera C, Stănică P, Yan H, Zhow Z (2020) Investigations on c-(almost) perfect nonlinear functions, manuscript
18. Peng J, Tan CH (2017) New differentially 4-uniform permutations by modifying the inverse function on subfields. Cryptogr Commun 9:363–378
19. Qu L, Tan Y, Tan CH, Li C (2013) Constructing differentially 4-uniform permutations over $\mathbb{F}_{2^{2k}}$ via the switching method. IEEE Trans Inf Theory 59(4):4675–4686
20. Qu L, Tan Y, Li C, Gong G (2016) More constructions of differentially 4-uniform permutations on $\mathbb{F}_{2^{2k}}$. Des Codes Cryptogr 78:391–408
21. Riera C, Stănică P, Investigations on c-(almost) perfect nonlinear functions. https://arxiv.org/abs/2004.02245

22. Stănică P (2020) Investigations on *c*-boomerang uniformity and perfect nonlinearity. https://arxiv.org/abs/2004.11859

23. Stănică P (2020) Using double Weil sums in finding the Boomerang and the c-boomerang connectivity table for monomial functions on finite fields. https://arxiv.org/abs/2007.09553

24. Stănică P, Geary A, The *c*-differential behavior of the inverse function under the *EA-equivalence*. Cryptogr Commun. https://arxiv.org/abs/2006.00355

25. Tokareva N (2015) Bent functions. In: Results and applications to cryptography. Academic Press, San Diego, CA

26. Yu Y, Wang M, Li Y (2013) Constructing differentially 4 uniform permutations from known ones. Chin J Electron 22(3):495–499

27. Yan H, Mesnager S, Zhou Z, Power functions over finite fields with low c-differential uniformity. https://arxiv.org/pdf/2003.13019.pdf

28. Wu Y, Li N, Zeng X, New P*c* N and AP*c* N functions over finite fields. https://arxiv.org/abs/2010.05396

29. Zha Z, Hu L, Some classes of power functions with low *c*-differential uniformity over finite fields. https://arxiv.org/abs/2008.12183

30. Zha Z, Hu L, Sun S (2014) Constructing new differentially 4-uniform permutations from the inverse function. Finite Fields Appl 25:64–78

Post-Quantum Secure Identity-Based Encryption from Multivariate Public Key Cryptography

Nibedita Kundu, Kunal Dey, Pantelimon Stănică, Sumit Kumar Debnath, and Saibal Kumar Pal

1 Introduction

In the modern era, we are very much dependent on the use of public key cryptography. Identity-Based Encryption (IBE) systems are well-known advanced candidates of public key cryptosystem. In IBE, a user's public key is some unique information about the user's publicly known identity, which may be an arbitrary string (like an email address). A general IBE system is a tuple of four algorithms:

1. Setup phase produces master public key and master secret key;
2. Extraction contains the generation of the recipient's private key using the master secret key and identity of the recipient;
3. Encryption procedure can be used for encrypting messages corresponding to the receiver's identity and master public key;

N. Kundu (✉)
Department of Mathematics, The LNM Institute of Information Technology,
Jaipur 302031, India
e-mail: nknkundu@gmail.com

K. Dey · S. K. Debnath
Department of Mathematics, National Institute of Technology Jamshedpur,
Jamshedpur 831014, India
e-mail: kunaldey3@gmail.com

S. K. Debnath
e-mail: sdebnath.math@nitjsr.ac.in

P. Stănică
Department of Applied Mathematics, Naval Postgraduate School, Monterey,
CA 93943, USA
e-mail: pstanica@nps.edu

S. K. Pal
SAG Lab, Defense Research & Development Organization, Delhi 110054, India
e-mail: skptech@yahoo.com

© The Author(s), under exclusive license to Springer Nature Singapore Pte Ltd. 2021
P. Stănică et al. (eds.), *Security and Privacy*, Lecture Notes in Electrical Engineering 744,
https://doi.org/10.1007/978-981-33-6781-4_12

4. **Decryption** allows to decrypt the ciphertext using the user's identity and secret key.

The concept of IBE was developed by Shamir [20] in 1984 for simplifying the certificate management process in e-mail systems. His aim was to make sure that when a sender desires to send a message to a receiver at "**receiver@gmail.com**" through email, there should not be any requirement for the receiver's public key certificate. Rather, the sender uses a public identity string of the receiver, such as **receiver@gmail.com**, for encrypting the message. In the following, the receiver decrypts the email by using his secret key which he obtains from a trusted third party, namely Key Generation Center (KGC), by authenticating himself to KGC. Then only the receiver can read the message. It is notable that KGC has knowledge of the receiver's private key, which means key escrow is inherent in identity-based email systems. Moreover, in contrast to the existing secure email infrastructure, the sender is able to send an encrypted email to the receiver even if the receiver's public key certificate is not set up yet.

So far, most of the research that has been done in the context of IBE systems are relying on the hardness of number theoretical problems, such as the factorization problems [18] and discrete logarithm problems [12, 13]. These number theoretic assumption-based IBE systems are vulnerable to attacks in polynomial time due to Shor's algorithm [21], provided efficient quantum computers are designed. To overcome this threat, finding an alternative, i.e., designing quantum computers immune IBE systems becomes an urgent issue. The construction of these quantum computer resistant IBE systems falls under post-quantum cryptography (PQC) [1]. In the context of PQC, multivariate public key cryptography (MPKC) is one of the most promising candidates, where a system of multivariate polynomials works as a public key. In the current state of the art, there are several constructions of encryption and signature schemes based on MPKC. However, exploring IBE systems through MPKC is at the beginning stage. Thereby, the development of a secure and efficient multivariate IBE becomes an interesting direction for further research.

There is only one multivariate IBE in the literature, which was developed by Samardjiska and Gligoroski [19] in 2012. Apart from the multivariate IBE, there are several other designs of post-quantum IBE systems [2, 6–8, 11, 14–16, 22, 23] based on other candidates of PQC.

2   Our Contribution

This paper deals with the design and analysis of post-quantum secure identity-based encryption schemes relying on multivariate cryptography. We are motivated by the work of [5], which concentrates on the construction of multivariate identity-based signatures. The technique of [5] has been utilized to develop our proposed identity-based encryption scheme, namely MU-IBE. It is quite efficient, as only modular multiplications and modular additions are responsible for generating the computation overhead of the proposed IBE. Our scheme attains IND-ID-CCA security under the hardness of the MQ problem (assuming the number of polynomials is $m = O(n)$, where n is the number of involved variables) in the random oracle model. Moreover, our proposed IBE is immune against collusion attack (in spite of the fact that it was believed that such an MQ-based IBE scheme that is immune against collusions is very hard to construct), while the only existing multivariate IBE of [19] does not achieve CCA or even CPA security. Further, the collusion attack is possible in the scheme of [19]. Thus, from a security point of view, our scheme performs better over the IBE of [19].

3 Preliminaries

Firstly, we introduce the basic notations. In this paper, the "security parameter" is represented by κ, where $x \in_R S$ stands for "x is chosen uniformly at random from a set S", $\mathbb{F}_q$ represents a finite field of order q (a power of a prime p), a π degree extension field of $\mathbb{F}_q$ is denoted by $\mathbb{F}_{q^\pi}$ and $(\mathbb{F}_q)^\pi$ is a vector space, defined as $\{\mathbf{x} = (x_1, \ldots, x_\pi) | x_i \in \mathbb{F}_q \text{ for } i = 1, \ldots, \pi\}$ with the known element-wise inherited operations.

Negligible function: We say that a function $\varphi(\kappa)$ is negligible in κ if for all $\lambda > 0$, we have $\varphi(\kappa) < \kappa^{-\lambda}$, for sufficiently large κ.

3.1 Hardness Assumption

MQ Problem [17]: Given a system of δ quadratic multivariate polynomials $\{p_1(x_1, \ldots, x_\pi), \ldots, p_\delta(x_1, \ldots, x_\pi)\}$ of π variables $x_1, \ldots, x_\pi$ over $\mathbb{F}_q$, it is proven that finding a solution $\mathbf{x} = (x_1, \ldots, x_\pi)$ of the system of equations $p_1(\mathbf{x}) = \cdots = p_\delta(\mathbf{x}) = 0$ is NP-hard even for polynomials of degree 2 over $\mathbb{F}_2$ [9], if $\delta = O(\pi)$ (recall that the big-Oh complexity class Landau notation $f = O(g)$ means that $|f(x)| \leq cg(x)$ for some constant $c > 0$, whenever $x \geq x_c$).

3.2 General Multivariate Encryption [17]

A general MPKC Encryption Scheme contains the following three algorithms:

- Key Generation : This algorithm generates a secret key $(\mathcal{L}, \mathcal{F}, \mathcal{T})$ and a public key $\mathcal{P} = \mathcal{L} \circ \mathcal{F} \circ \mathcal{T}$, where $\mathcal{L} : \mathbb{F}_q^m \to \mathbb{F}_q^m$ and $\mathcal{T} : \mathbb{F}_q^n \to \mathbb{F}_q^n$ are two invertible affine maps, and $\mathcal{F} : \mathbb{F}_q^n \to \mathbb{F}_q^m$ is an easily invertible function, known as "Central Map". Thereby, $\mathcal{P}$ is a system of $m \in \mathbb{Z}$ number of multivariate polynomials in $n \in \mathbb{Z}$ number of variables.

- Encryption : Given a message $\mathbf{x} \in \mathbb{F}_q^m$ and a public key $\mathcal{P} = \mathcal{L} \circ \mathcal{F} \circ \mathcal{T}$, the encryptor derives the ciphertext $\mathbf{y} = \mathcal{P}(\mathbf{x}) \in \mathbb{F}_q^m$.
- Decryption : To decrypt a ciphertext $\mathbf{y} \in \mathbb{F}_q^m$ using the secret key $(\mathcal{L}, \mathcal{F}, \mathcal{T})$, the decryptor recursively calculates $\mathbf{z} = \mathcal{L}^{-1}(\mathbf{y}) \in \mathbb{F}_q^m$, $\mathbf{w} = \mathcal{F}^{-1}(\mathbf{z}) \in \mathbb{F}_q^n$ and $\mathbf{x} = \mathcal{T}^{-1}(\mathbf{w}) \in \mathbb{F}_q^n$. Finally, it outputs $\mathbf{x} \in \mathbb{F}_q^n$ as the plaintext corresponding to the ciphertext $\mathbf{y} \in \mathbb{F}_q^m$.

3.3   General Identity-Based Encryption [10]

Setup, Extraction, EncryptionandDecryption are the four specified randomized algorithms for a general IBE scheme.

- Setup : It takes a security parameter κ as input and KGC runs these algorithms to create the master public key $\mathcal{MPK}$ and the master secret key $\mathcal{MSK}$ as output, along with the corresponding message space $\mathcal{M}$ and ciphertext space $\mathcal{C}$.
- Extraction : KGC runs this algorithm at the user's request to generate user's private key. This algorithm accepts $\mathcal{MPK}$, $\mathcal{MSK}$ and $ID_i \in \{0, 1\}^*$ as inputs and returns a secret key Sk_{ID_i} as output, where ID_i is the identity parameter of the ith user.
- Encryption : This algorithm is run by an encryptor. It takes $\mathcal{MPK}$, ID_i and message Mg as inputs, and computes output ciphertext Ct.
- Decryption : A user with (Sk_{ID_i}, ID_i) runs this algorithm to original plaintext Mg by decrypting the ciphertext Ct. The plaintext Mg should satisfy the correctness proof:

$$\text{Decryption}(Sk_{ID_i}, ID_i, \text{Encryption}(\mathcal{MPK}, ID_i, \text{Mg})) = \text{Mg}, \forall \text{Mg} \in \mathcal{M}.$$

3.4   CCA Security Model for Identity-Based Encryption [3, 4]

Let us consider an IBE consisting of Setup, Extraction, Encryption and Decryption. The chosen ciphertext security for IBE systems under a chosen identity attack is defined by Boneh and Franklin [3, 4] via the following game between a challenger Ch and an adversary Ad.

Setup : In this phase, Ch runs Setup to generate $(\mathcal{MPK}, \mathcal{MSK})$ and sends $\mathcal{MPK}$ to Ad.

Phase1 : Ad adaptively makes a polynomial number of queries $Q_1, \ldots, Q_{qe}$ to Ch, where Q_i is one of the following:

Extract query: For $ID_i \in \{0, 1\}^*$, Ad queries for the corresponding secret key.

The challenger Ch generates the corresponding secret key Sk_{ID_i} by running the Extraction algorithm and sends it to Ad.

Decryption query: For $ID_i \in \{0, 1\}^*$, Ad queries for the decryption of Ct_i. The challenger Ch first generates the corresponding secret key Sk_{ID_i} by running the Extraction algorithm. It then uses Sk_{ID_i} to decrypt Ct_i and sends the output message Mg_i to Ad.

Challenge : Ad submits two messages Mg_0, Mg_1 and an identity ID. Note that ID must not have appeared in any extract query of Phase 1. In the following, Ch chooses $b \in_R \{0, 1\}$, sets $Ct_b = Encryption(\mathcal{MPK}, ID, Mg_b)$ and sends Ct_b to Ad as challenge ciphertext.

Phase2 : This phase is similar to Phase 1, except that Ad is not allowed to make an extract query for ID or decryption query for (ID, C).

Guess : Ad outputs $\bar{b} \in \{0, 1\}$ and wins if $b = \bar{b}$.

An adversary Ad in the aforementioned game is called IND-ID-CCA adversary (IND stands for *indistinguishability*; ID stands for *full-identity attack*; and CCA stands for *chosen-ciphertext attack*).

Definition 1 An IBE is said to be $(\tau, Q_{ID}, Q_{Ct}, \nu)$ IND-ID-CCA secure if for any τ-time, IND-ID-CCA adversary that makes at most Q_{ID} extract queries and at most Q_{Ct} decryption queries has advantage at most ν in winning the aforementioned game.

4 Proposed Multivariate Identity-Based Encryption (MU-IBE)

We now discuss the construction of our proposed MU-IBE scheme. It is a tuple of four algorithms: (i) Setup, (ii) Extraction, (iii) Encryption and (iv) Decryption. Let us assume that the system contains d number of users $u_1, u_2, \ldots u_d$ and a trusted Key Generation Center (KGC). In Setup, the KGC generates master public key ($\mathcal{MPK}$) and master secret key ($\mathcal{MSK}$). During Extraction, the KGC generates secret key Sk_{ID_i} with the help of $\mathcal{MSK}$ and ID_i for the user u_i with identity ID_i. In Encryption, the Encryptor encrypts a message $Mg \in \{0, 1\}^\lambda$ using the master public key $\mathcal{MPK}$ and identity ID_i of an user u_i to obtain a ciphertext Ct, where $\lambda \in \mathbb{N}$ is the length of the message. A user u_i with identity ID_i runs the algorithm Decryption with the help of Sk_{ID_i} and ID_i to extract the message Mg from a ciphertext Ct.

Protocol MU-IBE

Setup(1^κ): The KGC, by taking input 1^κ, generates $\mathcal{MPK} = \mathcal{P}^{(v)} = \mathcal{L}^{(v)} \circ \mathcal{F}^{(v)} \circ \mathcal{T}^{(v)} : \mathbb{F}_q^n \to \mathbb{F}_q^m$ and $\mathcal{MSK} = \{\mathcal{L}^{(v)}, \mathcal{F}^{(v)}, \mathcal{T}^{(v)}\}$, where

1. $\mathcal{L}^{(v)} : \mathbb{F}_q^m \to \mathbb{F}_q^m$ is an invertible affine map with

$$\mathcal{L}^{(v)}(x_1, \ldots, x_m) = (L_1^{(v)}(x_1, \ldots, x_m), \ldots, L_m^{(v)}(x_1, \ldots, x_m))$$

and

$$L_i^{(v)}(x_1, \ldots, x_m) = \sum_{j=1}^{m} L_{i,j}(v_1, \ldots, v_\delta)x_j + L_{i,0}(v_1, \ldots, v_\delta),$$

for $i = 1, \ldots, m$, where each $L_{i,j} : \mathbb{F}_q^\delta \to \mathbb{F}_q$ is a linear function.

2. $\mathcal{T}^{(v)} : \mathbb{F}_q^n \to \mathbb{F}_q^n$ is an invertible affine map with

$$\mathcal{T}^{(v)}(x_1, \ldots, x_n) = (T_1^{(v)}(x_1, \ldots, x_n), \ldots, T_n^{(v)}(x_1, \ldots, x_n))$$

and

$$T_i^{(v)}(x_1, \ldots, x_n) = \sum_{j=1}^{n} T_{i,j}(v_1, \ldots, v_\delta)x_j + T_{i,0}(v_1, \ldots, v_\delta),$$

for $i = 1, \ldots, n$, where each $T_{i,j} : \mathbb{F}_q^\delta \to \mathbb{F}_q$ is a linear function.

3. $\mathcal{F}^{(v)}(x_1, \ldots, x_n) = (F_1^{(v)}(x_1, \ldots, x_n), \ldots, F_m^{(v)}(x_1, \ldots, x_n))$ is a system of quadratic multivariate polynomials with

$$F_i^{(v)}(x_1, \ldots, x_n) = \sum_{1 \le j \le k \le n} \phi_{i,j,k}(v_1, \ldots, v_\delta)x_j x_k + \sum_{j=1}^{n} \psi_{i,j}(v_1, \ldots, v_\delta)x_j$$

$$+ \zeta_i(v_1, \ldots, v_\delta),$$

for $i = 1, \ldots, m$, where $\phi_{i,j,k}(v_1, \ldots, v_\delta)$, $\psi_{i,j}(v_1, \ldots, v_\delta)$ and $\zeta_i(y_1, \ldots, y_\delta)$ are linear functions from $\mathbb{F}_q^\delta$ to $\mathbb{F}_q$.

4. The public key $\mathcal{P}^{(v)} : \mathbb{F}_q^n \to \mathbb{F}_q^m$ takes the form

$$\mathcal{P}^{(v)}(x_1, \ldots, x_n) = (P_1^{(v)}(x_1, \ldots, x_n), \ldots, P_m^{(v)}(x_1, \ldots, x_n))$$

with

$$P_i^{(v)}(x_1, \ldots, x_n) = \sum_{1 \le j \le k \le n} C_{i,j,k}(v_1, \ldots, v_\delta)x_j x_k + \sum_{j=1}^{n} D_{i,j}(v_1, \ldots, v_\delta)x_j$$

$$+ E_i(v_1, \ldots, v_\delta),$$

for $i = 1, \ldots, m$, where $C_{i,j,k}(v_1, \ldots, v_\delta)$, $D_{i,j}(v_1, \ldots, v_\delta)$ and $E_i(v_1, \ldots, v_\delta)$ are functions of $(v_1, \ldots, v_\delta)$ of degree 4 from $\mathbb{F}_q^\delta$ to $\mathbb{F}_q$.

Extraction($\mathcal{MSK}, ID_i$) : In this phase, the following steps are performed.

1. Each user u_i is registered to KGC. The KGC generates a unique public identity $ID_i \in \{0, 1\}^*$ for each u_i and computes $\mathsf{Hash}(ID_i) = \mathbf{b}_i = (b_{1i}, \ldots, b_{\delta i}) \in$

$\mathbb{F}_q^\delta$, using some cryptographically secure collision-free hash function Hash : $\{0, 1\}^* \to \mathbb{F}_q^\delta$.

2. Putting the value of $\mathbf{b}_i = (b_{1i}, \ldots, b_{\delta i})$ in $\mathcal{L}^{(\mathbf{v})}, \mathcal{F}^{(\mathbf{v})}, \mathcal{T}^{(\mathbf{v})}$, the KGC obtains $\mathcal{L}^{(\mathbf{b}_i)}, \mathcal{F}^{(\mathbf{b}_i)}, \mathcal{T}^{(\mathbf{b}_i)}$, which are functions depending upon $x_1, \ldots, x_m$.

3. Given $\mathcal{MSK}$ and the identity vector $\mathbf{b_i} \in \mathbb{F}_q^\delta$, the KGC needs to randomly choose two invertible affine maps $L_i : \mathbb{F}_q^m \to \mathbb{F}_q^m$ and $T_i : \mathbb{F}_q^n \to \mathbb{F}_q^n$ such that $\widehat{\mathcal{F}}^{(\mathbf{b}_i)} = L_i \circ \mathcal{F}^{(\mathbf{b}_i)} \circ T_i$ can easily be inverted. The KGC also derives $\widehat{\mathcal{L}}^{(\mathbf{b}_i)} = \mathcal{L}^{(\mathbf{b}_i)} \circ L_i^{-1}$ and $\widehat{\mathcal{T}}^{(\mathbf{b}_i)} = T_i^{-1} \circ \mathcal{T}^{(\mathbf{b}_i)}$.

It is clear that $\mathcal{P}^{(\mathbf{b}_i)} = \mathcal{L}^{(\mathbf{b}_i)} \circ \mathcal{F}^{(\mathbf{b}_i)} \circ \mathcal{T}^{(\mathbf{b}_i)} = \widehat{\mathcal{L}}^{(\mathbf{b}_i)} \circ \widehat{\mathcal{F}}^{(\mathbf{b}_i)} \circ \widehat{\mathcal{T}}^{(\mathbf{b}_i)}$ since

$$\mathcal{L}^{(\mathbf{b}_i)} \circ \mathcal{F}^{(\mathbf{b}_i)} \circ \mathcal{T}^{(\mathbf{b}_i)} = \mathcal{L}^{(\mathbf{b}_i)} \circ L_i^{-1} \circ L_i \circ \mathcal{F}^{(\mathbf{b}_i)} \circ T_i \circ T_i^{-1} \circ \mathcal{T}^{(\mathbf{b}_i)} = \widehat{\mathcal{L}}^{(\mathbf{b}_i)} \circ \widehat{\mathcal{F}}^{(\mathbf{b}_i)} \circ \widehat{\mathcal{T}}^{(\mathbf{b}_i)}.$$

The KGC sends $Sk_{ID_i} = (\widehat{\mathcal{L}}^{(\mathbf{b}_i)}, \widehat{\mathcal{F}}^{(\mathbf{b}_i)}, \widehat{\mathcal{T}}^{(\mathbf{b}_i)})$ along with identity ID_i to the user u_i.

Encryption(ID_i, Mg, $\mathcal{MPK}$): To encrypt a message Mg $\in \{0, 1\}^\lambda$, the encryptor, with access to ID_i and $\mathcal{MPK}$, performs the following steps:

1. Derives $\mathbf{b}_i = $ Hash(ID_i) $= (v_1, \ldots, v_\delta)$.
2. Chooses $\mathbf{r} = (\alpha_1, \ldots, \alpha_n) \in_R \mathbb{F}_q^n$.
3. Computes $\mathcal{P}^{(\mathbf{b}_i)}(\mathbf{r}) = \mathcal{P}^{(\mathbf{b}_i)}(\alpha_1, \ldots, \alpha_n) = (\beta_1, \ldots, \beta_m) = \chi$, where

$$\beta_j = P_j^{(\mathbf{b}_i)}(\alpha_1, \ldots, \alpha_n) \text{ for } j = 1, \ldots, m.$$

4. Evaluates $H_1(\mathbf{r})$ and $H_2(\text{Mg}, \mathbf{r})$, for some publicly known collision-resistant hash functions $H_1, H_2 : \{0, 1\}^* \to \{0, 1\}^\lambda$.
5. Outputs the corresponding ciphertext as Ct $= (\chi, \xi, \theta)$, where $\chi = \mathcal{P}^{(\mathbf{b}_i)}(\mathbf{r}), \xi = H_1(\mathbf{r}) \oplus$ Mg and $\theta = H_2(\text{Mg}, \mathbf{r})$.

Decryption(ID_i, Ct, Sk_{ID_i}): To decrypt the ciphertext Ct $= (\chi, \xi, \theta)$, n user u_i with identity ID_i and secret key Sk_{ID_i} executes the following steps:

1. Computes $\mathbf{b}_i = $ Hash(ID_i) $= (v_1, \ldots, v_\delta)$.
2. Evaluates $(\widehat{\mathcal{L}}^{(\mathbf{b}_i)})^{-1}(\chi) = (\widehat{\mathcal{L}}^{(\mathbf{b}_i)})^{-1}(\beta_1, \ldots, \beta_m) = \mathbf{w} = (w_1, \ldots, w_m)$.
3. Calculates the pre-image of $\widehat{\mathcal{F}}^{(\mathbf{b}_i)}$ on a particular value of $\mathbf{x}$, which means

$$(\widehat{\mathcal{F}}^{(\mathbf{b}_i)})^{-1}(\mathbf{w}) = \mathbf{y} = (y_1, \ldots, y_n).$$

4. Evaluates $(\widehat{\mathcal{T}}^{(\mathbf{b}_i)})^{-1}(\mathbf{y}) = \mathbf{z}$.
5. Computes $H_1(\mathbf{z}), \overline{\text{Mg}} = \xi \oplus H_1(\mathbf{z})$ and $\overline{\theta} = H_2(\overline{\text{Mg}}, \mathbf{z})$.
6. Checks whether the equality $\overline{\theta} = \theta$ holds. If it holds then the user outputs $\overline{\text{Mg}}$ as the message. Otherwise, again it starts from step 2. Note that H_1 and H_2 are collision-resistant hash functions. Thus, $\overline{\theta} = \theta$ implies $\overline{\text{Mg}} = $ Mg.

5   Security

Theorem 1 *If the hash functions H_1 and H_2 are designed as random oracles, then the proposed scheme* MU-IBE *is IND-ID-CCA secure under the hardness of the MQ problem.*

Proof Let $Ct_b = (\chi_b, \xi_b, \theta_b)$ be the challenge ciphertext received by Ad for the identity ID, where $\chi_b = \mathcal{P}^{(\text{Hash}(ID))}(\mathbf{r}_b)$, $\xi_b = H_1(\mathbf{r}_b) \oplus Mg_b$ and $\theta_b = H_2(Mg_b, \mathbf{r}_b)$. Here, the random oracle H_2 is a collision-resistant hash function. As a consequence, it is not feasible to find two distinct pairs $(Mg, \mathbf{r})$ and $(Mg', \mathbf{r}')$ such that $H_2(Mg, \mathbf{r}) = H_2(Mg', \mathbf{r}')$. At each decryption query step and for every $\theta \in \{0, 1\}^\lambda$, we define $H_2^{-1}(\theta) = (Mg, \mathbf{r})$ if H_2 was queried before $(Mg, \mathbf{r})$, and θ was returned as output; otherwise, $H_2^{-1}(\theta) = \perp$. Note that a ciphertext $Ct = (\chi, \xi, \theta)$ is completely determined by a pair $(Mg, \mathbf{r})$, while (χ, ξ) completely determines $(Mg, \mathbf{r})$. Let us simulate the extract query as follows: the response to the extract query for an identity ID is set as $\{S_1, S_1^{-1} \circ \mathcal{P}^{(ID)} \circ S_2^{-1}, S_2\}$ for randomly chosen invertible affine maps. Note that $S_1 \circ S_1^{-1} \circ \mathcal{P}^{(ID)} \circ S_2^{-1} \circ S_2 = \mathcal{P}^{(ID)}$. Clearly, $S_1 \circ S_1^{-1} \circ \mathcal{P}^{(ID)} \circ S_2^{-1} \circ S_2 = \mathcal{P}^{(ID)}$. Thereby, the simulated view and the real view are indistinguishable. Furthermore, simulate the decryption query in the following way: the response to the decryption query of a ciphertext $Ct = (\chi, \xi, \theta)$ is set as Mg if there exists some $(Mg, \mathbf{r})$, such that $H_2^{-1}(\theta) = (Mg, \mathbf{r})$; otherwise, the response is set as $\perp$, where $\perp$ signifies "failure" or "invalid input". Then the difference between the simulated game and the real game is that the simulated decryption oracle may answer $\perp$, while the real decryption oracle would provide an actual output. However, one may claim that the difference cannot be detected by the Ad with non-negligible probability. Particularly, there may be a difference if Ad can manage to ask a query for $Ct = (\chi, \xi, \theta)$, satisfying the following:

- $\theta \neq \theta_b$. This is because if $\theta = \theta_b$ then $H_2^{-1}(\theta) = (Mg_b, \mathbf{r}_b)$ and thereby Ad either asked a query that both oracles respond with $\perp$ or it asked the disallowed query $(\chi_b, \xi_b, \theta_b)$.
- Output of none of the previous queries $(Mg, \mathbf{r})$ to $H_2(\cdot)$ made by Ad is θ.
- $(Mg^*, \mathbf{r}^*)$ is determined by χ, ξ such that $H_2(Mg^*, \mathbf{r}^*) = \theta$.

However, θ is not the output of any previous query to $H_2(\cdot)$, i.e., no $(Mg, \mathbf{r})$ was asked before, such that $H_2(Mg, \mathbf{r}) = \theta$. Thus, the probability of the aforementioned circumstance is $2^{-\lambda}$, which is negligible in λ (sufficiently large). In other words, Ad cannot detect the difference between the simulated game and the real game with non-negligible probability. Thus, the decryption box of Ad can be simulated without having the knowledge of $(\mathcal{P}^{(\text{Hash}(ID))})^{-1}, Mg_b, \mathbf{r}_b$. In other words, Ad has no use for the decryption box.

Claim: We now claim that the probability that Ad queries $\mathbf{r}_b$ to the random oracles $H_1(\cdot)$ and $H_2(\cdot)$ is negligible.
We will argue that below, by considering the following simulation: substitute $\xi_b = H_1(\mathbf{r}_b) \oplus Mg_b$ by $\xi_b = k_1 \oplus Mg_b$ and $\theta_b = H_2(Mg_b, \mathbf{r}_b)$ by $\theta_b = k_2$, for some

random elements k_1, k_2, which are uniformly chosen from $\{0, 1\}^\lambda$. The simulated game may be distinguished from the real game by Ad only if it queries $\mathbf{r}_b$ to the random oracles $H_1(\cdot)$ or $H_2(\cdot)$ and observes that the outputs are different from k_1 and k_2, but then we already lost. Hence, the probability that Ad queries $\mathbf{r}_b$ in the simulated game is the same as the probability that it queries $\mathbf{r}_b$ in the real game.

However, in the simulated game, the only information Ad obtains about $\mathbf{r}_b$ is $\mathcal{P}^{(\mathsf{Hash}(ID))}(\mathbf{r}_b)$. As a consequence, Ad queries $\mathbf{r}_b$ to the random oracles $H_1(\cdot)$ or $H_2(\cdot)$ in the simulated game implies that it inverts $\mathcal{P}^{(\mathsf{Hash}(ID))}$. In other words, it breaks the MQ problem which is assumed to be NP-hard. This leads to a contradiction. Thus, it is possible to ignore the probability that Ad queries $\mathbf{r}_b$.

Utilizing the aforementioned claim, we can consider that $\xi_b = k_1 \oplus \mathsf{Mg}_b$ and $\theta_b = k_2$ for $k_1, k_2 \in_R \{0, 1\}^\lambda$. However, this implies that Ad does not obtain any information about Mg_b. Thereby, Ad will be unable to guess if Mg_b is equal to Mg_0 or Mg_1 with probability greater than $1/2$. $\qquad\square$

Theorem 2 *The proposed IBE is resistant to the collusion attack.*

Proof In this attack, one needs to check whether the collusion of a polynomial number of users will allow extracting the knowledge of $\mathcal{MSK}$ or other users' secret keys. The additional randomly chosen linear transformations L_i, T_i, used in the construction of users' secret keys, protect our proposed scheme against collusion attack. On the other hand, if we do not bring L_i, T_i into the construction of users' secret keys, then each coefficient of $\mathcal{MSK}$ is just a linear combination of $(v_1, \ldots, v_\delta)$. As a consequence, if an adversary gets δ secret keys corresponding to δ different IDs, then it can solve these obtained linear equations. In other words, if δ many users collude then they would be able to extract $\mathcal{MSK}$. Due to the involvement of L_i, T_i into Sk_{ID_i}, the form of Sk_{ID_i} becomes random, totally different from earlier. Thereby, a collusion attack is not possible in our scheme. $\qquad\square$

6 Complexity

The communication and computation overheads of the proposed MU-IBE are discussed below.

$\mathcal{MPK}$ size: The size of $\mathcal{MPK}$ is $m\binom{n+2}{2}\binom{\delta+4}{4}$ field ($\mathbb{F}_q$) elements.

$\mathcal{MSK}$ size: The size of $\mathcal{MSK}$ is $\left[m(m+1) + n(n+1) + m\binom{n+2}{2}\right]\delta$ field ($\mathbb{F}_q$) elements.

Sk_{ID_i} size: The size of Sk_{ID_i} is $\left[m(m+1) + n(n+1) + m\binom{n+2}{2}\right]$ field ($\mathbb{F}_q$) elements.

Ct size: The size of ciphertext Ct is m field elements $+ 2\lambda$ bits.

Encryption cost: $m\binom{n+2}{2}\sum_{i=1}^{4} i\binom{\delta+i-1}{i} + m\left[n + \binom{n+1}{2}\right]$ field multiplications and 3 hash function evaluations are required.

Decryption cost: $m^2 + n^2$ field multiplications, 3 hash function evaluations and computation cost due to evaluations of $(\widehat{\mathcal{F}}^{(\mathbf{b}_i)})^{-1}(\mathbf{w}) = \mathbf{y}$ are required.

7 Conclusion

We presented a multivariate IBE system that achieves IND-ID-CCA security under the hardness of the MQ problem in the random oracle model. Our scheme performs better over the only existing multivariate IBE of [19] from the security point of view, since [19] doses not incur CCA security and cannot resist collusion attack, unlike ours. In particular, the proposed IBE is the *first multivariate* IBE that achieves *IND-ID-CCA* security. It will be an interesting direction of future research to extend our work in the standard model (without random oracles).

Acknowledgements This work is supported by DRDO (ER & IPR) under File No: ERIP/ER/202005001/M/01/1775.

References

1. Bernstein DJ (2009) Introduction to post-quantum cryptography. In: Post-quantum cryptography. Springer, pp 1–14
2. Bert P, Fouque P-A, Roux-Langlois A, Sabt M (2018) Practical implementation of ring-SIS/LWE based signature and IBE. In: International conference on post-quantum cryptography. Springer, pp 271–291
3. Boneh D, Franklin M (2001) Identity-based encryption from the Weil pairing. In: Annual international cryptology conference. Springer, pp 213–229
4. Boneh D, Franklin M (2003) Identity-based encryption from the Weil pairing. SIAM J Comput 32(3):586–615
5. Chen J, Ling J, Ning J, Ding J (2019) Identity-based signature schemes for multivariate public key cryptosystems. Comput J 62(8):1132–1147
6. Duong DH, Le HQ, Roy PS, Susilo W (2019) Lattice-based IBE with equality test in standard model. In: International conference on provable security. Springer, pp 19–40
7. Emura K, Katsumata S, Watanabe Y (2019) Identity-based encryption with security against the KGC: a formal model and its instantiation from lattices. In: European symposium on research in computer security. Springer, pp 113–133
8. Gaborit P, Hauteville A, Phan DH, Tillich J-P (2017) Identity-based encryption from codes with rank metric. In: Annual international cryptology conference. Springer, pp 194–224
9. Garey MR, Johnson DS (1979) Computers and intractability, vol 174. Freeman San Francisco
10. Gentry C (2006) Practical identity-based encryption without random oracles. In: Annual international conference on the theory and applications of cryptographic techniques. Springer, pp 445–464
11. Katsumata S, Matsuda T, Takayasu A (2020) Lattice-based revocable (hierarchical) IBE with decryption key exposure resistance. Theor Comput Sci 809:103–136
12. Koblitz N (1987) Elliptic curve cryptosystems. Math Comput 48(177):203–209
13. Kravitz DW (1993) Digital signature algorithm. US Patent 5,231,668
14. Lee K (2020) Efficient identity-based encryption from LWR. In: Information security and cryptology-ICISC 2019: 22nd international conference, Seoul, South Korea, vol 11975. Springer Nature, p 225

15. McCarthy S, Smyth N, O'Sullivan E (2017) A practical implementation of identity-based encryption over NTRU lattices. In: IMA international conference on cryptography and coding. Springer, pp 227–246
16. Nguyen K, Wang H, J Zhang (2016) Server-aided revocable identity-based encryption from lattices. In: International conference on cryptology and network security. Springer, pp 107–123
17. Patarin J (1996) Hidden fields equations (HFE) and isomorphisms of polynomials (IP): two new families of asymmetric algorithms. In: International conference on the theory and applications of cryptographic techniques. Springer, pp 33–48
18. Rivest RL, Shamir A, Adleman L (1978) A method for obtaining digital signatures and public-key cryptosystems. Commun ACM 21(2):120–126
19. Samardjiska S Gligoroski D (2012) Towards a secure multivariate identity-based encryption. In: International conference on ICT innovations. Springer, pp 59–69
20. Shamir A (1984) Identity-based cryptosystems and signature schemes. In: Workshop on the theory and application of cryptographic techniques. Springer, pp 47–53
21. Shor PW (1999) Polynomial-time algorithms for prime factorization and discrete logarithms on a quantum computer. SIAM Rev 41(2):303–332
22. Takayasu A, Watanabe Y (2017) Lattice-based revocable identity-based encryption with bounded decryption key exposure resistance. In: Australasian conference on information security and privacy. Springer, pp 184–204
23. Zhang X, Tang Y, Wang H, Chunxiang X, Miao Y, Cheng H (2019) Lattice-based proxy-oriented identity-based encryption with keyword search for cloud storage. Inf Sci 494:193–207

Provably Insecure Group Authentication: Not All Security Proofs are What they Claim to Be

Chris J Mitchell

1 Introduction

A paper presented at ICICS 2019 [8] describes a protocol designed to enable members of a group to authenticate one another in a group-wise fashion. The paper also presents a formal security model for such 'group authentication' schemes, and provides proofs of security for the protocol. Unfortunately, as we describe in this paper, the protocol is completely insecure, allowing an outsider to masquerade as any group member and set up contradictory views of group authentication membership within a set of participating entities.

The fact that a fundamental flaw exists in a provably secure scheme is perhaps surprising. However, as we discuss in greater detail below, the examination of the main theorems reveals that they do not establish that the protocols are secure in any practical sense.

It turns out that the ICICS 2019 scheme is related to a scheme presented in 2013 [4] by one of the authors of the 2019 paper. As we discuss below, this earlier scheme is also completely insecure. Since the 2013 scheme is slightly simpler than the 2019 scheme, we present it and its flaws first, before doing the same for the 2019 scheme. We observe that the 2013 scheme has been cryptanalysed previously by Ahmadian and Jamshidpur [1], although the attack we describe here is very much simpler than the previously published attack.

The remainder of the paper is structured as follows. In Sect. 2, the 2013 protocol is described, and the goals of, and security claims for, the protocol are summarised. This leads naturally to Sect. 3 in which it is shown that the claimed security properties do not hold by describing a very simple attack; the 'proofs' of the failed theorems are also examined to see why an apparently provably secure scheme is fundamentally flawed. Section 4 presents the ICICS 2019 protocol, together with a summary of

C. J. Mitchell (✉)
Information Security Group, Royal Holloway, University of London, London, UK
e-mail: me@chrismitchell.net
URL: http://www.chrismitchell.net

© The Author(s), under exclusive license to Springer Nature Singapore Pte Ltd. 2021
P. Stănică et al. (eds.), *Security and Privacy*, Lecture Notes in Electrical Engineering 744,
https://doi.org/10.1007/978-981-33-6781-4_13

its design goals and security claims. This is followed by Sect. 5, where we show why it also possesses fundamental flaws; again the security theorems are examined. Conclusions are drawn in Sect. 6.

2   The 2013 Harn Scheme

2.1   Goals of the Scheme

In the context of the schemes considered in this paper, a *group authentication protocol* is one in which 'each user acts both roles of the prover and the verifier, and all users in the group are authenticated at once' [8]. The primary goal of such protocols is speed and efficiency, and not privacy (since all users in such a protocol are identified to each other). As discussed, for example, by Yang et al. [9], this contrasts with the use of the same or similar terms elsewhere in the literature, where protocols are considered which allow an entity to authenticate to another party as a member of a group, without revealing his or her identity.

The main goal for a group authentication protocol as considered here is to enable all members of a defined group to be given assurance, by executing the protocol, that the specified members are all present and actively involved in the protocol, and that no other parties are involved. A review of recent work on the design of such protocols can be found in Sect. 1.1 of Xia et al. [8].

Unfortunately, the precise threat model for which the protocol was designed is not clear from the 2013 paper [4]. References are made to both insider and outsider attacks, i.e. the protocol is intended to be secure against both of these classes of attacks. However, no reference is made to the trust assumptions for the broadcast channel used for communication between the parties. However, it is standard practice when analysing authentication protocols to assume that an attacker can manipulate the communications channel, including to intercept, delete, insert and modify messages (see, for example, Boyd et al. [2], Sect. 1.5.1). We therefore assume this in our analysis of the scheme. Indeed, it is hard to imagine a practical situation where it would not be possible for a determined attacker to modify messages; certainly, there are many real-world examples of message manipulation attacks on the broadcast channels used in mobile telephony—see, for example, the rich literature on IMSI catcher attacks [3, 5, 7].

2.2   Operation

Harn [4] actually presents three distinct protocols. The first, the 'basic scheme', is intended to demonstrate the main ideas; however, it requires information to be divulged simultaneously by all parties and hence would not be secure in practice.

The second and third schemes are elaborations of the basic idea designed to allow for asynchronous information release. In the second scheme, participant credentials can only be used once, whereas the third scheme allows multiple uses of credentials. However, since the second and third schemes are very similar in operation, for simplicity we focus here on the second scheme.

Initialisation This scheme, like all the schemes in both papers, involves a *Group Manager* (GM) trusted by all participants, which pre-equips all participants with credentials used to perform the group authentication process. We suppose that there are n participants $\mathcal{U} = \{U_1, U_2, \ldots, U_n\}$.

To initialise the protocol, the GM performs the following steps.

- The GM chooses parameters t and k, where t determines the resistance of the scheme to insider adversaries—that is, the scheme is designed to be secure so long as at most $t - 1$ insiders collaborate. No explicit guidance on the choice of k is given except that it must satisfy $kt > n - 1$, and hence here we assume $k = \lceil n/t \rceil$.
- The GM chooses a large prime p. All calculations are performed in $\mathrm{GF}(p) = \mathbb{Z}_p$.
- The GM chooses a cryptographic hash function H with domain $\mathbb{Z}_p$.
- The GM chooses a secret $s \in \mathbb{Z}_p$, and computes $H(s)$.
- The GM selects a set of k polynomials $\{f_1(x), f_2(x), \ldots, f_k(x)\}$ over $\mathbb{Z}_p$ of degree $t - 1$, where the coefficients are chosen uniformly at random from $\mathbb{Z}_p$.
- The GM selects two sets of k integers $\{w_1, w_2, \ldots, w_k\}$ and $\{d_1, d_2, \ldots, d_k\}$ with the property that

$$s = \sum_{j=1}^{k} d_j f_j(w_j),$$

where the values $\{w_1, w_2, \ldots, w_k\}$ are all distinct.
- The GM computes a set of k tokens $\{f_1(x_i), f_2(x_i), \ldots, f_k(x_i)\}$ for each participant U_i ($1 \leq i \leq n$), where $x_i \in \mathbb{Z}_p$ is a unique identifier for U_i.
- Using an out-of-band secure channel, the GM equips participant U_i ($1 \leq i \leq n$) with t, k, p, H, the identifiers $\{x_1, x_2, \ldots, x_n\}$, the integers $\{w_1, w_2, \ldots, w_k\}$ and $\{d_1, d_2, \ldots, d_k\}$, $H(s)$, and the participant's collection of k secret tokens $\{f_1(x_i), f_2(x_i), \ldots, f_k(x_i)\}$.

Group Authentication We now suppose that some subset $\mathcal{U}' \subseteq \mathcal{U}$ of the participants (where $|\mathcal{U}'| = m \leq n$) wish to authenticate each other in a group-wise fashion. Suppose $\mathcal{U}' = \{U_{z_1}, U_{z_2}, \ldots, U_{z_m}\}$. We suppose every participant in $\mathcal{U}'$ is aware of the membership of $\mathcal{U}'$. Each participant $u_{z_i} \in \mathcal{U}'$ now proceeds as follows.

- Compute

$$c_{z_i} = \sum_{j=1}^{k} d_j f_j(x_{z_i}) \prod_{\substack{r=1 \\ r \neq i}}^{m} \frac{(w_j - x_{z_r})}{(x_{z_i} - x_{z_r})}$$

.
- Broadcast c_{z_i} to all members of $\mathcal{U}'$.

– Once all the values $\{c_{z_1}, c_{z_2}, \ldots, c_{z_m}\}$ have been received, compute

$$s' = \sum_{r=1}^{m} c_r.$$

– If $H(s') = H(s)$ then the protocol succeeds, i.e. all users have been successfully authenticated.

Note that the protocol can only be executed once per initialisation, as the secret s is revealed to anyone receiving the messages sent on the broadcast channel. The third scheme removes this limitation.

2.3 Security Claims

A number of claims are made with respect to the security properties of the protocol. In particular the *security* property is claimed, namely that any outside adversary cannot impersonate … a member … after knowing at most $n - 1$ values from other members. The meaning of impersonation in this context is not clear, but we assume that this means that, following the completion of the protocol, legitimate participants cannot end up with differing beliefs about who are the participants in a group authentication. Sadly, as we show below, this property does not hold.

3 Analysis of the 2013 Scheme

3.1 Previous Results

As noted in Sect. 1, this scheme has previously been cryptanalysed by Ahmadian and Jamshidpour [1]. Their approach involves performing computations using broadcast values intercepted during protocol execution, and requires certain conditions to be satisfied to succeed. The attack we describe below is almost trivially simple, and works regardless of group size.

3.2 Preliminary Observation

The attack we propose below relies on a very simple fact. From the description in Sect. 2.2, it should be clear that participant U_{z_i} will accept that the group authentication has succeeded if and only if the sum of the $m - 1$ received values c_{z_j} $(j \neq i)$

and the value c_{z_i} it computed is equal to s. That is, the correctness of individual c_{z_j} values is not checked.

3.3 An Outsider Impersonation Attack

Suppose an (insider) adversary controls the broadcast channel with respect to the 'victim' participant U_{z_i}, i.e. the adversary can (a) prevent messages sent by other legitimate participants from reaching U_{z_i}, and (b) send messages to U_{z_i} on this channel that appears to have come from other legitimate participants. Since the protocol makes no assumptions about the trustworthiness of the communications channels (see Sect. 2.1), this assumption is legitimate (indeed, if the broadcast channel was completely trustworthy, then the security protocol would not be needed).

The adversary does two things. Firstly, it legitimately engages in the protocol with an arbitrary subset $\mathcal{U}''$ of the legitimate participants, where $U_{z_i} \notin \mathcal{U}''$. As a result of completing this protocol, the adversary now knows s. During the execution of the protocol, the adversary prevents any of the broadcast messages from reaching U_{z_i}. The adversary now engages with the 'victim' participant U_{z_i}, suggesting that a group authentication is to be performed by the members of an arbitrary set of participants $\mathcal{U}' \subseteq \mathcal{U}$, where $U_{z_i} \in \mathcal{U}'$ and $|\mathcal{U}'| = m$, say. This may involve sending 'fake' messages to U_{z_i} that apparently originate from the other members of $\mathcal{U}'$.

The adversary now chooses values c_{z_j} ($j \neq i$) for $U_{z_j} \in \mathcal{U}'$, and starts sending them to U_{z_i} as if they come from the members of $\mathcal{U}'$. The only condition the values must satisfy is that they sum to $s - c_{z_i}$. Of course, this means that the adversary cannot send all $m - 1$ values to U_{z_i} until c_{z_i} is sent by U_{z_i}, but the protocol is meant to be used 'asynchronously', i.e. where not all participants send their messages at the same time. It should be immediately obvious that U_{z_i} will accept the success of the protocol, although clearly the group authentication that U_{z_i} believes has occurred has not actually occurred.

Note that the third scheme in the 2013 paper [4] suffers from a precisely analogous attack.

3.4 What About the Security Theorems?

The fact that the protocol is so fundamentally flawed is perhaps surprising given Theorem 2, [4], which asserts that the scheme 'has the properties of the t-secure m-user n-group authentication scheme ... if $kt > n - 1$'. This appears to contradict the simple attack we have just described. The answer is simple—the 'proof' of Theorem 2 only attempts to show that an adversary cannot forge legitimate values c_{z_j}, but the attack does not require this. Thus it is clear that the 'proof' is making unwarranted assumptions about how an attack might be launched, and as such Theorem 2 is demonstrably not a theorem at all.

To be fair, this shortcoming was already noted by Xia et al. [8], who observe that the security properties of the 2013 scheme 'are only justified by heuristic arguments rather than formal security proofs'. Unfortunately, despite a much more formal approach, we show below that the Xia et al. scheme is also completely insecure, and that the threat model underlying the security arguments is not adequate to reflect real-world attacks.

4   The Xia-Harn-Yang-Zhang-Mu-Susilo-Meng Scheme

4.1   Goals of the Scheme

The second protocol we consider here, [8], is also an example of a group authentication protocol in the sense given in Sect. 2.1. Xia et al. [8] go much further than much of the prior art in attempting to formalise the goals and security model for a group authentication scheme. However, even here the specific objectives of such a protocol are left a little vague. The following statement is the closest to a formal definition.

> In general, a group authentication scheme works as follows. The group manager (GM) generates a number of credentials, and sends each of these credentials to a user in the group. In the authentication stage, every participating user uses her credential to compute a token and broadcasts it. Subsequently, every user can use the revealed information to verify whether all users are belonging to the same group.

However, as was the case with the 2013 paper analysed above, no explicit references are made to the trust assumptions applying to the channel used for communications. As a result, when analysing the protocol below, we make the same (standard) assumptions about this channel as were made for the 2013 protocol, namely that messages are subject to interception, insertion, deletion and/or modification. As stated in Sect. 2.1, it is hard to imagine a real-world deployment scenario where this would not be possible. However, as we discuss below, the security *proof* implicitly assumes that the attackers are restricted to being passive interceptors ('honest but curious'), which is why it is possible to construct a security proof for a protocol that under reasonable real-world assumptions is subject to a fundamental attack.

4.2   Operation

As is the case for the 2013 protocol, the scheme can be divided into two phases: initialisation, when the GM equips each participant with the credentials needed to perform group authentication, and the group authentication phase where a subset of the participants simultaneously authenticate each other as a group.

Initialisation Again as before we suppose that there are n participants $\mathcal{U} = \{U_1, U_2, \ldots, U_n\}$. To initialise the protocol, the GM performs the following steps.

- The GM chooses parameters t and ℓ, where the scheme is designed to be secure as long as at most $t - 1$ insiders collaborate, and ℓ determines the number of group authentication sessions that can be performed before new credentials need to be issued.
- The GM chooses a cyclic group G (expressed multiplicatively) with order a large prime q, and randomly selects $g_1, g_2, \ldots, g_\ell$ to be ℓ independent generators of G.
- The GM chooses a cryptographic hash function H with domain G.
- The GM chooses a secret $s \in \mathbb{Z}_q$, and computes the ℓ values $H((g_i)^s), 1 \leq i \leq \ell$.
- The GM randomly selects a polynomial $f(x) = \sum_{i=0}^{t-1} a_i x^i$ over $\mathbb{Z}_q$ of degree $t - 1$, where $a_0 = s$.
- The GM computes a credential $s_i = f(x_i)$ for each participant U_i ($1 \leq i \leq n$), where $x_i \in \mathbb{Z}_p$ is a unique identifier for U_i.
- Using an out-of-band secure channel, the GM equips participant U_i ($1 \leq i \leq n$) with t, G, q, H, the identifiers $\{x_1, x_2, \ldots, x_n\}$, the generators $\{g_1, g_2, \ldots, g_\ell\}$, the hash codes $\{H((g_1)^s), H((g_2)^s), \ldots, H((g_\ell)^s)\}$ and the participant's own secret credential $s_i (= f(x_i))$.

Group Authentication Just as in the 2013 scheme, we now suppose that some subset $\mathcal{U}' \subseteq \mathcal{U}$ of the participants (where $|\mathcal{U}'| = m \leq n$) wish to authenticate each other in a group-wise fashion. Suppose $\mathcal{U}' = \{U_{z_1}, U_{z_2}, \ldots, U_{z_m}\}$. We suppose every participant in $\mathcal{U}'$ is aware of the membership of $\mathcal{U}'$. We further suppose that the set of participants has reached session number σ in the period of use of a particular credential set, where $1 \leq \sigma \leq \ell$. Note that each session must be conducted using a new value of σ, and σ determines which generator g_σ from the set of generators will be used in this particular protocol instance.

Each participant $u_{z_i} \in \mathcal{U}'$ proceeds as follows.

- Choose $u_{z_i} \in \mathbb{Z}_q$ uniformly at random, and broadcast it to all other participants.
- Once the set of values $\{u_{z_1}, u_{z_2}, \ldots, u_{z_m}\}$ has been received, compute

$$\gamma_i = \prod_{\substack{j \in \{1,2,\ldots,m\} \\ z_j < z_i}} (g_\sigma)^{u_{z_j}} \prod_{\substack{j \in \{1,2,\ldots,m\} \\ z_j > z_i}} (g_\sigma)^{-u_{z_j}},$$

$$L_i = \prod_{\substack{j \in \{1,2,\ldots,m\} \\ z_j \neq z_i}} \frac{x_{z_j}}{x_{z_j} - x_{z_i}},$$

and

$$c_{z_i} = (g_\sigma)^{s_{z_i} L_i} (\gamma_i)^{u_{z_i}}.$$

- Broadcast c_{z_i} to all members of $\mathcal{U}'$.
- Once all the values $\{c_{z_1}, c_{z_2}, \ldots, c_{z_m}\}$ have been received, compute

$$\prod_{r=1}^{m} c_{z_r}.$$

– If $H(\prod_{r=1}^{m} c_{z_r}) = H((g_\sigma)^s)$, then the protocol succeeds, i.e. all users have been successfully authenticated.

4.3 Security Claims

We first observe that Xia et al. [8] make the following statement about the assumed properties of the broadcast channel.

> Note that the broadcast channel is only assumed to be asynchronous, such that messages sent from the uncorrupted users to the corrupted ones can be delivered relatively fast, in which case, the adversary can wait for the messages of the uncorrupted users to arrive, then decide on her computation and communication, and still get her messages delivered to the honest users on time.

The security model of Xia et al. [8] gives the *No impersonation* property as follows.

> The outside adversary A_O cannot impersonate a group member without being detected, even if A_O computes her token after seeing all other users' tokens in the asynchronous networks.

5 Analysis of the ICICS 2019 Scheme

5.1 Preliminary Observation

We consider what can be learnt by observing a single value c_{z_i} in a single instance of the protocol, together with the initial broadcasts of the values $\{u_{z_1}, u_{z_2}, \ldots, u_{z_m}\}$. We suppose that the (outside) observer has access to the system parameters, i.e. the values provided by the GM to all participants, namely t, G, q, H, the identifiers $\{x_1, x_2, \ldots, x_n\}$, the generators $\{g_1, g_2, \ldots, g_\ell\}$ and the hash codes $\{H((g_1)^s), H((g_2)^s), \ldots, H((g_\ell)^s)\}$.

As defined in Sect. 4.2,

$$c_{z_i} = (g_\sigma)^{s_{z_i} L_i} (\gamma_i)^{u_{z_i}}.$$

Now, again as defined above

$$\gamma_i = \prod_{\substack{j \in \{1,2,\ldots,m\} \\ z_j < z_i}} (g_\sigma)^{u_{z_j}} \prod_{\substack{j \in \{1,2,\ldots,m\} \\ z_j > z_i}} (g_\sigma)^{-u_{z_j}},$$

i.e. computing γ_i does not involve any secret credential values and hence is simple to derive for anyone with access to the system credentials. Since we also supposed that u_{z_i} has been intercepted, the observer can thus compute

$$c_{z_i} \cdot (\gamma_i)^{-u_{z_i}} = (g_\sigma)^{s_{z_i} L_i}.$$

Next observe that, yet again as defined above,

$$L_i = \prod_{\substack{j \in \{1,2,\dots,m\} \\ z_j \neq z_i}} \frac{x_{z_j}}{x_{z_j} - x_{z_i}},$$

and hence L_i is also available to anyone with access to the system credentials.

Having derived L_i, the observer now computes a value M such that $M L_i \equiv 1$ (mod q), a calculation which is simple to perform given that q is known (see, for example, Algorithm 2.142 of Menezes et al. [6]). Note that M is guaranteed to exist since q is prime (see, for example, Fact 2.119 [6]).

It then follows immediately that

$$[c_{z_i} \cdot (\gamma_i)^{-u_{z_i}}]^M = (g_\sigma)^{s_{z_i} L_i M} = (g_\sigma)^{s_{z_i}}.$$

That is, an observer of c_{z_i} and the values $\{u_{z_1}, u_{z_2}, \dots, u_{z_m}\}$ can compute $(g_\sigma)^{s_{z_i}}$.

5.2 An Outsider Impersonation Attack

The above observation leads to a very simple and powerful attack, enabling the impersonation of a participant in any group. The attack scenario is very similar to that described in Sect. 3.3. We suppose an (outsider) adversary controls the broadcast channel with respect to the 'victim' participant U_{z_i}, i.e. the adversary can (a) prevent messages sent by other legitimate participants from reaching U_{z_i}, and (b) send messages to U_{z_i} on this channel that appears to have come from other legitimate participants. Finally, we assume that it is 'time' for a session using the group generator g_σ.

We first suppose the adversary observes a group of participants $\mathcal{U}'' \subseteq \mathcal{U}$ (where $U_{z_i} \notin \mathcal{U}''$) engaging in the protocol. The adversary

- intercepts all the u_{z_j} and c_{z_j} values sent by each $U_{z_j} \in \mathcal{U}''$;
- uses these intercepted values, together with the system parameters, to compute $(g_\sigma)^{s_{z_j}}$ for each $U_{z_j} \in \mathcal{U}''$;
- prevents any of the messages reaching U_{z_i}.

We now suppose that the adversary persuades the victim participant U_{z_i} that it is being invited to join a group of participants $\mathcal{U}' \subseteq \mathcal{U}'' \cup \{U_{z_i}\}$, where $U_{z_i} \in \mathcal{U}'$, e.g. by sending 'fake' messages from members of $\mathcal{U}''$ to U_{z_i}. The adversary chooses arbitrary values u_{z_j} for every $U_{z_j} \in \mathcal{U}' - \{U_{z_i}\}$, and sends these values to U_{z_i} as if they come from U_{z_j}. Once U_{z_i} sends its value u_{z_i}, the adversary can use the complete set of values

$\{u_{z_j}\}$ and the computed values $(g_\sigma)^{s_{z_j}}$ (which it has for every $U_{z_j} \in \mathcal{U}' - \{U_{z_i}\}$) to compute the 'correct' values c_{z_j} for every $U_{z_j} \in \mathcal{U}' - \{U_{z_i}\}$, which it sends to the victim participant U_{z_i}. Since all the received values are 'correct', the victim will falsely believe that it is part of a group authentication with a set of participants, of whom none believe they are being authenticated to the victim.

5.3   Other Possible Attack Scenarios

There are many other scenarios in which the observation in Sect. 5.1 could be used to launch an attack on the protocol. For example, if an attacker could control the broadcast network with respect to two victims, a range of conflicting beliefs about who has been authenticated to whom could be established. That is, once an attacker has observed a participant U_{z_j} output a value c_{z_j}, this can be used to impersonate U_{z_j} in any group the attacker chooses (assuming control over the broadcast channel).

5.4   What About the Proof of Security?

The attack described above clearly breaks the 'no impersonation' property given in Sect. 4.3. However, Theorem 4 [8] states that 'The proposed group authentication scheme satisfies the no impersonation property, assuming that H is a preimage resistant hash function and the DDH assumption holds in G'. The attack does not invalidate the assumptions of the theorem, and hence the theorem must be false.

How can this be true? Well, the examination of the proof of Theorem 4 suggests why. The proof apparently only deals with the 'honest but curious' case, where all participants are assumed to follow the protocol correctly. The sort of manipulation of messages and beliefs involved in the attack do not appear to be covered by the proof. That is, while the mathematics may be correct, the result does not establish that the protocol would actually be secure in a real-world deployment (which, of course, it is not).

Indeed, this is partly admitted by Xia et al. [8]. In the concluding section of their paper, it is stated that 'There are two distinct approaches to defining security for cryptographic protocols: simulation proof and reduction proof. The former is more intuitive because it models security of the targeted problem via an ideally trusted third party. However, the definitions will become complicated once all details are filled in. In contrast, the reduction proof yields definitions that are simpler to describe and easier to work with. However, the adequacy for modelling the problem is less clear. In this paper, we followed the latter approach, and it is still open how to provide formal security treatment for group authentication using the simulation proof.'

6 Conclusions

We have examined two different group authentication protocols, and found that both possess fundamental flaws. Clearly, this means that neither of them should be used in practice. Fortunately, there are many well-established and relatively efficient means of performing authentication—see, for example, Boyd et al. [2].

The fundamental flaws in the protocols exist despite the fact that in both cases theorems are provided asserting their security. Indeed, in the more recent case, the theorems are given within the context of a formal security model. This is clearly worrying—modern cryptography takes as a fundamental tenet that 'proofs of security' are necessary, but clearly they are not of much value if the proofs are false.

Of course, mistakes in proofs are commonplace, but in these cases the issue is clearly not just a mistake. In the earlier paper, there is no formal security model, and the theorems are simply heuristic arguments. Even in the more recent paper, where the results may well be valid, the authors themselves admit that the security model used is not sufficient to establish security other than in a case where the attackers are restricted to behaving in an 'honest' fashion. This clearly suggests that reviewers need the time to carefully review proofs (and the precise details of claims of security) for adequacy. This flies in the face of the modern obsession with speedy publication, both for conferences and many journals (e.g. *IEEE Access* which allows referees only a week to complete a review). Perhaps we, as the research community, need to think more carefully about finding ways to allow reviewers the time and space to write carefully considered and detailed reviews.

References

1. Ahmadian Z, Jamshidpour S (2018) Linear subspace cryptanalysis of Harn's secret sharing-based group authentication scheme. IEEE Trans Inf Forensics Secur 13(2):502–510. https://doi.org/10.1109/TIFS.2017.2757454
2. Boyd C, Mathuria A, Stebila D (2020) Protocols for authentication and key establishment. In: Information security and cryptography, 2nd edn. Springer. https://doi.org/10.1007/978-3-662-58146-9
3. Dabrowski A, Pianta N, Klepp T, Mulazzani M, Weippl ER (2014) IMSI-catch me if you can: IMSI-catcher-catchers. In: CNP Jr, Hahn A, Butler KRB, Sherr M (eds) Proceedings of the 30th annual computer security applications conference, ACSAC 2014. ACM, New Orleans, LA, USA, pp. 246–255. https://doi.org/10.1145/2664243.2664272.
4. Harn L (2013) Group authentication. IEEE Trans Comput 62(9):1893–1898. https://doi.org/10.1109/TC.2012.251
5. Khan MSA, Mitchell CJ (2017) Trashing IMSI catchers in mobile networks. In: Noubir G, Conti M, Kasera SK (eds) Proceedings of the 10th ACM conference on security and privacy in wireless and mobile networks, WiSec 2017. ACM, Boston, MA, USA, pp. 207–218. https://doi.org/10.1145/3098243.3098248
6. Menezes AJ, van Oorschot PC, Vanstone SA (1997) Handbook of applied cryptography. CRC Press, Boca Raton
7. Mjølsnes SF, Olimid RF (2017) Easy 4G/LTE IMSI catchers for non-programmers. In: Rak J, Bay J, Kotenko I, Popyack L, Skormin V, Szczypiorski K (eds) Computer network security—

7th international conference on mathematical methods, models, and architectures for computer network security, MMM-ACNS 2017, Warsaw, Poland, August 28–30, 2017, Proceedings, vol 10446. Lecture Notes in Computer Science. Springer International Publishing, Cham, pp 235–246

8. Xia Z, Harn L, Yang B, Zhang M, Mu Y, Susilo W, Meng, W (2020) Provably secure group authentication in the asynchronous communication model. In: Zhou J, Luo X, Shen Q, Xu Z (eds) Information and communications security—21st international conference, ICICS 2019, Beijing, China, Lecture Notes in Computer Science, vol 11999. Springer, pp 324–340. https://doi.org/10.1007/978-3-030-41579-2_19

9. Yang H, Jiao L, Oleshchuk VA (2014) A general framework for group authentication and key exchange protocols. In: Danger J, Debbabi M, Marion J, García-Alfaro J, Zincir-Heywood AN (eds) Foundations and practice of security—6th international symposium, FPS 2013, La Rochelle, France, Lecture Notes in Computer Science, vol 8352. Springer, pp 31–45. https://doi.org/10.1007/978-3-319-05302-8_3

Terahertz Communication: Merits, Demerits, and Future Challenges Regarding 6G Wireless Networks

Nira and Aasheesh Shukla

1 Introduction

Bill Clinton stated that "four years ago, no one knew about the Internet except for 2 nuclear fascists, but today my cat also has a web page, and when I used to talk to children on video calls, my cat was also present on the video call". So from these things, we can understand from where technology has reached in today's time. What really happens is that as the needs of people increase, so too do the changes in technology. Initially, Communicating with people was a very difficult task, then it marked the first beginning of the 1G technology era. Then the demand of people increased and it was like sending photos or documents from one place to another, and how to make the Internet better [2]. Then came the question of how to speed up the Internet, so in a few years, the generation of technology such as CDMA, FDMA, and TDMA, 3G, improved and has a lot of technology that works [7]. It is not that 3G is bad or it was bad at that time, but the needs of the people increased day by day, which was not easy to complete 3G. Because of this, technology was changed every time. Now, 4G comes in the same sequence, so the same thing is also in 4G. Now there is also some deficiency in 4G which 5G has to overcome. Now, we also know about 5G, as we can see that many telecom companies are working to bring their mobile network to 5G. Actually, 5G has many advantages. In this way, we can get many users to provide good Internet with very little delay simultaneously. And many people connect multiple devices together with high efficiency. And in 5G, the speed from one device to another is 15 Gbps to 20 Gbps, which itself is considered a very good speed [7, 13]. But it is said that the needs of the people are

Nira (✉) · A. Shukla
GLA University, Mathura 281406, (U.P), India
e-mail: nirasingh096@gmail.com

A. Shukla
e-mail: aasheesh.shukla@gla.ac.in

© The Author(s), under exclusive license to Springer Nature Singapore Pte Ltd. 2021
P. Stănică et al. (eds.), *Security and Privacy*, Lecture Notes in Electrical Engineering 744,
https://doi.org/10.1007/978-981-33-6781-4_14

Fig. 1 Characteristics of 6G

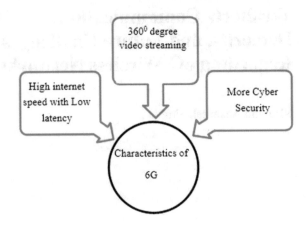

never met; their needs always increase day by day, so it is imperative to say that by 2030 the whole world will be hit by Artificial Intelligence. In the future, there will be many tools of Artificial Intelligence and all this will be very much dependent on Internet speed. Therefore, to run devices of Artificial Intelligence, good Internet speed would be required, which 5G would not be able to accomplish [12]. To meet this demand, Researchers have already started working on 6G. 6G (6th Generation) is the replacement for 5G cell innovation. One of the major roles of 6G is that it is more secure than previous generations. 6G organizations will have the option to use higher frequencies than the 5G network and have a generously high range and very little laziness. One of the objectives of the 6G Internet would be to help with one-microsecond inertia correspondence, many times faster than one-millisecond throughput, or speaking for 1/1000th of inactivity. 6G innovation is dependent on encouraging huge growth in the areas of market imaging, presence innovation, and sector mentality. Work related to computerized logic (AI) will be the option to decide the best field to be independently registered in the computational foundation of 6G [5, 10]. This information includes options about stockpiling, preparation, and sharing. So it is about the next generation of wireless communication called 6G. Earlier, people did not know much about the Internet, due to which cybercrimes were also very less and people did not give much attention to it, but today people are more active on social media, due to which Cybercrime and Hackers have also increased. So whether it is a personal or official document, we should keep our documents carefully so that they are saved from theft because criminals and hackers can misuse them. Now since crime has increased so much, think what will happen by 2030. This means that by the time 6G comes, there will be a lot of increase in cybercrime.

Because of this, a lot of attention has to be paid to cybercrime. A lot of Researchers work on 6G and their key technologies such as Terahertz Communication (0.3–10 THz), Visible Light Communication (400–800 THz), etc. [12]. In this paper, Terahertz Communication is explained in detail. A study has been done. So first let's know what are Terahertz Waves or Radiation. Terahertz Radiation—also called Sub-Millimeter Radiation, T-Waves, T-Light, T-Lux, or THZ—consists of Electromag-

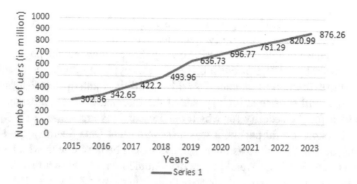

Fig. 2 Waveform between the number of mobile users versus years

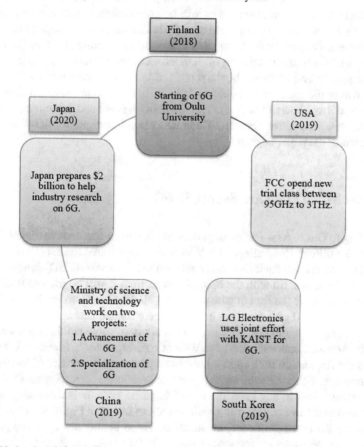

Fig. 3 Nation-insightful research activities to accomplish 6G

netic Waves inside an ITU-assigned band, ranging 0.3–3 Terahertz (THz). These are bands of Frequencies. Indeed, all Frequencies below the Terahertz Frequency have been used because people are increasing day by day. So now that the population will increase further by 2030, it needs a higher frequency; so by 2030, there will be an attempt to use Terahertz Frequency. And by 2030, it is anticipated that more and more devices will operate at high speeds of the Internet. So for that reason, it will have to wait for the security for which our Researchers are working [3, 9]. After studying through several papers, it was discovered that Data Security would be an important topic in the future as many hackers would be born due to which our data could be stolen. For that, several papers have studied on how to secure data. As you know, there are many changes in the generation after every 2–3 years [15], so 6G is likely to come out by 2030; then through this paper, in the next part, we will show how data in 6G and Confidential data will be protected from hackers, and why 4G would be more effective in protecting data. So in this paper, first, we will discuss 5G, then after that study about 6G in detail as to how many securities are there in it. After that, we will study in the briefing of Terahertz Communication why to use such a large frequency, and what will be the profit and loss and its effect on our health [1].

The rest of the paper is contained as follows. In the second section, a brief Introduction of 6G and how much data are secure in 6G is given and the third section will study the new innovative Terahertz Communication technique for 6G. Finally, the conclusion of the paper is given.

2 How Much Data are Secure in 6G

According to Cisco, Asia-Pacific organizations receive 6 consecutive digital threats. A Frost & Sullivan study alleged by Microsoft revealed that the expected financial misfortune in the Asia-Pacific region could fight $1.745 trillion (USD) due to network protection incidents. So with the help of this section, it will be tried to understand how safe and secure the data in wireless 6G is [7]. Wireless Communication invents new things every 10 years, such as better QoS, distributed new assets, the latest initiative leading Technologies. Although 5G is not despicable at this point, scientists have directed their concentration toward the 6G correspondence framework, because 5G lays the foundation for a special need to empower an assortment of innovations, for example, self-driving vehicles, AI, portable broadband correspondence, IoT, and savvy urban areas. In any case, the use of fantastic gadgets is increasing steadily each year and the use of data traffic will be seen as fast as in Fig. 1, which is imperative in the 5G correspondence organization. These boundaries open the gateway to another correspondence framework that includes greater range, surprisingly low laziness, high information transmission, secure mess-free correspondence, and complete remote inclusion. Table 1 analyzes the primary specifications of citations and innovations in both 5G and 6G. 6G will have the option to associate everything and coordinate various advances. Not only phones but many Internet of Things different devices will also use 6G. There are various advantages of 6G, such as providing

Table 1 Differentiation of 4G, 5G, and 6G

Characteristics of generation	4G	5G	6G
Introduced	2009	2019	2030
Bandwidth of Data	1Gbps	10Gbps	10Tbps
Standards	LTE Advanced, ITU-R, UMB	IMT-2020 Standards	MIIT and FCC
Major companies	Bharti Airtel, Telia Sonera	Ericsson, Nokia 8.3, Qualcomm	Huawei, Nokia, Samsung
Multiple access used	CDMA and OFDMA	NOMA, RSMA, SCMA	D-OMA

very good Internet speed for Smart Devices. If the speed a 6G smart device is good, then we can keep our data safe and secure. This is because if the speed is good, they will lock the data sooner than hackers and no one will be able to access our file. But little has been known on this, such as how to implement network security, and later, new security processes with creative cryptographic strategies to be considered, including physical layer security Technology and union security with negligible diligence. Methods include low volatility and high security. For example, the Web is a dangerous place for information. If you talk about the device, if the device gets hacked, you can take a lot of human personal data, which is a big thing in itself. So this is a problem that will have to be faced in 2030, but by then the arrival of 6G will solve all these problems [14]. So for this, a different kind of major techniques have to be studied. In this paper, of all the major technologies, only Terahertz will study the communication technology in detail (Figs. 2 and 3).

3 Terahertz Communication: Major Technology for 6G

By 2030, a High-Performance fundamental Technology is indispensable for using 6G and Beyond Wireless Communication Networks. Towards this path, examination exercises around the world are proceeding with bunch ICT-09-2017 funded by Europe Horizon 2020, a major undertaking supported by the Chinese Ministry of Technology and Science and various Sustainable NSF Awards in the United States. Reference [5] consists of electromagnetic waves within the ITU-allotted band of 0.3–3 Terahertz (THz) frequencies. A Terahertz is 1012 Hz or 1000 GHz. The radiation frequency in the Terahertz band ran from 1.0 mm to 0.1 mm, respectively. Figure 4 is the spectrum of Electromagnetic waves in which it can show that there are several Frequency Ranges.

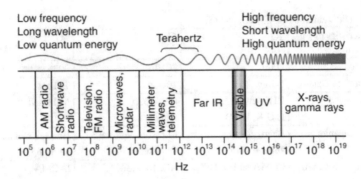

Fig. 4 Spectrum of electromagnetic waves

3.1 Why Terahertz Frequencies are so Helpful?

The Terahertz Frequencies are so helpful because of the following reasons:

1. Vast Energy of Terahertz Frequency: Electromagnetic radiation at Terahertz Frequencies has far less vitality than Electromagnetic Radiation at higher Frequencies (for instance, X-rays). The Electromagnetic Radiation Energy is given by

$$E = hf \tag{1}$$

where E is the photon vitality, f is the Recurrence of radiation, and h is Planck's constant. In fact, Terahertz radiation is important because the vitality of Terahertz waves is too low to think of knocking electrons off particles, for example, they cannot possibly ionize the material, and thus survive does not damage the tissue. This makes them extremely attractive for clinical use.

2. Higher determination than other safe Frequency: Electromagnetic Radiation in the range can be used to make images. The X-beam is a natural model. The degree of detail of a photograph will depend on the Frequency of Electromagnetic Radiation used. Lesser Frequency, better target. Terahertz Waves may not have the same Degree of settling power as X-Beams or noticeable light, yet they are preferable to using Microwave or Radio Waves.

3. Numerous normal materials are straightforward to terahertz radiation: Many materials that are mistaken for noticeable light are direct to Terahertz radiation, including many materials, paper, and cardboard. For example, this potentially opens up for security applications, as Terahertz radiation can filter individuals for disguised weapons without using an X-beam. This innovation is being used in some air terminals in the Netherlands Incorporating Schiphol.

4. Transfer of data and bandwidth: The terahertz fragment of the electromagnetic range offers gigantic potential for high information transmission rates. Information rates are obliged by the accessible data transmission, and the terahertz fre-

quencies offer wide transfer speeds in an uncrowded aspect of the electromagnetic range.

3.2 Innovative Devices for Terahertz Communication

The thing is that by 2030, the population of people will be very large, as of today, because of which, today's communication channel will be very less for people then. So Researchers are working on many high frequencies for people such as Terahertz Frequency, Mm Wave, and Microwave Frequency. But new innovative devices are implemented in previous terahertz frequencies, which are believed to be one of the key technologies for 6G. So for this, we will learn about all the devices one by one.

1. **Transceivers** In fact, Terahertz Frequency Research work began in 1990. Terahertz Communication requires an excessive power signal transmitter and a high-vulnerability detector that only works at room temperature, with innumerable headways operating in diverse innovation ways simultaneously reducing the purported THz gap. Therefore, two types of techniques can be used for this: Electronic Technology and Photonic Technology [5]. Both these techniques are described one by one. Silicon is used for electronic technologies such as CMOS technology, heterojunction bipolar junction (HBJ), and Shotsky diodotechnics, which have achieved state of the art and can be found based on the formula, and to operate the mixer at frequencies of 1 THz are ready for. All this is only about Electronic Technology. If talking about Photonic Technology, there are also different types of antennas such as Photo-mixer and Photoconductive antennas which use nearby 1THz. Unique in relation to the Electronic or Photonic advances already mentioned, the ongoing reception of nanomaterials has opened up another way to create novel Plasmonic gadgets for the THz interchange, for example, the use of graphene.

2. **Antennas and Arrays**: Speaking of antennas and arrays, 6G has many antennas that use Terahertz Frequency. The low transmission intensity of THz handsets persuades them to be used as directional antennas, such as Horn antenna, Common antenna design, Lens antennas, etc., which are available within 1 THz. The short wavelength of THz signals (3 millimeters to 100 GHz to 30 film to 10 THz) takes care of these radio wires to be minuscule. This property likewise allows for more imaginative schemes, including multi-ray app hector reception apertures and focal point coordinated receive strings, all slight impressions. Similarly, based on the THz handset, new nanomaterials can be used to plan antennas newly [4].

3. **Terahertz Re-configurable Intelligent Surfaces**: In addition to using the performance of the received wire in transmission and assembly, novel reconfigurable clever surfaces (RIS), or evenly encapsulating hypersurfaces, can be used to control the propagation of THz signals, EM waves. Blasting, polarization and stage moving, collimation, and concentrating, among others. In contrast with the traditional transfer, RIS conclusively and powerfully considers adaptation to the laws

of electromagnetic propagation, accepted by a lot of conductive meta-particles, and switch components on a dielectric substrate [11].

So all these changes were in devices, due to which the Terahertz frequency is used in 6G wireless communication.

3.3 Merits and Demerits of Terahertz communication

The Terahertz (THz) band (0.1–10 THz) highlights its potential as a key remote innovation to meet future requests for the 6G remote framework because of its four properties: (1) Hundred GHz transfer of Asset's property, (2) Pico-second level image duration, (3) Thousands of submillimeter long-wire receive strings coordinated, and (4) Frail constraint without complete inheritance guideline. Known as the THz hole for a long time, the THz band is one of the least investigated repetition groups in the electromagnetic (EM) range for the absence of efficient THz handsets and radio wires. In any case, practical THz correspondence frameworks are empowered by significant advances in the most recent 10 years [1]. The THz range can resolve the issue of range constraints and upgrade the current remote framework range. Different promising applications are envisioned, for example, Tbps WLAN Framework (Tera-WiFi), Tbps Internet of Things (Tera-IoT), and Tbps Access Backhaul (Tera-IAB) remote in remote server farms. The organization and super broadband THz Incorpo-201 evaluated the space paper (Tera-space-communication). At microwave frequencies, the THz frequency provides greater communication bandwidth. Terahertz (THz) has the following burdens: (1) It does not retain long-distance correspondence due to cloud, dust, downpour, and so on, spreading and assimilating. (2) It exhibits less penetrating proficiency than microwave radiation. In addition, it restricts entry through mists and fog. THz waves cannot intrude into liquid, water or metal. (3) Terahertz frequencies are difficult to detect because dark-colored radiation at room temperature is exceptionally solid at these frequencies. (4) Sources, locators, and modulators are not accessible at a reasonable cost which impedes its commercial access as a correspondence framework. (5) The problem with Terahertz is the extremely high prevalence of misfortune and forced correspondence isolation.

The disadvantage of communicating with the Terahertz Frequency is that there is strong absorption from the atmosphere. Like the efficacy affecting 1-mW source and 1 PW detection, the working unique range is 60 dB, allowing for interchanges in the range of 500 m in the climate transmission window with a fading of 100 dB/km. With the help of Fig. 5 waveform, it will be necessary to believe that even though the absorption will be high, and the Terahertz frequency is less efficient, the Communication will be better. One thing is that there is very little or more absorption, but it will not affect the satellite communication process to the satellite, but little difference is seen due to the Earth's environment. By the way, another advantage of Terahertz is that its bandwidth is large. Therefore, the transmission rate is good

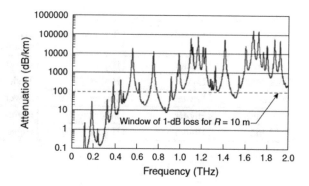

Fig. 5 Climatic attenuation versus frequency in the range of THz

compared to the Microwave Frequency. And the size of the Antenna can also be kept small, due to which it can easily handle Satellite Communications for 6G.

3.4 Health Issues Regarding Terahertz Communication

Not in the slightest degree like X-radiates, Terahertz radiation is not radiating and has low photon energy which is believed to not injure all living tissues and DNA. A pair of frequencies of the thirteenth radiation can penetrate the tissue with a millimeter less water content (e.g., oily tissue) and the extravaginal can be behind the extravagant. Terahertz Radiation can likewise distinguish contrasts in the watery matter and tissue thickness. Such a methodology may allow the solid revelation of epithelial damage with an imaging system that is non-mediated, and easy. Primary images created using Terahertz Radiation date back to 1960. In any case, the 1995 photographs were given using Terahertz time-zone spectroscopy, which generated much interest. A pair of frequencies of Terahertz Radiation can be used for 3D imaging of teeth and perhaps more careful than ordinary X-bar imaging in dentistry.

THz-band applications raise various richness and assurance concerns [1]. International Commission on Non-Ionizing Radiation Protection (ICNIRP) is an essential risk factor for THz radiation. Since THz radiation does not enter the body, this risk is limited to the heating of skin tissue. In light of everything, beyond the question of whether THz radiation can cause dermatitis, for example, given the trademark density and high radio wire gain in THz, appreciating the valid effect of THz radiation for enhancement. It is necessary to assess the guidance for. Overriding, an assurance concern leads to negligible standard detection, imaging, and suppression. With the high irradiance advantage, precise bar control limits and stunning imaging can be coordinated in a decent way, possibly by methods for direct imaging, such as in THz-based air terminal scanners. This can happen at the customer end (if a customer's device has been hacked) or at the organization (as compared to a network-driven arrangement). For achieving this with AI processes, security concerns are certain. Such concerns should be linked to both programming and equipment. Table 2 is a

Table 2 Comparison table of existing frequencies

Origin	Lucidity	Resoluteness	Safety and security	Sensibility
X-Beam	Higher	Higher	Lower	Lower
Ultraviolet	Lower	Higher	Moderate	Moderate
Infrared	Lower	Higher	Lower	Moderate
Mm Wave	Higher	Moderate	Higher	Lower
Terahertz	Higher	Higher	Higher	Higher

survey of Sci-Direct, which shows that the results obtained by Terahertz are better than other sources in the parameters of Lucidity, Resoluteness, Security, and Sensibility. Various promising applications are envisioned, for example, in the Tbps WLAN Framework (Tera-WiFi), Tbps Internet of Things (Tera-IoT), Tbps Unified Backhaul (Tera-IAB) remote organizations, and remote server farms. Supercomputer Broadband coordinated THz space paper (Tera-SpaceCom), THz, and VLC (visible light communication) are almost the only solutions that work on both micro- and macro-scales.

3.5 Database Security by Using Terahertz

We know as a whole that the fear of the country knows no borders and is currently on the ascent. Furthermore, dangerous tactics are getting smarter with shroud weapons and threats that are difficult to detect. Security-related applications can be divided into two important subcategories, which are illustrated as follows.

I. Security screening of letters, envelopes, and small bundles: The identification of numerous hazards in powders, liquids, explosives and small bundles and exhibitions has become significant. After finding characters with Bacillus anthracis, such new threats are seen as CBREs (synthetic, biological, and radiological components) that are real and require new and viable recognition methods to combat them. With the aim of reviewing level articles (envelopes, letters, and small bundles), our Terahertz imaging scanner gives security screening goodness and openness as far as goodness, openness, and discovery are concerned.

II. Security screening of individuals (Body Scanner): Unlike X-beam machines, Terahertz-waves are completely innocuous to people and have no ionized radiation, although there may be intrusive fabric without stretch and a few different nooks [6]. These properties make THz-based individual screening systems very important for applications where human welfare and safety are of utmost importance. The Tera-Sense Security Body Scanner operates in reflection mode and is proposed to detect weapon deadlock, including cold steel and guns, bombs and projectiles, and dangerous belts.

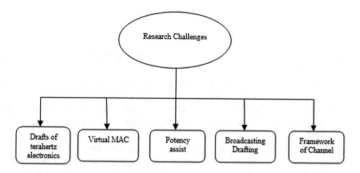

Fig. 6 Climatic attenuation versus frequency in the range of THz

4 Research Challenges

If we talk about Research Challenges, there are many Advanced Research topics in this field which are very important to work on. For example, thinking about using Terahertz for 6G, what effect will the Terahertz frequency have on Electronics, because any frequency Electronics Characteristic is very important. Second, it is very important to see how this will affect the virtual medium access control (MAC) [8]. And everyone knows that Communication is not possible without a channel, then it will be very important to look at the modeling of the channel. It was mentioned earlier that Terahertz has much higher absorption than the Microwave Frequency, but even then, Satellite-to-Satellite Communication is not a problem; it should also be noted how broadcast formatting will be affected. Last but not least, there is a lot to think about the purpose of Security for Database and Network-based Security. And hopefully, many researchers will get a lot of help through this paper. They can consider all things which is mentioned in (Fig. 6).

5 Conclusion

This paper gave information on why Terahertz Communication is called an important technology for 6G and also discussed its properties, merits, demerits, and its applications like Tera-IoT, Tera-Wi-Fi, etc. To use Terahertz Devices in 6G, what has been amended? It has been shown that Terahertz waves have a very high defect like strong absorption but provide an unrelated spectrum that is more adequate for IoT devices by 2030. It has also been studied that 6G is safer than 4G and 5G in terms of Data security. Here is a waveform indicating that the attenuation of the Terahertz frequency is very low. This paper also concludes how health issues arise when working at high frequency, like Terahertz waves. Hence, it concludes that Terahertz Communication Technology is a very good Technology for 6G and provides greater security in terms of Wireless, Network-Based, and Database Systems.

References

1. Akyildiz IF, Jornet JM, Han C (2014) Terahertz band: next frontier for wireless communications. Phys Commun 12:16–32
2. Akyildiz IF, Kak A, Nie S (2020) 6G and beyond: the future of wireless communications systems. IEEE Access 8:133995–134030
3. Alsharif MH, Kelechi AH, Albreem MA, Chaudhry SA, Zia MS, Kim S (2020) Sixth generation (6G) wireless networks: vision, research activities, challenges and potential solutions. Symmetry 12(4):676
4. Basar E, Di Renzo M, De Rosny J, Debbah M, Alouini MS, Zhang R (2019) Wireless communications through reconfigurable intelligent surfaces. IEEE Access 7:116753–116773
5. Chowdhury MZ, Shahjalal M, Ahmed S, Jang YM (2020) 6G wireless communication systems: applications, requirements, technologies, challenges, and research directions. IEEE Open J Commun Soc 1:957–975
6. Crowe TW, Deal WR, Schröter M, Tzuang CKC, Wu K (2017) Terahertz RF electronics and system integration [scanning the issue]. Proc IEEE 105(6):985–989
7. Giordani M, Polese M, Mezzavilla M, Rangan S, Zorzi M (2020) Toward 6G networks: use cases and technologies. IEEE Commun Mag 58(3):55–61
8. Han C, Wu Y, Chen Z, Wang X (2019) Terahertz communications (teracom): challenges and impact on 6G wireless systems. arXiv preprint arXiv:1912.06040
9. Khan LU, Yaqoob I, Imran M, Han Z, Hong CS (2020) 6G wireless systems: a vision, architectural elements, and future directions. IEEE Access 8:147029–147044
10. Lu Y, Ning X (2020) A vision of 6g–5g's successor. J Manag Anal 7(3):301–320
11. Nagatsuma T, Ducournau G, Renaud CC (2016) Advances in terahertz communications accelerated by photonics. Nat Photonics 10(6):371–379
12. Petrov V, Pyattaev A, Moltchanov D, Koucheryavy Y (2016) Terahertz band communications: applications, research challenges, and standardization activities. In: 2016 8th international congress on ultra modern telecommunications and control systems and workshops (ICUMT). IEEE, pp 183–190
13. Rappaport TS, Xing Y, Kanhere O, Ju S, Madanayake A, Mandal S, Alkhateeb A, Trichopoulos GC (2019) Wireless communications and applications above 100 GHZ: Opportunities and challenges for 6G and beyond. IEEE Access 7:78729–78757
14. Strinati EC, Barbarossa S, Gonzalez-Jimenez JL, Kténas D, Cassiau N, Dehos C (2019) 6G: The next frontier. arXiv preprint arXiv:1901.03239
15. Viswanathan H, Mogensen PE (2020) Communications in the 6G era. IEEE Access 8:57063–57074

Author Index